Qualitative Data Analysis with ATLAS.ti

Qualitative Data Analysis
with ATLAS.ti Susanne Friese

**$SAGE

Los Angeles | London | New Delhi
Singapore | Washington DC

First published 2012

Apart from any fair dealing for the purposes of research or private study, or criticism or review, as permitted under the Copyright, Designs and Patents Act, 1988, this publication may be reproduced, stored or transmitted in any form, or by any means, only with the prior permission in writing of the publishers, or in the case of reprographic reproduction, in accordance with the terms of licences issued by the Copyright Licensing Agency. Enquiries concerning reproduction outside those terms should be sent to the publishers.

SAGE Publications Ltd
1 Oliver's Yard
55 City Road
London EC1Y 1SP

SAGE Publications Inc.
2455 Teller Road
Thousand Oaks, California 91320

SAGE Publications India Pvt Ltd
B 1/I 1 Mohan Cooperative Industrial Area
Mathura Road
New Delhi 110 044

SAGE Publications Asia-Pacific Pte Ltd
3 Church Street
#10–04 Samsung Hub
Singapore 049483

British Library Cataloguing in Publication data

Library of Congress Control Number: 2011920595

A catalogue record for this book is available from the British Library

ISBN 978-0-85702-130-4
ISBN 978-0-85702-131-1

Typeset by C&M Digitals (P) Ltd, India, Chennai
Printed by MPG Books Group, Bodmin, Cornwall
Printed on paper from sustainable resources

To John Seidel, where it all began

Contents

About the author

Susanne Friese started working with computer software for qualitative data analysis in 1992. She was introduced to CAQDAS tools during her time at QualisResearch in the USA, between 1992 and 1994. In subsequent years, she worked with the CAQDAS Project in England (1994–6), where she taught classes on The Ethnograph and Nud*ist. Two additional computer programs, MAXQDA and ATLAS.ti, followed shortly thereafter as the respective Microsoft Windows versions of these programs. During her dissertation and later as an Assistant Professor at the Copenhagen Business School in Denmark, she carried out a variety of research projects using both qualitative and quantitative methods. Dr Friese used SPSS software to analyse quantitative data, and the ATLAS.ti. program to support her work with qualitative material. She has taught qualitative and quantitative research methods in the Sociology Department at Leibniz University Hanover, Germany, at both undergraduate and graduate level. Today, she runs courses in ATLAS.ti. and computer-assisted qualitative data analysis (see http://www.quarc.de). In addition, she has assisted on numerous projects around the world in a consulting capacity and has authored didactic materials and works for ATLAS.ti at the intersection of developers and users.

Introduction

ATLAS.ti belongs to the genre of CAQDAS programs. CAQDAS stands for computer-aided qualitative data analysis software. It is a somewhat lengthy acronym as compared to 'QDA software', which can also be found in the literature. The latter stands for qualitative data analysis software and the apparent similarity may be responsible for some of the misunderstandings and misperceptions related to CAQDAS.[1] ATLAS.ti – like any other CAQDAS program – does not actually analyze data; it is simply a tool for supporting the process of qualitative data analysis. Computers are generally very good at finding things like strings of characters or coded data segments in a large variety of combinations, but the researcher first needs to tell the computer, by way of coding, which data segment has what kind of meaning (see also Konopásek, 2007). This prerequisite is used by some people as an argument against using software, asking: if the computer doesn't do the coding, then what it is good for? And without 'test driving' a CAQDAS package, they judge the software to be inadequate in a qualitative research context and return to their manual methods of colored pencils and filing cabinets. Welsh (2002) describes two camps of researchers: those who see software as central to their way of analyzing data and those who feel that it is peripheral and fear that using it leads to a 'wrong' way of analyzing data. Smith and Hesse-Biber (1996) found that software is used mainly as an organizing tool. However, technology has advanced considerably since 1996 and I propose that software can be used for much more than just organizing data.

Software frees you from all those tasks that a machine can do much more effectively, like modifying code words and coded segments, retrieving data based on various criteria, searching for words, integrating material in one place, attaching notes and finding them again, counting the numbers of coded incidences, offering overviews at various stages of a project, and so on. By using ATLAS.ti, it becomes much easier to analyze data systematically and to ask questions that you otherwise would not ask because the manual tasks involved would be too time consuming. Even large volumes of data and those of different media types can be structured and integrated very quickly with the aid of software. In addition, a carefully conducted computer-assisted qualitative data analysis also increases the validity of research results, especially at the conceptual stage of an analysis. When using manual methods, it is easy to 'forget' the

---

1 The acronym CAQDAS was developed by the directors of the CAQDAS networking project at the University of Surrey, Guildford, UK (http://caqdas.soc.surrey.ac.uk/).

raw data behind the concepts as it is quite laborious to get back into the data. In a software-supported analysis, the raw data are only a few mouse clicks away and it is much easier to remind yourself about them and to verify or falsify your developing theoretical thoughts.

Your ideas about the data are likely to be different three or six months into the analysis as compared to the very early stages, and modification of codes and concepts is an innate part of qualitative data analysis. With the aid of computers, this process can also easily be documented. The steps of analysis can be traced and the entire process is open to view. For a more extensive discussion on the advantages as well as the disadvantages of using computers for qualitative data analysis, see Fielding and Lee (1998).

Even if some of the information in this book applies to all CAQDAS packages, you will learn in particular how to carry out a project with ATLAS.ti. Like a lot of other software, ATLAS.ti offers many functions and options but it does not explain what you actually need do to in order to conduct your analysis. Looking back at my own experience, when I started to use software to analyze qualitative data in 1992, I did what most novices probably do: I looked at the features, played around a bit, muddled my way through the software and the data, gained some insights and wrote a report. It worked – somehow. But it wasn't very orderly or systematic.

Since then, my way of working with ATLAS.ti has gradually become much more systematic and – to a certain point – even standardized. This did not happen overnight: it took many years of working with the software and teaching it, as well as involvement in many project consultations. As each qualitative research project is to an extent unique, this allowed me to test my ideas in different contexts and to develop a method of computer-assisted analysis.[2] Lewins and Silver (2007), in their book on using software in qualitative research, take a different stance. They are afraid that the use of software conventionalizes data and leads to expectations and assumptions about how the data should be analyzed (p. 57); therefore they make suggestions but leave it up to the users to find their way through a software package.

However, I often see users struggling instead of finding their own way of working with a particular software package. They are overwhelmed by its many functions and sometimes don't even know where to start. They appreciate very much having someone to guide them through the analytical process, advising them which function to use when and at which stage.

What is fundamentally lacking in the literature is a data analysis method for computer-assisted data. A number of books and articles have been written about the general use and usefulness of software for qualitative data analysis,

---

2 The term 'method' is used here in an epistemological sense as a set of steps and procedures by which to acquire knowledge, as distinct from the more encompassing term 'methodology' which includes the entire research process starting with ontological consideration of what there is that can be studied (Blumer, 1969; Hug, 2001; Strübing and Schnettler, 2004).

the early ones often expressing concern as well as enthusiasm about how software can help (Barry, 1998; Hinchliffe et al., 1997; Morrison and Moir, 1998; Richards and Richards, 1994; Seidel, 1991). At times, a chapter on computer-assisted analysis is included at the end of qualitative data analysis books (e.g. Silverman, 2000; Mayring, 2010), or you might find short descriptions and screenshots showing how certain analysis steps could be implemented (Corbin and Strauss, 2008). I was very surprised, however, to read descriptions of pile sorting and other manual methods of data analysis in a book first published in 2010 (Bernard and Ryan, 2010). The authors point out that the various procedures they describe can also be accomplished using a software package, but they do not explain how. Maybe the assumption is that it goes without saying: you simply load the software and it is immediately obvious how to adapt your old manual procedures.

I argue that (1) it is not and (2), more importantly, an exactly equivalent step-by-step process is not even desirable. Today, with the new possibilities available, we can approach data analysis in different ways. Therefore analysis methodology needs to be rewritten to exploit the benefits of a software-supported approach. Software changes the way we build up coding systems. The process becomes much more exploratory due to the ease of renaming and modifying codes. Computers also change the ways we ask questions about the data. Data analysis procedures have become much more sophisticated, because for a computer it is much easier to find things in the data and to output results. Also, CAQDAS makes it easier to combine qualitative and quantitative methods, which of course does not preclude a purely qualitative approach. It allows qualitative researchers to move out of the black box of analysis and to make the entire analytic process more transparent. And it allows them to work in teams, even across geographical boundaries. This creates new opportunities and also new challenges.

This book, in addition to teaching you how to work with ATLAS.ti, proposes a method for computer-assisted data analysis. The method is called 'computer-assisted NCT analysis'. This process of Noticing, Collecting and Thinking will be explained in more detail starting with Chapter 5. As the name indicates, the focus of the method is on data analysis and not on the entire research process. Thereby it is possible to integrate it into various methodologies; you don't need to subscribe to a particular world view in order to use it, and it doesn't prescribe how you should tackle your analysis. If the overall methodological approach or the research questions require an inductive approach, you can work inductively; if it makes more sense to work deductively, you can do that as well, or use a mixed approach. You can work purely qualitatively or, if applicable, quantify some of the findings. Whether you come from an ethnographic, a phenomenological or a grounded theory tradition, whether you have conducted action research, narrative interviews, focus groups or biographical research, whether you have structured or unstructured data, observational data or audio-visual material, I am interested in teaching you how to approach the analysis of your data in a systematic computer-assisted way.

The book can be followed as a guide and I make specific suggestions about when to do what and why. If you find these suggestions useful for your purposes, you are welcome to follow the suggested methodological steps as well. If you view ATLAS.ti as a tool for managing your data, you can focus on the technical instructions. You will find both methodological and technical advice in this book.

Computer-assisted analysis is like exploring a data landscape

Computer-assisted analysis can be thought of as a journey. Think of your ATLAS.ti project as an excursion into unknown territory. The data material is the terrain that you want to study; the chosen analytic approach is your pathway through it. The tools and functions provided by ATLAS.ti tools are your equipment to examine what there is to discover. In Chapters 1 to 3 we prepare for the journey. The preparation of the data material can be compared to selecting the right time of the year for the excursion. Ice and snow may hinder the success of our excursion, so can a careless transcription or wrongly chosen data file formats. A well-thought-out project setup is like planning your excursion carefully and not just running off up the first dirt track you see: that might turn out to be a dead end. Learning the technical aspects of coding in Chapter 4 is essential before you can make progress. With that knowledge, you will be well prepared to embark on the journey. Along the way you will improve your coding skills and learn further skills, like developing a system for all the interesting things you observe; how to write notes on them (writing comments); how to write a diary that documents the excursion and your major insights and findings on the way (writing memos); and how to examine specific characteristics of certain objects and their relations to other objects in depth, using the query tool, the co-occurrence explorer and other helpful functions.

Let's think of our data as a landscape that we want to explore (Figure I.1). The nature trail that I will take you on will take a couple of days and we will naturally take some breaks (e.g. to rest, to play games or to listen to a story around the camp fire in the evening), and I have more metaphors in store that will help you to understand better why some paths are dead ends or detours and why some tools should be used in particular ways to best achieve what we are aiming for – that is, a meaningful and comprehensible representation of the terrain we are examining.

As your tour guide, I will call a last preparatory team meeting before we embark on the journey. The aim of the meeting is to outline what lies ahead and explain to you the route I plan to take. In order to make this meeting more fun, we will play a game. As part of the game, you will learn about the NCT model of software-supported qualitative data analysis.

Then it will be time to gain your first hands-on experience. You will begin by observing the terrain, spotting things that might be interesting, collecting them and putting your coding skills into practice. The aim of this first day of the

Figure I.1 Looking at data like a landscape to be explored

journey is to become familiar with the terrain, to observe and then to write down notes and first coding ideas. We will meet up later to discuss what you have found. I will show you that other people found very similar things on their first day. You may already be starting to structure your thoughts about the things you have noticed, or at least wondering how to do so. I will explain it using the terrain of the example data provided, but I will also draw on other examples to show how their investigators managed to add more structure to their enquiries.

This calls for another day of skills training and some storytelling, where you will learn first how best to describe surface observations (developing subcategories) and secondly how to pull together very detailed observations by recognizing common characteristics (developing categories). Most people are likely to find examples of both when they look at their coding after the first day of the journey. A few will find that they have so far paid attention only to surface characteristics or the smallest details. Equipped with some new skills, you can move on to explore more of the data landscape until you feel that it is mapped out well and that you can describe what the terrain looks like. At this stage, the development of the coding system is more or less finished.

For some the journey will end here, as this is all they want to achieve. Maybe it was a first excursion into qualitative data analysis as part of a qualitative methodology course or a first independent project in the form of an undergraduate thesis. Others will want to continue the journey, to dig a bit deeper and find out how all the different observations relate to each other and whether some causal relations can be discovered – perhaps to develop a theory about what was discovered in the field. In order to do this, we will need to learn to handle new tools like the query tool, the co-occurrence explorer and the network views. Thus, the journey needs to be halted for a few days to acquire some new knowledge. With these new skills, you will no longer need a tour guide to accompany your journey. You can take it from there, gaining your own experiences and maybe becoming a tour guide yourself one day.

For whom did I write the book?

I wrote this book for new users as well as for more experienced users of ATLAS.ti who would like some guidance on how to work with the software. In it, I have answered a lot of questions that are asked again and again at the ATLAS.ti help desk. These are often questions that cannot be answered by a technically oriented software manual. They relate to project management issues, how to organize team work, methodological issues on how to build up a good coding system and what to do with the data once coded.

I also wrote the book for teachers of qualitative data analysis. My personal conviction is that, in the twenty-first century, qualitative data should be analyzed with the support of software. It is time that what has long been standard practice in quantitative statistical research is applied to qualitative data analysis as well.

As methodological training is quite diverse, the book can be used for undergraduate as well as postgraduate courses. It is suitable for undergraduates where method training comprises a large part of their study program. My aim for those students is to teach them descriptive-level analysis and thus they could work productively up to Chapter 5 in this book. The course can be continued in postgraduate study to include second-level conceptual analysis. At PhD level, the aim should be to go through the full cycle of the analytic process. From the book's companion website (www.quarc.de/qualitative-analysis-with-atlasti. html), lecturers can download presentations and sample data for use in tutorials, etc. The samples contain raw as well as coded data, and projects which follow up the skills training sessions in the book.

Chapter overview

In Chapter 1, I introduce the ATLAS.ti interface and the terminology used by the software. There is unfortunately no common language when you look at the different CAQDAS packages. What is called a variable in one software package is an attribute in another. Codes might be referred to as keywords or as nodes. In ATLAS.ti, however, a node is a nodal point in a network view, and so on. Thus, it is first necessary to learn the language of the software. With time, this will enable you to sound like a pro, to become a member of the ATLAS.ti community where talk is about HUs, families, managers, P-Docs and the like. If you already have some experience of working with ATLAS.ti, you will probably be familiar with the terminology and can skip Chapter 1 on getting to know the interface.

In Chapter 2, data preparation is discussed. You get to know the data file formats that ATLAS.ti supports, you learn when and for what purpose to choose which file format and how to prepare data transcripts so that you can best utilize software features later on. Miscellaneous settings like language support are also discussed, as ATLAS.ti users are spread around the globe and speak and use a variety of languages.

In Chapter 3, we are ready to rock – and to begin an ATLAS.ti project. It is a very important chapter: data management issues are often dismissed as boring and thus get neglected, and this frequently leads to difficulties, time wasting and sometimes data loss further down the line. I therefore explain the basic principles of data management in ATLAS.ti; they are not difficult to understand but you need to know them. Then I explain various project setup scenarios for single user and team situations. Here you can choose any scenario that applies to you. There is no need to read through all of them.

In Chapter 4 I explain the technical aspects of coding. You will find out about all the options for the variety of data file formats available. This is followed by a chapter on the methodological aspects of coding. Coding on the simplest level refers to the process of assigning a label to a data segment that the analyst deems to be relevant for some reason. Whether the code is mere description, just a paraphrase of the text or a concept or category on an abstract level makes no difference to the software. Software offers the option to code; what users do with this option is up to them. Starting with Chapter 5, the book moves away from considering only technical aspects and introduces a method of data analysis, namely computer-assisted NCT analysis.

In Chapter 6 the idea of second-level conceptual analysis is introduced. This chapter combines an explanation of the memo function with a description of the analysis tools offered by ATLAS.ti. The two topics are discussed side by side, because querying data and writing memos are related analytic procedures. Describing them as separate entities would not adequately reflect the methodological process of this stage of the analysis.

Chapter 7 is about visualizing ideas and findings in the form of network views and hyperlinks. These are tools that enable you to create links within and across data. If you don't yet know what network views look like, think of them as concept maps. As in previous chapters, there is a mix of technical explanations and methodological considerations.

The aim of Chapter 8 is to summarize all methodological aspects presented throughout the various chapters and to provide a coherent picture of the proposed method of computer-assisted NCT analysis.

At the end of the book, you will find some addenda providing further information on data and project management. They include topics such as what you should know about editing documents, how to merge projects, how to create backups and what to do when in trouble.

Background reading

Bourdon, Sylvain (2002). The integration of qualitative data analysis software in research strategies: resistances and possibilities [30 paragraphs]. Forum Qualitative Sozialforschung/Forum: Qualitative Social Research, 3(2), Art. 11, http://nbn-resolving.de/urn:nbn:de:0114-fqs0202118.

Fielding, Nigel G. and Raymond, M. Lee (1998). *Computer Analysis and Qualitative Research*. London: Sage.

Friese, Susanne (2005). Software and fieldwork, in R. Wright and D. Hobbs (eds.), Part Nine: Fieldwork, Science and Technology, *Handbook of Fieldwork*. London: Sage.

Gibbs, Graham R., Friese, Susanne and Mangabeira, Wilma C. (2002). The use of new technology in qualitative research. Introduction to Issue 3(2) of FQS [35 paragraphs]. Forum Qualitative Sozialforschung/Forum: Qualitative Social Research, 3(2), Art. 8, http://nbn-resolving.de/urn:nbn:de:0114-fqs020287.

Hahn, Christopher (2008). *Doing Qualitative Research Using Your Computer*. London: Sage.

Hesse-Biber, Sharlene (2003). Unleashing Frankenstein's monster? The use of computers in qualitative research, in S. N. Hesse-Biber and P. Leavy (eds.), *Approaches to Qualitative Research: A Reader on Theory and Practice*. Oxford: Oxford University Press. Chapter 25.

Hinchliffe, Steve, Crang, Mike, Reimer, S.M. and Hudson, Alan (1997). Software for qualitative research: 2. Some thought on 'aiding' analysis. *Environment and Planning A*, 29, 1109–24.

Mangabeira, Wilma C., Lee, Raymond M. and Fielding, Nigel G. (2004). Computers and qualitative research: adoption, use and representation. *Social Science Computer Review*, 22(2), 167–78.

Morrison, Moya and Moir, Jim (1998). The role of computer software in the analysis of qualitative data: efficient clerk, research assistant or Trojan horse? *Journal of Advanced Nursing*, 28(1), 106–16.

Muhr, Thomas and Friese, Susanne (2001). Computerunterstütze qualitative Datenanalyse, in *Wie kommt die Wissenschaft zu ihrem Wissen. Band 2: Einführung in die Forschungsmethodik und Forschungspraxis*. Hohengehrenpp: Schneider Verlag. S. 380–99.

Seidel, John (1991). Methods and madness in the application of computer technology to qualitative data analysis, in Nigel G. Fielding and Raymond M. Lee (eds.), *Using Computers in Qualitative Research* London: Sage. pp. 107–116.

Silver, Christina and Fielding, Nigel G. (2008). Using computer packages in qualitative research, in C. Willig and W. Stainton-Rogers (eds.), *The Sage Handbook of Qualitative Research in Psychology*. London: Sage.

Tesch, Renata (1990). *Qualitative Research: Analysis Types & Software Tools*. New York: Falmer Press.

ONE

Getting to know ATLAS.ti

For this chapter, we will work with the 'Jack the Ripper' sample project that was copied to your computer when you installed ATLAS.ti. You can play around with the project material and explore as many functions and possibilities as you like – you don't have to be afraid of causing any serious damage. It is just 'dummy' material!

Within this sample project you will get to know the main features of the user interface and the structure of the program as a whole. Please do not expect to learn about all the features and functions of the program at once. The aim is to give you a quick and easy insight into the possibilities of the software; to show you what a coded text or a network looks like; or how to use the context menus. The operational parts of the architecture are the same for all sorts of different functions, so having seen a few you will easily recognize others and find your way through the program.

This chapter also functions as an overview of what is to come. All subsequent chapters go into further detail regarding the various aspects and functions previewed here.

Some basic terms and concepts

To understand how ATLAS.ti handles data, think of your entire project as an intelligent 'container' that keeps track of all of your data. This container is the ATLAS.ti project file, called the **hermeneutic unit** or **HU** for short. The HU contains the analysis you carry out in ATLAS.ti. The term follows the tradition of hermeneutic sciences. It reminds us of Hermes, the divine messenger in Greek mythology and the god of fortune-tellers (and thieves!). Derived from it is the term 'hermeneutics' referring to the art of fortune-telling and text interpretation.

The ATLAS.ti HU can be understood as a container which holds everything you need for interpreting your data. This includes objects such as the link to your primary documents or the documents themselves, quotes, code words, notes, memos, links, code families, stored query results, supercodes, etc. You will learn more about these object types below and throughout this book. Opening a HU automatically activates all associated materials, thus streamlining your data and enabling you to work with a single entity.

Your source data can comprise text documents (such as interviews, articles, reports), images (photos, screenshots, diagrams), audio recordings (interviews, broadcasts, music), video clips (audio-visual material), PDF files (papers, brochures, reports) and geo data (locative data using Google Earth). Once you assign a data file to your project, it becomes a primary document which represents and contains additional information about its source counterpart (i.e. the assigned data file). Once your various documents are assigned and organized, your real work can begin.

Creating quotations and coding them is the basic activity you engage in when using ATLAS.ti and is the basis of everything else you will do. In practical terms, coding refers to the process of assigning categories, concepts or 'codes' (more generally speaking) to segments of information that are of interest to your research objectives. This function corresponds to the time-honored manual practice of marking (underlining or highlighting) and annotating text passages in a book or other documents.

In its conceptual underpinnings, ATLAS.ti has drawn from what might be called an earlier 'paper and pencil paradigm'. The user interface is designed accordingly and many of its processes are based on this analogy and thus can be better understood by it.

Because of this highly intuitive design principle, you will quickly come to appreciate the margin area as one of your most central and preferred workspaces – even though ATLAS.ti usually offers a variety of ways to accomplish any given task.

The ATLAS.ti user interface

At the top of the user interface (Figure 1.1) you have a title bar which displays the file name. Underneath you find the main menu, the toolbar and a number of drop-down menus. In addition, there is a vertical toolbar at the left margin. The rest of the screen is dedicated to displaying project data.

All materials for analysis must be available in digital format. In ATLAS.ti these become primary documents (P-Docs).

With progressive analysis, you code your primary documents, attach memos to data segments, link codes and other objects to each other, and so on. In contrast to manual ways of analyzing qualitative data, ATLAS.ti does not alter the original material, so the document files are not affected by your analysis. Instead you work with a virtual copy of a document (e.g. a transcribed interview). It is displayed on the left-hand side of your workspace. When you load another document, only the copy is removed from the screen. All notes, code words, memos, etc. are stored in the HU. The HU thus holds all materials and the results of your analysis in an 'electronic container'.

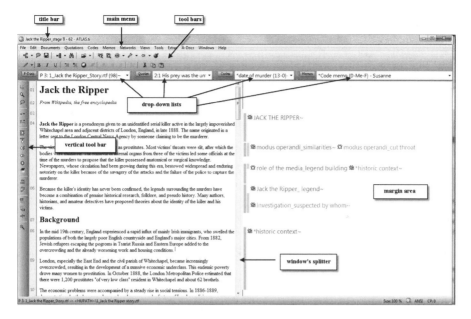

Figure 1.1 The ATLAS.ti. interface

Unlike confusing piles of paper with notes and references, the HU keeps growing but remains clearly arranged. Every step is documented according to strict rules so that the electronic HU means not only a tidier desk, but also a change from the art of fortune-telling to an understandable, verifiable technique of text interpretation. Keeping this background information in mind, let's now begin to work with the software.

Starting the program

When you open ATLAS.ti for the first time, click on the start button, then select All programs → Scientific Software → ATLAS.ti (Figure 1.2). To save a few clicks the next time you open it, drag the program icon to the desktop or right click on the program icon and select the option to attach it to the start menu or task bar.

When the program opens, you are greeted by the welcome wizard. You can continue to work with the wizard, or select the option 'Just continue' and 'Don't display this screen again'. Click on **OK**. Then you are offered the tip of the day. Select whether you want to see the tip every time you open the software; if not, deactivate the option.

If you have worked with ATLAS.ti on your computer before, the most recently used project is opened. Otherwise a new HU is loaded. Check the title bar to find out. Let's now open the sample project.

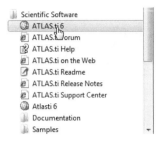
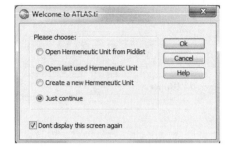

Figure 1.2   Starting the software

Opening the sample project

The sample project was copied to your computer during the installation process of ATLAS.ti.

- From the main menu select **HELP / QUICK TOUR / LOAD "JACK THE RIPPER STAGE II"**. This
  opens the coded version of the sample project.
- Look at the title bar. The name of the project is displayed there.

Before we begin to examine the sample project, I would like to introduce one
frequently used feature of ATLAS.ti – the context menus.

Context menus

In standard configuration, a context menu opens when you right click the
mouse. The context menu offers options and commands that only apply to the
area or object on which you click. Thus, when right clicking on the background
(e.g. in the middle of the screen), a context menu pops up exclusively for the
background.

    As a very first exercise we want to change the background of the HU editor
so that the codes of the currently loaded project are displayed:

- Right click on the background. The context menu opens, offering a number of options.
- Click on the option **DISPLAY WALLPAPER** to deactivate it. The background turns
  transparent.
- Right click again and click on the option **DISPLAY CODES**. You will now see the project
  codes displayed in a spiral around the center of the screen (Figure 1.3).

    The colors are dynamic and cannot be set by the user. You can tell that this
screenshot was taken at a weekend as it displays two colors, violet and green
(see companion website). On a weekday, you see one color and a light band,
similar to the violet one above. This indicates the hour of the day. Thus, the

Figure 1.3 Background displaying project codes (see website for clear image)

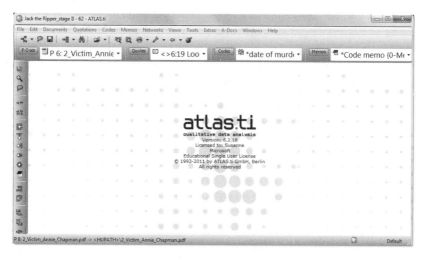

Figure 1.4 Default wallpaper as background

screenshot was taken at around midday (in fact, at 12:50). This is somewhat irrelevant to our task – teaching you to conduct a computer-assisted qualitative data analysis – but knowing it adds a bit of fun and color to a working day. We will find more of this sort of thing throughout the software.

If you are less playful and want a more professional-looking background, then select the wallpaper option and the wallpaper DEFAULT (Figure 1.4).

The drop-down menus and object managers

After opening the sample project file you will find a number of new entries on the screen but you cannot see the data yet. First, we want to take a look at the four drop-down lists (Figure 1.5).

Figure 1.5 Drop-down menus

On the left-hand side is the list of all documents assigned or imported to an ATLAS.ti project. They are called primary documents or P-Docs. Next to it is the list of all coded segments, or quotations, followed by the list of codes and the list of memos.

- The four drop-down menus can be moved by 'drag and drop' and their size can be adjusted by dragging the dotted line from right to left with the mouse. Try it!
- If you click on the down arrow to the right of a list, the list of objects is displayed. Open the list for all four object types and take a look.
- Open the list of documents (P-Docs) and select one document with a left click (e.g. **P3: 1_Jack the Ripper_story.rtf).** The selected primary document will be loaded and displayed on the screen with all related codings, hyperlinks and memos.

The object lists are convenient for some tasks but not for others. Therefore ATLAS.ti offers the possibility of opening all objects in a separate browser called the Object Manager.

- Open all four Object Managers by clicking on the icon to the left of the drop-down menu.

- Arrange them on your screen so that you can view them next to each other (Figure 1.6).

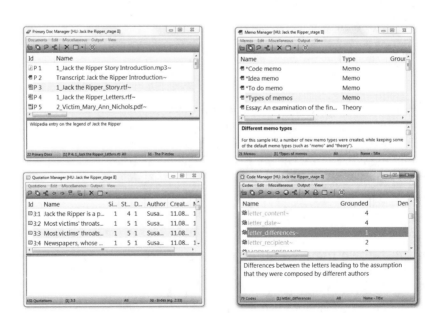

Figure 1.6 All four Object Managers side by side

In your everyday work with ATLAS.ti, you will probably not open all four managers at once. The purpose of this exercise is to show the commonalities of ATLAS.ti browsers that you will see throughout the program. Besides a mere list, the Object Managers also provide further information like author name, creation date or date of last modification. The different kinds of objects can be recognized by a specific symbol, as shown in Figure 1.7.

The first primary document P1 is an audio file. P2, the second one, is a memo assigned as a primary document. P3 and P4 are Word documents, P5 and P6 are PDF files, P7 is a video file, P15 a Google Earth document and P16 an image file. The symbols may vary depending on the multimedia software you have installed. The quotations also show the respective media format. Codes use a yellow diamond symbol and show a Post-it note when a definition has been entered. The memo symbol resembles a note booklet with a red cover.

Each Object Manager offers a **menu** and a **toolbar**. The menu options are the same as in the main and submenus. To spare you long treks with your mouse you can access them directly from here. In the space underneath the toolbar of the Object Manager you will find the objects and additional information in table format. The handling of this table is similar to other Windows programs such as Excel: every column has a header and the table can be sorted by a click on the column head; the width of the column can be adjusted by dragging the border (see figure 1.7).

Underneath the object list there are a **screen splitter** and a white area. The white area is a text editor in which you can write. By grabbing the splitter with your mouse you can adjust the size of the object list or editor respectively.

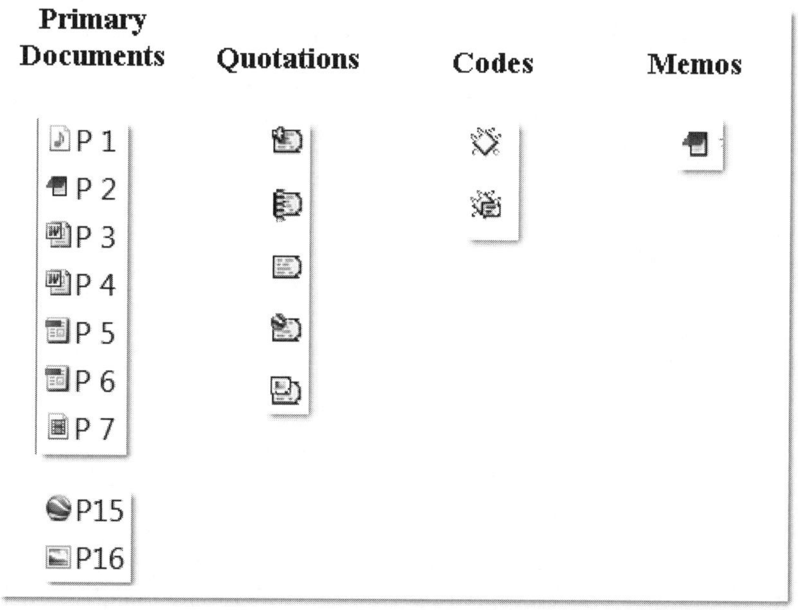

Figure 1.7 Symbols for the different kinds of objects: P-Docs, quotations, codes and memos

To train yourself in the use of the Object Manager, please carry out the following exercises:

- Sort the entries in the table with a click on the column header.
- Adjust the width of a column.
- Grab the splitter and move it up and down.
- Select an object from the list and write a comment about this object in the text editor (i.e. the white space). To save this new entry, click on another object in the list or open the context menu (right click) and click on **Accept**. Every entry for which you have created a comment carries a tilde symbol (~).

- For more comfort, the comment editor can be opened in a separate window. To do this, click on the third icon from the left in the toolbar of the manager (the speech bubble).

To prepare the screen for the next exercise:

- Close all object managers except the Code Manager.
- As in the Windows file manager, you can select different types of views. This applies to all Object Managers, but right now we only want to change the view for the Code Manager. Select **View / Single Column**. If you want, you can also try out the other options. Return to the single column view to finish this exercise.

You will now see only the code word and two numbers in brackets after them: e.g., *date of murder {13-0}. This is all you need to know when coding the data. This view allows you to resize the Code Manager to save space on your screen. The numbers in brackets are explained below.

Resize the Code Manager as shown in Figure 1.8 below, so that you see a long and narrow list of codes on the right-hand side of your screen. Your screen should be divided into three areas: the text of the loaded document on the left

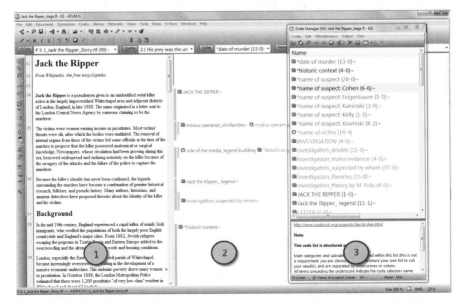

Figure 1.8 Preparing your screen for coding

side; the attached codes and possible other objects in the middle; and the Code Manager to the right of it.

ATLAS.ti remembers the views and position of its windows. This means that when you close and reopen the window or close and reopen ATLAS.ti, the Code Manager will be shown in the current view and in its current position.

Navigating the list of codes

For a regular project it is quite common to have between 120 and 200 codes. This is an average number based on experience that you can use as a rule of thumb. It can vary depending on the type of project and the type of analysis. This is discussed in more detail in Chapter 5 on the methodological aspects of coding.

For now the point is that code lists can become quite long and you won't see all the codes at once on your screen. Thus, you either need to scroll through the list or, easier, jump to a specific code by typing the first letter(s) of a code word. Try it out:

- The mouse pointer should be located somewhere within the Code Manager. Then click on the letter **m** on your keyboard. The focus of the code list moves to the code MODUS OPERANDI. Type the letters **mu**; you will then jump to the code word MURDER. Type the letter **v**; this bring you to the code word VICTIM and so on.

You may already be wondering what the numbers in brackets after the code words mean.

- Click on the code ***name of suspect: Cohen**.

🏆 *name of suspect: Cohen {6-6}~

The first figure shows how many times the respective code has been used: in this case, six times. It gives you some information on the **groundedness** of a code (i.e. how relevant this code is in the data). The second figure displays the so-called **density**, which is the number of links to other codes. The code ***name of suspect: Cohen** is linked to six other codes.

First, we want to take a look at the frequency of usage:

- Double click on the code. This opens a window showing the list of the six coded segments, the quotations.
- By left clicking on each quotation, it will be displayed or played in context. In this example, there are two text quotations and four audio quotations. The audio quotations show a loudspeaker symbol. View and listen to each quotation.

Next, we want to explore the second number and the term 'density'.

A preview of the network view function

- Close the list of quotations. Then click on the network button in the Code Manager toolbar. The network view for this code opens, showing the six links with other codes that have been created.

If you only see symbols for the description of the relation between two codes, then you need to change the display:

- Select **DISPLAY / LINK DISPLAY / MENU LABEL**.
- When the code labels are shown in black, you need to click on the colored circle in the toolbar and select the option **USE COLORED LABEL** (more on this in Chapter 7 on the network view function).
- Play around with the codes in the network view by dragging them to different positions (Figure 1.9).

By the way, the network views are not automatically created by the software; they are a result of the interpretation process and need to be created manually.

- Then close the network view window. When you are asked whether you want to save it, select **No**.

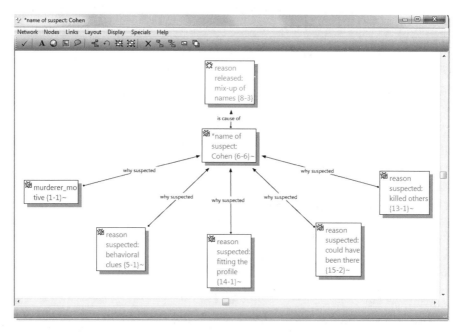

Figure 1.9   Focused network view on code *name of suspect: Cohen

A preview of the query tool

Here's what we have done so far. We learned about the four object types in ATLAS.ti and how they can be accessed via the four drop-down lists or via a

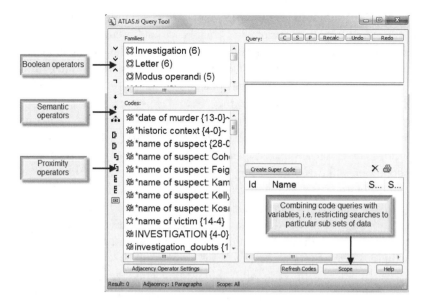

Figure 1.10 Previewing the query tool

manager window. We took a closer look at the Code Manager and learned what the terms 'groundedness' and 'density' mean. Double clicking on a code opens the list of all segments that have been coded with it. This is also referred to as **simple retrieval**, simple because it is based on just one code. We can, however, also ask more complex questions based on multiple codes. This is done using the query tool.

- To open the query tool (Figure 1.10), select the main menu option **TOOLS / QUERY TOOL** or click on the binoculars symbol in the main toolbar.

At this point we do not actually want to click a query, just to notice that there are 14 operators, organized into three groups (Boolean, semantic and proximity operators), which you can use to combine codes and groups of codes in order to ask questions about your data. In addition, you can use the query tool to restrict searches to particular subsets of data via the scope button. This allows you to set tasks like: 'Find all data segments that I have coded with "friendship" within "childhood", but only for married men between ages 31 to 40.' Thus, retrievals can become quite complex. The **query tool** will be discussed in detail in Chapter 6.

'Survival tips' to find your way around the main menu

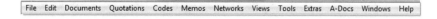

Figure 1.11 The main menu

There are 13 main menus (Figure 1.11) and each of them has submenus. At the time of writing, the total number of menus and submenus amounts to 443! This sounds frightening and you may think that you will never be able to learn each option. But there's no reason to panic: some menus are repetitive and you can find the same option in different places. Furthermore, here is an easy rule to help you to find your way around.

We have already learned about the four main object types: P-Docs, quotes, codes and memos. Take a look at the main menu bar. You will find a main menu option for each of these object types. When you need an option related to primary documents like assigning a new document or creating output, click on the main menu DOCUMENTS and your choices are already reduced.

When you want to do something related to codes, click on the main menu CODES and then you will find the option CODING with various suboptions. When you want to edit or rename a memo, click on the menu MEMOS. And when there is something to do involving a network view, click on the menu NETWORKS. To practice, find the following options. The solutions are provided at the end of this chapter.

- You want to create a group of documents. This is called a document family in ATLAS.ti. Where do you find this option? (a)
- Next, you want to create a group of codes. This is called a code family in ATLAS.ti. Where do you find the option? (b)
- In case this should be of relevance at some point, where do you find the option for creating a memo family? (c)

Do you get the point? It is not as difficult as it appears at first. Did you notice that within each submenu for documents, codes and memos you find a sort option, a filter option, a miscellaneous option and an output option?

- New users often ask whether it is possible to print the coded documents as they appear on the screen. Where would you look for this option? Just as a reminder, the part of the screen where the codes are displayed is called the margin area and what you are asked to do is to print documents. (d)

The toolbars

Many of the menu options can also be launched via the icons on the horizontal and vertical toolbars. When you move your mouse over the icon you will see a tool tip displaying a useful keyword or explanation (Figure 1.12).

Figure 1.12 Tool tip for icon 'assigning documents'

Of course, all these options can be launched via the text and context menus as explained above. Over time, you will develop your individual preferences about which ones you choose.

Summary

In this chapter you have learned about important terms and concepts used in ATLAS.ti, like the four main object types: primary documents, quotations, codes and memos. Then you previewed some of the major tools needed for a qualitative data analysis like the Code Manager, the query tool and the network view function; and you received some guidance on how to find menu options, even though you do not yet know all of them by heart.

Solutions to the 'survival' exercise

(a) DOCUMENTS / EDIT FAMILIES / OPEN FAMILY MANAGER

(b) CODES / EDIT FAMILIES / OPEN FAMILY MANAGER

(c) MEMOS / EDIT FAMILIES / OPEN FAMILY MANAGER

(d) DOCUMENTS / OUTPUT / PRINT WITH MARGIN ...

REVIEW QUESTIONS

1   What are the four main object types in ATLAS.ti?
2   What are Object Managers and what are they useful for?
3   What is the optimal position of the Code Manager to allow for maximum space and to have a free view of all relevant areas of the screen when coding or reviewing coding?
4   How can you navigate through a long list of codes?
5   What do the numbers mean that you see in brackets after the codes in the 'single column' view?
6   What is the query tool useful for?
7   How do you find your way around the many menu options?

GLOSSARY OF TERMS

Codes: Keywords that are generally linked to quotations, but don't have to be. You can also create free codes. When you link free codes to a number of different codes, then they are called abstract codes.

Hermeneutic unit (HU): A data file that stores everything you do to the data, but not the data themselves. An exception is when you work with internal text documents. Then the HU also contains your data. The HU data file has the file extension .hpr6 for version 6 files or .hpr5 for version 5 files. The file type is 'Hermeneutic Unit'. The file does not have to be stored at a specific location; you can store it wherever you want. The best option is to save it in the same folder as the documents you want to analyze. As the HU file is just a regular file, you can copy it, move it, delete or rename it in the file manager, just like any other file.

Memos: From a purely functional perspective, memos in ATLAS.ti consist of a title, a type and some text. They can be free or linked to other memos, to codes and to quotations. It is possible to attach a memo to a quotation as a means to comment on that quotation. In Chapter 6, however, I suggest a different way of using memos in ATLAS.ti. Memos are places to write down all sorts of ideas and thoughts. You can use them to remind you of things like what to do next week, what you wanted to ask your supervisor about, what you wanted to discuss with your team member. And you can use them as a place to write up your analysis and as building blocks for a later research report.

Network views: Network views offer a place for visualizing relations within your data. You can link almost all objects to each other; visualize your codings, visualize relationships between codes, relationships between quotations, relationships between memos and memos, relationships between memos and quotations, relationships between memos and codes, relationships between object families and their members. Network views can also contain unlinked objects, like thumbnail images of image PDs (for more detail, see Chapter 7).

Object Managers: The four main objects in ATLAS.ti are the primary documents, the quotations, the codes and the memos. The list of objects can be viewed by clicking on the down arrow to open the list field, or you can open a separate window for each object. These separate windows are called 'Object Manager'. The Object Managers have their own main menu and a toolbar. The options available are repetitions from the main menu, but with one slight difference. When selecting an object in the Object Manager and then one of the menu options, the option only applies to the selected object. Selecting the same option from the main menu has a global effect.

Primary documents (P-Docs or PD): When you assign, import or embed a document in HU, then ATLAS.ti creates a primary document. The primary document then becomes the container for the source file you assign, import or embed. Each primary document has a name and stores information about the author and when it was created and last modified. In addition, it has some information (e.g. a path reference) about where to access the source file. Only when the source is available can the primary document display the content. The name of the primary document can be changed within ATLAS.ti without affecting document access. The default name is the name of the source file. See also Chapter 3 on project management.

Query tool: The query tool allows you to retrieve quotations based on a combination of codes. It offers four Boolean operators, three semantic operators and seven proximity operators. Further, it allows you to combine code queries with variables; that is, you can ask for information such as: 'Find me all quotations that I have coded with code A and code B, but only for women between the age of 31 and 40.'

Quotations: Marked data segments that have a clearly defined start and end point. Often quotations are coded, but they don't have to be. You can also create so-called free quotations. Free or coded quotations can be used as a source or target to link data segments to each other. Linked quotations are called hyperlinks.

A quotation has an ID and a name. The ID consists of the primary document number that it belongs to and a number that indicates the sequence of when it was created. The quotation name is based on either the first 30 characters of a text quotation or the name of the primary document. This automatically generated name can be modified. If the default number of characters is not sufficient, it can be increased under EXTRAS/PREFERENCES/GENERAL PREFERENCES À LIST NAMES SIZE FOR QUOTES. The position where a quotation can be found within a primary document is indicated after the name.

TWO

Data preparation

This chapter provides an overview of the data file formats supported by ATLAS.ti and a few things you need to pay attention to. The recommendations and suggestions are derived from everyday user problems and questions that I have come across in the past. In addition, I include some transcription guidelines relating to the technicalities of the software. Following these guidelines will facilitate your work with ATLAS.ti at later stages of your analysis.

Supported file formats

In principle, most textual, graphical and multimedia formats are supported by ATLAS.ti (see Table 2.1).

Compatibility

Text documents

For some formats, their suitability depends on the version of your Windows system, particularly in regard to what other software is already installed. Doc and docx files, for example, are converted to rich text. For this process a doc(x) to rich text converter needs to be installed on your system. When you install an Office package, converters are installed as well; if, however, you get a project that contains Word 2007 or 2010 files and you still use Word 2003, then you may need to go online and download the latest converter pack.

PDF files

ATLAS.ti displays PDF files in their original layout, no formatting is lost. Misunderstandings sometimes happen in distinguishing between textual and image PDFs. When you scan a document, activate the character recognition option to turn the document into a text rather than an image PDF. Image

Table 2.1 Supported file format

Type of data	Format	Specific features/ considerations
Text	txt (plain text): rtf (rich text)	Can be modified within ATLAS.ti
	doc(x): converted to rich text by ATLAS.ti Native text PDF	cannot be modified[1]
Image	Over 20 different image file formats are supported. The most common are jpg, jpeg, bmp, tif(f), giv, png, jif(f), emf+ graphic PDF	Multi-page tiff images can also be used
Audio	The most commonly used formats are mp3, wma, midi, au, wav	When there is a problem in playing audio or video files, it is most likely due to a missing codec. You can find complete codec packages online that you can install on your computer.
Video	The most commonly used formats are mpeg, mpeg2, wmv, avi, mov	
Geo data	Google Earth as data source	
Survey data (Excel)	Results from an online survey can be imported as case based primary documents (commonly used for the analysis of open ended questions)[2]	
	Variables from surveys can be imported in the form of Primary Document families (= document attributes in ATLAS.ti)	

[1] Modification of doc and docx files will be possible with version 7.

[2] The specifics of preparing an Excel spreadsheet for import are not discussed in this book. Please take a look at the ATLAS.ti website and manuals for further details.

PDF files are treated like all other image documents by ATLAS.ti. You also need to be aware that all retrieved text from textual PDF files is rich text. You will lose the original layout when creating an output of coded PDF segments.

Audio and video files

A common problem with audio and video files is a missing codec. Audio and video files are usually compressed to use up less storage space, and for this process a codec is used. In order to read the files, the same codec that was used to 'pack' the files is needed to 'unpack' the files. Today you can find free codec packages online that you can download and install. Another video file-related problem I have come across was where the camcorder software installed on a computer was blocking everything else and not allowing the files to be played in ATLAS.ti. After uninstalling this software, everything worked fine. I generally advise that before you prepare all of your video files, create a short trial file for testing in ATLAS.ti. After you figure out the settings, appropriate format and file type, you can prepare the rest of the material.

Image files

When working with images, there is no point in assigning the full-quality image taken with a 14 million pixel camera to ATLAS.ti. The image won't fit on your screen as the resolution is way too high, so you end up resizing the images in ATLAS.ti to make them suitable for analytical purposes. I cannot provide a 'one-size-fits-all' figure regarding the optimal image size as it depends on the resolution and size of the screen. However, a good starting point would be 1024 × 768 pixels.

Excel files

You need to follow a specific syntax when preparing an Excel file for import. Special characters indicate to the software which part of the spreadsheet should be assigned as document, as variable or as code. Please refer to the documentation provided by ATLAS.ti on how to prepare such documents. It is straightforward and easy to implement.

For Mac users

If you use ATLAS.ti on a Mac, you should install OpenOffice (or Microsoft Office) for Windows as well, otherwise some components that ATLAS.ti draws upon will be missing. It is also recommended that you move the files that you want to analyze in ATLAS.ti to the Windows environment of your Mac before assigning them to an ATLAS.ti project.

Size

Theoretically, size restriction is not an issue because of the way ATLAS.ti handles PDs (see Chapter 3, 'Data handling in ATLAS.ti'). However, you should bear in mind that your computer's processing speed and storage capacity affect its performance. Excessively large documents can be uncomfortable to work with, even if you have an extremely sophisticated computer. The crucial issue is not always the file size, but rather, in the case of multimedia files, the length of playing time. For text documents, the number and size of embedded objects may cause extraordinarily long load times. There is a high likelihood that if a text document loads slowly in ATLAS.ti, it will also load slowly in other applications like Word.

Choosing between different text formats

As shown in Table 2.1, you can choose between four different text file formats: plain text, rich text, doc or docx files and textual PDF documents. **Plain text** does not include any formatting such as different font types and sizes, bold or italic characters or colors. As the name says, these text files are plain. You still find them today in emails or online texts like blogs and in forums. If your primary data are in this format, there is no need to save them in a different one. You can assign them just as they are to an ATLAS.ti project. As soon as you go into edit mode to modify some file content, the texts are enriched and saved in rich text format by ATLAS.ti.

When preparing your own data (e.g. transcribing recorded data), my recommendation is to store the files as **rich text in order to avoid conversion**. This assures the greatest compatibility across platforms and various versions of Word and Windows. You will find this file type option in any word processing program. The advantage over doc and docx files is that rich text is the standard format used by ATLAS.ti: no conversion is necessary and, if needed, the documents can be modified at a later point in time even after coding. **Doc and docx files** need to be converted by the software. As this does not always work smoothly because of differences in the various versions of Word and changes over time, newer versions of ATLAS.ti (later than 6.2) will introduce a new way of handling data. Then doc or docx files will still be converted to rich text, but only once. The rich text version will then be stored in a packaged format by ATLAS.ti and the doc or docx file is no longer used.

PDF files are a choice when the original layout is important for analysis purposes or when the documents are already available as PDFs. ATLAS.ti supports native PDF; this means the files are displayed within ATLAS.ti just as they look in their native PDF environment. The content is not converted. Thus, nothing is lost and the full information is available to you when coding the data.

Language support

It is possible to use documents in ATLAS.ti that are not in English or other European languages. For Western languages, usually nothing has to be changed in ATLAS.ti for the characters to be displayed correctly. A basic requirement is that language-specific fonts are installed on the computer. Displaying text in different languages in the HU editor does not require any specific attention. You may however experience difficulties in displaying a 'right to left' and a 'left to right' language in one document in a Western language similarly do not require specific attention. If the text is not displayed correctly in your language, check the default language settings by clicking on the **Default** field at the bottom right-hand side of the ATLAS.ti main window. You may also need to change the default if you experience a problem in displaying special characters in Western languages, like the German ä, ü, ö or letters like à, ñ, ŷ, etc. You do, however, need to configure the font settings and possibly your Windows settings if you want to use Cyrillic, Hebrew, Arabic, Thai, Chinese characters and the like for all other text fields in ATLAS.ti. This applies to code and other object labels, comment fields, memos, quotation IDs and network view entries. In order for the language to be displayed correctly, you need to set the appropriate font and script and sometimes also code page in ATLAS.ti. For Thai and East Asian language support, you may first of all need to install the appropriate language files on Western European and US Windows systems.

Font settings

- Select **Extras / Preferences / General Preferences** and then the **Font** tab.
- Select one or more object types for which you want to change the font.
- Select a font and appearance (bold, italic) for these object types.
- If you use ATLAS.ti in different contexts, you can specify different font themes.

In case your language requires a specific code page:

- Select the **Text Editor tab** in the General Preferences window, and then the code page for the language you want to use.

System settings for Thai and Asian language support on Western European and US Windows systems

The prerequisite is that a language pack is installed on your computer.

- Log in to your computer with full administrative rights.
- Select **Start / Control Panels / Regional and Language Options**.
- Select the **Languages** tab and then the option to install the appropriate language files that you need.
- Under the **Advance** tab, select the language in the field 'Language for non-Unicode programs'.

Preparing documents

Transcription

A very nice new option in version 6 of ATLAS.ti is the association between transcripts and the original audio or video recording. This allows access to the original recording via the transcript. When you want to make use of this option, a requirement is that you use either ATLAS.ti or the free software f4 to transcribe your data (importing transcripts based on other software like Express Scribe or InqScribe is in the pipeline but not yet implemented at the time of writing). During transcription you enter timestamps (or, as known in ATLAS.ti, association anchors). It is also possible to enter these anchors later when you have a transcript without timestamps and the

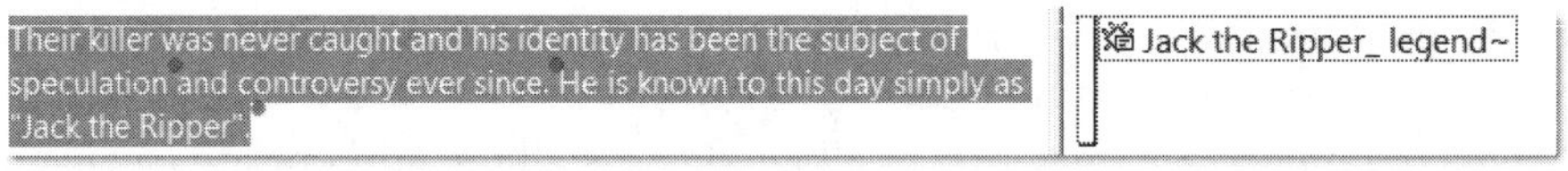

> Their killer was never caught and his identity has been the subject of speculation and controversy ever since. He is known to this day simply as "Jack the Ripper".

> 🔊 Jack the Ripper_ legend~

Figure 2.1 Associated text

recording is still available in digital format. Let's try it out so you can see the benefit of associated documents:

- Make sure the sound is turned on.
- Open the sample file 'Jack the Ripper stage II' via **HELP / QUICK TOUR**.
- **LOAD P2: TRANSCRIPT: JACK THE RIPPER INTRODUCTION** by clicking on the down arrow in the P-Docs drop-down list. Select P2 with a left mouse click.
- In the margin area, click on the code 'Jack the Ripper_legend'. The coded segment is highlighted.
- From the main menu either select **A-DOCS / PLAY SELECTED TEXT** or press **CTRL+P**. This activates the associated audio file and you will hear the voice of Martin Fido speaking the text (Figure 2.1).

The red dots in the text show the association anchors (timestamps). I usually set them quite frequently – basically every time I stop the recording when transcribing. The closer the anchors are set, the more accurately the associated segments can be played. A standard option in transcription software is that a timestamp is set after each paragraph. If paragraphs are long and you want to play just a specific section, the software needs to interpolate between the available anchor points, calculating the start and end positions as best as possible. Setting timestamps manually does not take much effort: in ATLAS. ti or f4 you just need to hit the F8 key. It is well worth doing.

In this book I won't describe the technical aspects of transcribing data in ATLAS.ti as it is easier to follow the instructions in the manual. You will also find some instructions in the primary document P14 on the 'Jack the Ripper' sample project. Setting up a project based on associated documents is described in Chapter 3, 'Scenario 3'.

Preparing textual documents

Avoid tables

As mentioned above, textual documents, apart from textual PDFs, are displayed in rich text format. The rich text format, however, is not as 'rich' as the name suggests. ATLAS.ti does not use the newest rich text protocol in order for older projects to still be readable and compatible with newer versions. Reusability has always been an important aspect in the development of ATLAS. ti (Muhr, 2000). A side effect is that in most cases, tables in Word documents will not be converted properly to rich text. Text in table cells that spread over multiple lines is shown as one line, thus not remaining within the cell boundary as shown in Figure 2.2. Therefore, the advice is not to use tables. If it is important to include tables, consider saving the document as a PDF file. Version 7

Type of data	format	specific features / considerations	
Text	txt (plain text): converted to rich text by ATLAS.ti after editing		can be modified
	doc(x): converted to rich text by ATLAS.ti		
	rtf (rich text)		
	Native text PDF	cannot be modified	
Image	Supported are over 20 different image file formats, most common ones are jpg, jpeg,		bmp, tif(f), giv, png, jif(f), emf + graphic PDF
	Multi-page tiff images can also be used		
Audio	Most commonly used formats are mp3, wma, midi, au, wav		When there is a problem in playing audio or
video files, it is most likely due to a missing codec. You find complete codec packages online that you can install on your computer.			
Video	Most commonly used formats are mpeg, mpeg2, wmv, avi, mov		
Geo data	Google Earth as data source		
Survey data (Excel)	Variables from surveys can be imported in form of Primary Document families (=document attributes in ATLAS.ti)		
	Results from an online survey can be imported as case based primary documents (commonly used for the analysis of open ended		
questions)			

Figure 2.2 Table converted to rich text

makes use of a new rich text protocol, which means the proper display of tables is no longer an issue. In order for all old projects to still function, the currently used rich text protocol will be kept. This means no one has to be afraid of ending up with misaligned coded segments because of the new protocol.

Transcription guidelines

In this section, I will provide some guidelines for structuring transcriptions of recorded data. In interview transcripts with one interviewee it helps you quickly recognize the different speakers and speaker units in the transcript. In transcriptions of group interviews or focus groups, it lets you automatically code all speaker units by adding attribute codes. This is how you need to prepare the transcript:

- Mark all speakers unambiguously and enter an empty line between each speaker in turn.

In the sample transcript to the right, the paragraph marker is visible, indicating when the Enter button was pressed. The two speakers in the transcript are marked clearly with unique identifiers: **INT:** is used for the interviewer and **AL:** for Alexander, the interviewee. 'Interviewer' or 'Alexander' would be impractical as markers because those words might appear in the text itself, but the character combination INT: and AL: is not likely to be found anywhere else. This is essential for using the auto coding tool.

- If one speaker talks for a long time period, break the speech into multiple paragraphs (see sample transcript).

INT: Ok. So how, how, how did you actually um meet him? You met him in class I guess? ¶
¶
AL: In class yeah, and we were in the same form as well so. ¶
¶
INT: How, how do you sort of um ... how do you sort of pass the time with him, you know when you guys are together? ¶
¶

(Continued)

(Continued)

AL: Both, well I suppose we just sat about sometimes, we also sort of played footie as you do and uh um ... he um, after our GCSEs, we um he had a villa in er Minorca um so there was a group of us planning to go out so we basically, we sat in er, during lunchtime planning what we were going to do, and we just sort of went to the pub. ¶

I mean my mum kicked me out at the age of sixteen and told me to go to the pub with the lads, and it's like 'Er yeah cheers mum' [laughs]. Er so you know we went to the pub every Friday and yeah just general stuff, you know just hanging around, meet up with some girls and stuff. ¶

¶
INT: ...

The reason for this is the ATLAS.ti referencing system for quotations. Each quotation has an ID, and paragraph numbers are used to indicate where it starts and finishes – so if you code just one sentence in a longer paragraph, the reference for the resulting quotation might not be precise enough.

This way of organizing the transcript can be used for any documents that include structuring elements, like dates in historical documents, emails or letters. The automatic coding tool can also be useful, and even though you may not know at this point whether you will want to use it, it is sensible to get used to all the above formatting rules as early as possible. Although neglecting these 'best practice rules' will not have a negative effect in the initial phase, you may later regret not having used them from the beginning.

In order for you to understand better why these transcription rules are recommended, here is a brief preview of the auto coding procedure:

- Open the HU 'Example Transcript' provided on the companion website.
- Open the auto coding tool via the main menu: **CODES / CODING / AUTO CODING**
- Enter one or more codes that you want to use for automatically coding all hits (Figure 2.3). A search term based on a string of characters or using regular expressions (GREP) is possible.
- Select where you want to search (in the currently selected document/in a selected group of documents based on a document family/in all documents).
- Select the length of the segment to be coded: the entered search term (it must be an exact match), the complete word, the sentence, the paragraph (single hard return), the text up to the next blank line (multiple hard returns) or the entire document (all text).
- Check whether the search should be case sensitive, whether GREP expressions are included in the term, and whether you want to confirm the coding of each hit.

In order to automatically code all of Alexander's speaking parts with his name, gender and student status, 'AL:' is used as the search term. The scope is set to the selected PD and the length of the segment to be coded is the speaker unit.

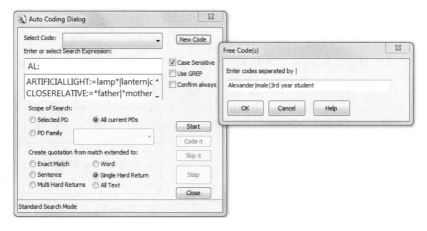

Figure 2.3   Preparing your data for getting maximum benefit from the auto coding tool

As each speaker unit is separated by a blank line, the option 'Multi Hard Returns' (¶) can be used here.

Best practice rules and solutions in a nutshell

Related to data file formats:

- When choosing a text format other than PDF, prepare your documents as rich text files in order to avoid conversion.
- In case your project includes doc or docx files, make sure that the latest doc(x) to rtf converter pack is installed on your computer.
- When considering PDF documents as primary data, pay attention to whether these are image or text PDFs.
- If you experience a problem in playing audio or video files, check the codec and – if necessary – install a complete codec pack.

Related to transcription:

- In Versions 5 and 6 avoid working with tables, since they are not properly displayed in rich text format in most cases.
- Clearly mark speakers or other text features by using unique identifiers.
- Separate the change of speakers and other divisions with blank lines (= two hard returns).
- Break long paragraphs into smaller units (but keep the units together by not entering a blank line). This results in more exact quotation references.

If you are interested in specific notations for preparing transcripts, see Jefferson (1984) or Kallmeyer and Schütze (1976).

1   Which data file formats can be analyzed with the support of ATLAS.ti?
2   What do you need to pay attention to when choosing a specific format for textual files?
3   What is important for Mac users to know when they want to work with ATLAS.ti?
4   What do you need to do if you want to work with non-Western languages?
5   What do you need to pay attention to when transcribing data? What are the recommended guidelines?

THREE

Project management: project setup for single users and teams

ATLAS.ti project management entails an understanding of how ATLAS.ti handles and accesses documents. It involves decisions regarding where HUs and documents are to be stored. Most problems can be avoided by a little informed planning about issues such as file locations and paths, and the need to copy, move and transfer ATLAS.ti projects across disks, networks and computers. For more general considerations in designing and conducting qualitative research in a software environment, see di Gregorio and Davidson (2008).

The most frequently asked support question related to project management is, 'Help, where are my documents?' You can imagine the panic that arises when, after months of coding, a user opens his or her project and cannot see the coded data on the screen: the entries in the drop-down lists are visible but the HU editor is empty. In most cases, I can help you to find the data again. However, there are situations where work is lost altogether. This is very rarely caused by the software itself; usually it is due to a lack of information. After reading this chapter and the addenda on further project management-related issues, you will most likely never have to ask, 'Where are my documents?'

In Version 7, project management will be less of an issue as ATLAS.ti will offer the option to manage the documents for the user. Currently, the users have to take care of data and project management themselves. This will still be possible in version 7 and is recommended, for example, when working with large video files. But for most projects the managed version will be suitable. It cannot hurt, however, to learn about a few technical issues that happen behind the scenes in terms of data and project management. It will also help you to better understand what it means to work with a managed project in Version 7.

Working with ATLAS.ti involves users, files and computers. An ATLAS.ti project can be as simple as a single person working with one HU and a few primary documents (P-Docs) on a stand-alone computer. It can be as complex as large teams working on different computers in a network or at different geographic locations; working on several projects at once; moving files between users, computers and networks; merging partial projects into compiled projects, and many other conceivable scenarios.

First, however, you need to know a few basics about how ATLAS.ti handles data and to understand that a well-managed project begins even before you enter any data: that is, when thinking of names for your files. After this, you will be ready to look at the three different project setup scenarios.

- Scenario 1 covers the largest variety of possible project situations and also works best for most users. It allows for easy transfer of projects and for data sharing. You can use it for small or for large-scale projects whether working on your own or in teams, either locally or widespread.
- Scenario 2 is for those that only want to analyze text files. It can be used by single users or teams. It explains a project setup where all files are created as internal documents. Thus, it is applicable for small to medium-sized projects with up to 100 documents.
- Scenario 3 applies to small-scale interview studies when you want to make use of the association function, linking transcripts with the original audio or video recordings.
- Scenario 4 has been included to cover very specific project situations. It applies to only a few cases. An example would be a project based on archive data stored in separate folders which cannot be incorporated under a common root folder.

The scenarios are written as hands-on exercises that you can follow either by using your own data or by downloading sample data from the companion website (http://www.quarc.de/qualitative-analysis-with-atlasti.html)

What you need to know before setting up a project

Each computer user, I assume, has a preferred way of organizing files and folders. When working with ATLAS.ti, you don't have to get used to a different way of handling or storing them. In that respect, ATLAS.ti is like any other Windows software you know. It may happen that users do not know where they have stored their ATLAS.ti project file simply because they have allowed ATLAS.ti to determine the location. They wouldn't do that when using Word, for instance; when they create a Word document and save it, they normally select a specific location where they want it to be stored. If they don't do that, Word saves the file to its default location – the My Documents or My Files folder – and the process is no different in ATLAS.ti. The default location for saving project files in ATLAS.ti is the so-called TextBank folder. It can be found under My Documents\Scientific Software\ATLAS.ti. You can save your project data at this location if you want to, but you don't have to. As in Word or Excel or any other application, you have a choice where to store your files.

Data handling in ATLAS.ti

Let's assume that you conduct an interview study with 20 audio-recorded interviews. You transfer the audio files to your computer and begin to transcribe and save the resulting text files somewhere on your computer, using your own system for organizing and storing them. Next, you want to analyse the data with the help of ATLAS.ti. You open ATLAS.ti and begin to add data to

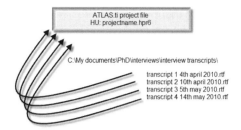

Figure 3.1 Explaining the ATLAS.ti referencing model

your project. You have read or seen somewhere that you can easily do that by dragging your data files from the file manager into the drop-down list for P-Docs. You begin to code and at some point you save your project via FILE/ SAVE, enter a project name and click on the Save button. This is what most new ATLAS.ti users do.

Now let's consider what happens 'behind the scenes'.

Figure 3.1 shows some transcript files stored in a subfolder called interview transcripts. The name of the file comprises the word 'transcript', a consecutive number and the date of transcription: 'transcript 1 4th April 2010.rtf'. As I will explain further, this is not a very good choice because the name does not include any information that could be helpful for the analysis. For the moment, we'll continue to work with this example. The blue arrows indicate the process of adding documents to an ATLAS.ti project. The word used in ATLAS.ti for this process is **assigning**.

Your ATLAS.ti project, the HU, is also a data file. It has the file extension hpr6. This stands for hermeneutic (h), project (pr), ATLAS.ti version 6 (6). The moment you assign a file, the HU stores the reference of the assigned document. For transcript 1 this reference is:

C:\My documents\PhD\interviews\interview transcripts\transcript 1 4th April 2010.rtf

For transcript 2 this reference is:

C:\My documents\PhD\interviews\interview transcripts\transcript 2 10th April 2010.rtf

And so on. The name of the function already indicates that the files are **assigned** to a project and not imported. They stay where they are on the hard disk. After assigning a file to a HU, you will find a shell for each document. The general name for this shell is **primary document**. The primary document has a name which is by default the name of the assigned data file; it contains the reference where the file is stored, the file type, date of creation and modification and the name of the ATLAS.ti user who has assigned it. Also, you have the option to add a comment to each shell. I will return to this later in the chapter. The important thing to remember is that the shell itself does not contain the assigned file. It can only load the file into the HU editor, based on the reference it has.

D:\My documents\PhD\interviews\interview transcripts\transcript 2 10th April 2010.rtf

What happens when you open the ATLAS.ti project and want to load one of the transcripts? Take a moment to think about it before I tell you.

The answer is that the HU goes looking for the files on the C drive, trying to follow the path that is stored as reference, but cannot find the document there. Thus, the document cannot be loaded and all you see are the drop-down lists and an empty HU editor. At the bottom of the screen, in the gray and unimposing status bar, the message 'file not found' is shown, followed by the full path reference. However, it is seldom that the file is truly lost. It simply cannot be found because it is no longer stored at the expected location. You can think of the reference as a kind of address for the file.

Let's assume we have met at some point somewhere on this globe. We liked each other and exchanged addresses just in case one of us was in the neighborhood at some point in time. As life goes on, you happen to visit Hanover and remember that I live nearby. You check my address on your mobile phone, call a taxi and tell the taxi driver to take you there.

Unfortunately, I recently moved and the address is no longer correct. You will no longer find my name at the door. This is exactly what happens when you move a document that you have assigned to a HU – and as HUs are not human beings, they cannot ask a neighbor if I left a new address. Nor do they feel sad (or panicky, or frustrated, or angry) that they were unable to find what they were looking for: that's only the users!

What can be done? You can either move all files back to the location where the HU expects them to be, or be a friendly neighbor and tell the HU about the new address; or – and this is what I recommend – you simply set up your project in a different way so that lost documents will never become an issue. You need to be in charge, and not let ATLAS.ti decide where to store your project files.

When the project is set up as shown in Figure 3.1, then the HU file ends up being stored in the TextBank folder and the data remain somewhere in your usual file system. The reference that is stored in this case is termed an 'absolute path reference'. As we have seen, this is not very flexible. If you want to move your project data or transfer a project to a different computer, it won't work without taking steps like renaming all path references. A better and much easier project setup is to store all data, including the HU file, in one folder. The main project folder can also contain subfolders in case you work with lots of data. This setup is called the HUPATH setup. Basically, what it means is that the path references are determined by the location of the HU. As long as all data *and* the HU are stored within a common folder, all documents can be accessed, no matter where the project folder is stored on your computer, flash drive, USB stick or server. Figure 3.2 shows a one-folder setup and a setup where subfolders are used.

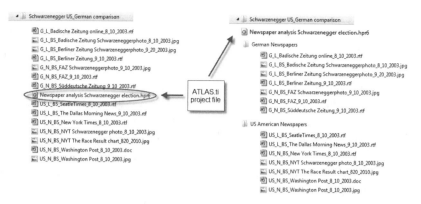

Figure 3.2 Recommended project setup – the HUPATH setup options

The project folder in this example is called **Schwarzenegger US_German comparison**. The documents are newspaper articles collected on the day and one day after the election of Arnold Schwarzenegger as governor in California in October 2003. In the sample setup to the left, all files are stored within one folder. A newspaper analysis, though, might easily contain a couple of hundred files and it could get a bit crowded if you store all of them in one folder. Instead, you can create subfolders based on countries or even smaller units within countries, like subfolders for local and national newspapers, broadsheets and tabloids, etc. For ATLAS.ti the number of subfolders does not matter; however, do not overdo the level of structuring at this point. You can group the data within the software as well, and only this will allow you to ask comparative questions. An elaborate subfolder structure in the file manager will not help you to accomplish this task. It is okay to store 100 or more files *plus* the HU file in one folder without using subfolders.

It is important to store a file in the project folder *before* you assign it. Assigning documents can be done at any point during the course of a project. When new data are added over time, give the file a good analytic name and then save it to its intended location in the project folder, either on the main level or in a subfolder. Then proceed to assign it.

Reasons for handling data via external file references

You may already have asked yourself why ATLAS.ti uses this way of handling data. There are good reasons for it:

- When data are not being imported, the size of a document does not affect the size of the HU to which it is assigned. This is a prerequisite for working with audio and video files, which are usually quite sizable. It also offers the possibility of working with a large set of data. Comparable software packages which import files often become quite slow or even crash when a larger data set is analyzed.
- A single data source file can be used by more than one project file. It may even be assigned to the same project multiple times, to allow for different angles of analysis.
- Team members can share data files. If the project is set up properly, changes to data sources (editing) are broadcast to all sub projects that use the files, keeping everyone up to date.

By the way, ATLAS.ti is not the only software that handles data in such a way. It is in fact a procedure common to many professional applications when things get large or complex. Video editing software, for instance, also manages its files in the form of one central project file and a number of dependent sub documents like snapshots, overlays, music or special effects. The objective is to reduce the overall size of the main document and make handling easier and faster. Word offers a similar option for managing large numbers of documents when writing a book, for example. An Internet link works on the same basis as well. When you click on a link, your browser loads and displays the linked page. A Web link is really nothing but a reference to another Web page. Such a reference is very much like a file name, except that the former is unique in the 'namespace' of the whole world, while a simple file name is unique only on a certain computer. However, if the linked page has ceased to exist, or has been moved or renamed, or if a connection to the site where the file resides can simply not be established, you will get a message that the page cannot be loaded. The same is true in ATLAS.ti.

About 'good' data file names

When storing your data within a common project folder alongside your HU, most 'Help, where are my documents?' questions will not be necessary unless you rename the files. Renaming files within your project folder will also result in your HU not finding the documents. Therefore it is a good idea to think about a good data file name before you assign documents, so there is no need to rename them later.

What I mean by 'good' is that the name should assist the analytic process. If you just use the first name you think of it won't actually hinder your analysis, but why not do yourself a favor by making it a bit easier? Naming a transcript 'transcript' – as in the example above – is only useful if you're working with other data sources as well. Numbering them consecutively and adding the date of transcription is useful for the process of transcription, but not for your analysis. More informative are names that include criteria which you already know are important for your analysis, like gender, age, profession, location and date of interview. This may not be the case for all studies and for all data analyzed in ATLAS.ti, but it does apply to a large number of projects. To prevent the data file names getting too long by adding all this information, my suggestion is to use a code as shown in Figure 3.2 and below:

G_N_BS_Süddeutsche Zeitung_9_10_2003

G_L_BS_Badische Zeitung_8_10_2003

US_N_New York Times_8_10_2003

Code:

G:	Germany
US:	US American

N:	national paper
L:	local
BS:	broadsheet
B:	tabloid
9_10_2003:	9th October 2003

In a real project, probably more than one article from a newspaper would be analyzed. In this case, the name of the newspaper could also be abbreviated to leave some space for adding the article's title.

Naming your files in this way has the advantage that the documents are already sorted by these criteria before assigning them. This facilitates creating subgroups of your documents in ATLAS.ti for analytical purposes when retrieving data and, overall, in adding transparency to your project.

Description of the sample data set

The data material provided on the companion website (www.quarc.de/qualitative-analysis-with-atlasti.html) consists of newspaper articles and pictures that were published on the day or the day after Arnold Schwarzenegger was elected Governor of California for the first time, in October 2003. The English-only version of the sample data contains nine documents, the English/German version 12 documents. I will continue to use this data set as an example throughout the book.

The sample data set has been chosen for use by people from a variety of disciplines and countries. The data files are short – the longest one is six pages – and fairly quick to read. Another advantage of this data set is that most readers probably remember the occasion due to worldwide press coverage. Also, it is not too difficult to find it vaguely interesting as nearly everyone has heard of Arnold Schwarzenegger and has some kind of opinion of him. I have used this data set as sample material since 2003, along with a few others; this is the one that has proved to work best.

The main issue to investigate in this project is how the news that Arnold Schwarzenegger was elected Governor of California was portrayed in the media. Did all newspapers report the same thing? Were there differences? In order to examine this rather general question, we need to look at smaller issues: how the reports differed in terms of the topics covered, the evaluation of the event, the language used, the style of reporting, the layout of the article, the use of headings and subheadings, the use of photographs and images, and the type of sources drawn upon. Can the differences be explained by the type of newspaper, its political orientation, its readership or nationality?

Let's start setting up this project in ATLAS.ti so that we can find some answers to these questions in later chapters.

Setting up a project

There are more possible ways to set up a project than are described here. My aim, however, is not to confuse you with too many options but, rather, to provide you with straightforward instructions that probably cover 99 percent of conceivable circumstances. Generally it can be stated that project management is least complex if you can store all project-related documents in the same folder along with the HU itself or in sub folders (scenarios 1 and 2). ATLAS.ti can also handle situations where files are distributed across the file system and across networks. Then other considerations will apply (see scenario 3).

Scenario 1: the one folder setup – for single users and teams

Storing all data files to be analyzed and the ATLAS.ti project file in one folder – as shown in Figure 3.2 – is the easiest and most flexible way to set up a project. Even when working with video files or other sizable data sets that you may store on an external hard disk or server, you can still use this setup. You just need to save the ATLAS.ti project file (the HU) on the external disk or server as well. This scenario also works well for team projects. Each team member stores the project folder with all of the data on his or her computer, or the project folder is kept on a server. In the team project case a few more issues need to be considered, like working with user accounts and different sub-HUs. Teams can follow the instructions for the sample data set and then continue to read the add-ons for team projects.

Project setup

- Download and unzip the sample data set. The name of the unzipped project folder is 'Newspaper analysis Schwarzenegger election'.
- Store the project folder at any location on your computer. For ease of explanation, let's assume that the project folder is stored on the desktop. The project folder already contains all data that we want to analyze – no subfolders are used.
- Open ATLAS.ti. Check the title bar. If the last used HU is open and not a new one, select the main menu option **FILE / CLOSE**. The text in the title bar should read: New Hermeneutic Unit.

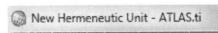

- Select the main menu option **DOCUMENTS / ASSIGN**.
- A file loader window opens. Navigate to the desktop and then to your project folder. Select all documents in the folder (Figure 3.3). If you are working with the ATLAS.ti demo version, select only 10 documents, as this version won't allow you to save more than that when it comes to saving the project. To select all documents, you can use the key combination **CTRL+A**.
- Click on the Open button (it will appear in the language of your Windows system).
- You can now see some entries in the P-Docs field (Figure 3.4). Open the list to check it. All documents are numbered consecutively.
- Left click on each document to find out whether you can load the documents on your computer.

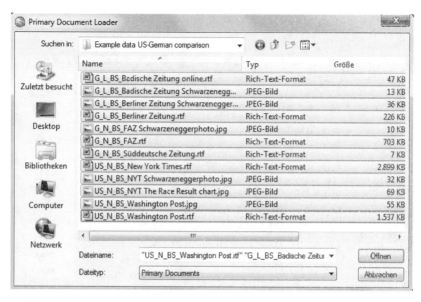

Figure 3.3   Loading primary documents

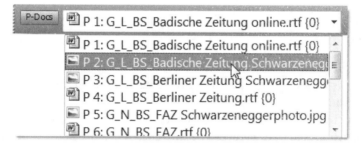

Figure 3.4   Assigned documents in the P-Docs drop-down list

Documents are assigned in alphabetical order as listed in the file manager, and each document name starts with the country code; so the documents are sorted first by country, then by local and national paper, then by type of paper (all broadsheets here) and finally by newspaper title.

Open the Primary Document Manager by clicking on the P-Docs button.

I am often asked how to present and report on a project that has been analyzed with the assistance of ATLAS.ti. Look at the list of document names in the P-Doc Manager (Figure 3.5). This is where to start – use the P-Docs Manager to explain your sampling. If well chosen, the names will already include some of the major sampling criteria. In addition, such criteria are often useful in making comparisons later on. This means we need to create subgroups of data and this is also facilitated when the names already contain analytically important information.

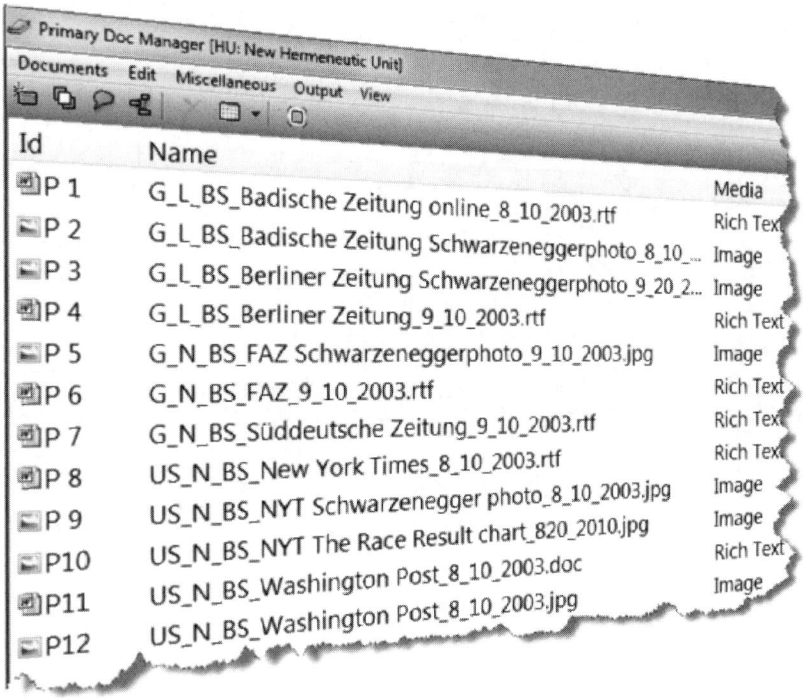

Figure 3.5 Using the PDoc Manager for presentation purposes

In case the alphabetical order is not useful for your purposes, or if you do not assign all the data at once, you can always drag and drop a document to a different location.

It may not always be possible to know from the very beginning what might be a good analytical name – or perhaps you have already created a project before reading my suggestions. In that case, you have the option to rename each primary document (right click on a primary document in the P-Docs Manager and select the option **Rename**). Renaming a primary document does not affect the data file names on the hard disk. It is only an internal change reflected in the HU. Thus, the entries in the Name column in the P-Docs Manager will differ from the entries in the Origin column when you change the name of a primary document.

Let's save the project before we do anything else, as we do not want to risk losing anything:

- Move the slider in the P-Doc Manager over to the right so that you can see the column **Origin.** As we have not saved the HU yet, it shows a long absolute path reference for each document. In my case:

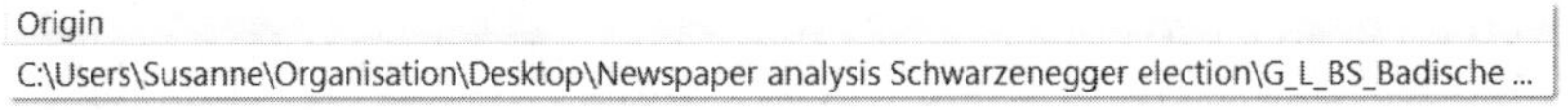

  Origin
  C:\Users\Susanne\Organisation\Desktop\Newspaper analysis Schwarzenegger election\G_L_BS_Badische ...

- Leave the P-Docs Manager at this position and proceed to save. Select the main option FILE / SAVE (or SAVE AS...).

Origin
<HUPATH>\G_L_BS_Badische Zeitung online_8_10_2003.rtf
<HUPATH>\G_L_BS_Badische Zeitung Schwarzeneggerphoto_8_10_2003.jpg
<HUPATH>\G_L_BS_Berliner Zeitung Schwarzeneggerphoto_9_20_2003.jpg
<HUPATH>\G_L_BS_Berliner Zeitung_9_10_2003.rtf

Figure 3.6 HUPATH entries in the Primary Document Manager

A window opens where you can specify the location of the HU file and its name. The default location is the TextBank folder. *Do not* save the HU there!

- Navigate to your project folder (in my case the desktop and then the folder 'Newspaper analysis Schwarzenegger election'). The folder appears empty, as only files of the type *.hpr6 are shown. You can see this at the bottom of the window, where there is a field for file types.
- Enter a name for the HU, your ATLAS.ti project file (e.g. 'My first test project' or 'Newspaper analysis of Schwarzenegger election').
- Click on the save button shown in the language of your Windows system.
- Now, take a look at the column '**Origin**' in the P-Docs Manager again. If you followed the instructions correctly, then all absolute path references are replaced with the entry <HUPATH> (Figure 3.6).

Congratulations. That was probably the biggest hurdle in terms of project management in ATLAS.ti. The project can now be moved to any location: you simply have to move the entire folder. If you have finished with the project for today, it is probably not a good idea to leave it on the desktop: just as with non-virtual desks, it's good practice to clear up the computer after work. Thus, you could move the project to a more secure place within your file system, store a copy of the project folder on a server or external device, or send a zipped version of the project folder (in case it is not too large) to yourself or another person via email.

As mentioned earlier, in Version 7 you will have the option that ATLAS.ti manages your project for you. Basically what happens is that ATLAS.ti will create the above described one folder scenario for you by copying the documents that you assign into a repository. ATLAS.ti then no longer needs the original files and you can do with them whatever you want. Even if you delete them, this won't destroy the integrity of your ATLAS.ti project. To transfer a project between computers you need to use the built-in copy bundle function (see addenda). The location of the repository can be defined by the user, e.g. if you prefer a location on a server when working on a team project.

Before I begin to present the next three scenarios, I would like to discuss two additional issues: (1) commenting on your primary documents and (2) organizing them. As a good practice rule I recommend performing these tasks as a part of the project setup whenever applicable.

Commenting on documents

It is possible to enter a comment for each document. This may not be necessary for all types of projects, but users often do not think of adding information to the HU that they already have. My advice is to include all information in the HU that is relevant for the analysis. When working with newspaper articles, as in our example, you could add information about each newspaper into the P-Docs comment field, such as a description of the newspaper, its circulation, readership, etc. When analyzing interview transcripts, researchers often write an interview protocol. But instead of adding it to their ATLAS.ti project they store the protocols as Word files in some other folder. The better option is to copy and paste the protocols into the comment field of the respective primary document. The likelihood that you will look at the protocols again is much greater when they become part of your ATLAS.ti project. This is how it works:

- Select a primary document in the P-Docs Manager. The white field (as you may remember from Chapter 1) is a text editor and thus the place where to enter a comment.
- Type text into the comment area or copy and paste text from Word.
- When you are finished, click on another document in the P-Docs Manager. This action automatically saves your entry. In addition you will see a tilde (~) after the document name (you may have to extend the name column a bit to see it) (Figure 3.7).

Organizing documents into groups (= creating variables)

Grouping documents as soon as you set up a project is a nice easy way to begin. Getting started is a whole task in itself, so adding some structure is a good way to add analytic content to an as yet 'empty' project. Document groups, also called P-Doc Families in ATLAS.ti, contribute to the clear organization of the data material. During later stages, they are used as filters and in queries. Although exactly when to create primary document families is a question of the personal preference of the analyst and also depends on the nature of the project.

Examples for document groups are the classic socio-demographic variables such as gender, age groups, material status, profession, location, etc. In our newspaper analysis, possible groups are: country, circulation, type of newspaper or media.

Documents in ATLAS.ti are grouped via the so-called document families. The term 'family' has been derived from the concept of code families used in grounded theory. A code family is basically a group of codes. This was adopted

P 4   G_L_BS_Berliner Zeitung_9_10_2003.rtf~

Figure 3.7   Commented primary document

in ATLAS.ti for primary documents and memos as well. The family managers are the places where to create, describe, modify and delete families.

- To open the family manager for primary documents, you can either use the main menu **Documents** / **Edit Families** / **Open Family Manager**, or – if the P-Docs Manager is already open – you can simply click on the family manager button (see right). You will find this button in all managers, and also for creating code families and memo families.
- On the lower right-hand side of the window, you will see the list of all documents that can be sorted into a family. The first step is to create a family. Again you can use the menu for this (**Families** / **New Family**) or click on the 'Create a new item' button. It is worthwhile remembering this button. It appears in all windows where new objects can be created.
- We want to create two families. If you're using the English/German data set, you can create a family **German Newspapers** and another **US American Newspapers**. If working with the English-only data set, create the two families **local** and **national**.
- Next, we need to add documents to each family (Figure 3.8). Highlight, for instance, the family 'German Newspapers'. Then select all documents that start with the letter G in the lower right hand corner of the window.

For selecting documents, common Windows procedures can be used, like holding down the Shift key to select a list of consecutive documents, or the Ctrl

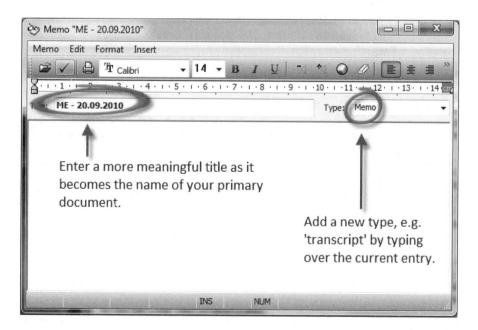

Figure 3.8 Adding documents to a family

key to select them one by one. Documents can also be selected and moved individually by double clicking on them.

- Click on the button with the left-pointing arrow to move the selected documents into the family.
- Next, highlight the document family 'US American Newspapers'. Select the suitable documents and add them to the family.
- You can write a description of each family in the lower part of the family manager in case the family name is not self-explanatory.

Did you notice, when selecting the second family, that all documents became available again for inclusion in the family? This suggests that it is possible to add each document to more than one family. It is not an exclusive either/or allocation. One document can be a member of the families 'German Newspapers', 'Local' and 'Broadsheet'. During the course of the analysis, families can be combined in a number of ways. For instance, you can compare all articles from local German newspapers to all articles from local US American newspapers. Or in a different data set, you may want to compare all comments made on a topic by all female elementary school teachers to all comments on the same topic made by female high school teachers. The document families in ATLAS.ti are a prerequisite for such questions being asked. It might also explain why the term 'family' is still used instead of attribute or variable, as is the case in other programs. As in real life, we are usually members of more than one family. We are born into a family of origin, we might get married and become part of the in-laws family; later we might get divorced, remarry and end up with kids in both families ... . The same is true for documents, codes and memos that you pull together using their respective object family.

A primary document can only be assigned reasonably to one or more families, if the mentioned characteristics refer to the whole of the document. For example, if you interview two people, a man and a woman, or conduct a group interview with 10 people, you can assign the interview neither to the family **male** nor to the family **female**. In this case, the variables **male** and **female** have to be assigned directly to the statements of each person via codes. This is easiest done by using the automatic coding function in combination with the transcription guidelines provided in Chapter 2.

Exporting and importing information on document groups

Outputting your document groups in the form of an Excel table is an interesting option, if you are working with a large number of families or your database consists of mixed quantitative and qualitative data. I insert a brief description of this option here as users often do not realize that it exists, discovering only later that it would have been useful for their projects.

The Excel table can appear in two ways, depending on the naming convention used for the families. Above, I used a simple descriptive name like 'German Newspapers'. In a quantitative sense, the appropriate variable label would be 'Country' with the two values Germany and USA. When using a descriptive label, each family is turned into a dichotomous variable with the values 0 and 1. When adding the variable label to the name using the following naming convention, **Country::Germany / Country::USA**, the Excel table will show **Country** as the variable label and the entries after the double column (::) as nominal labels in the cells.

To create such a table:

- Close the P-Docs Family Manager so that all entered information is saved. From the main menu select Documents / Miscellaneous / Export PD-Family Table.
- Next you need to select whether to create an Excel-compatible csv or an xls file.
- As output destination, select File & Run. Accept the suggested name or enter a new name. When entering a new name, you need to add the xls extension manually.
- Save the file. The default location is TextBank. A better location, however, is a subfolder within your main project folder. You may want to call it 'Output' and store there all the output files that you create during the course of the analysis. The file is directly opened in Excel, executed by the command **Run**.

Figures 3.9 and 3.10 show the two possible appearances based on the naming convention used.

PD-Family Tables can also be imported. This is a useful option in combination with survey data when information is already available in spreadsheet format. The easiest way to prepare such a table is to first export a table with no families entered. This way you don't have to create the document and name column yourself. The table usually also provides further information about path and origin. This information has been deleted in preparing the images for Figures 3.9 and 3.10. For further instructions on how to export and import tables, I refer you to the manual. Here I just want to point out that this option exists.

	A	B	C	D	E	F
			German	US American		
1	documents	Name	Newspapers	Newspapers	local	national
2	P 1	G_L_BS_Badische Zeitung onli	1	0	1	0
3	P 2	G_L_BS_Badische Zeitung Sch\	1	0	1	0
4	P 3	G_L_BS_Berliner Zeitung Schw	1	0	1	0
5	P 4	G_L_BS_Berliner Zeitung_9_1(	1	0	1	0
6	P 5	G_N_BS_FAZ Schwarzenegger	1	0	0	1
7	P 6	G_N_BS_FAZ_9_10_2003.rtf	1	0	0	1
8	P 7	G_N_BS_Süddeutsche Zeitung	0	0	0	1
9	P 8	US_N_BS_New York Times_8_	0	1	0	1
10	P 9	US_N_BS_NYT Schwarzenegge	0	1	0	1
11	P 10	US_N_BS_NYT The Race Resul:	0	1	0	1
12	P 11	US_N_BS_Washington Post_8_	0	1	0	1
13	P 12	US_N_BS_Washington Post_8_	0	1	0	1

Figure 3.9 PD-Family Table showing dichotomous variables

	A	B	C	D
1	documents	Name	#Circulation	#Country
2	P 1	G_L_BS_Badische Zeitung on	local	Germany
3	P 2	G_L_BS_Badische Zeitung Sch	local	Germany
4	P 3	G_L_BS_Berliner Zeitung Sch	local	Germany
5	P 4	G_L_BS_Berliner Zeitung_9_1	local	Germany
6	P 5	G_N_BS_FAZ Schwarzenegge	national	Germany
7	P 6	G_N_BS_FAZ_9_10_2003.rtf	national	Germany
8	P 7	G_N_BS_Süddeutsche Zeitun	national	Germany
9	P 8	US_N_BS_New York Times_8	national	USA
10	P 9	US_N_BS_NYT Schwarzenegg	national	USA
11	P 10	US_N_BS_NYT The Race Resu	national	USA
12	P 11	US_N_BS_Washington Post_8	national	USA
13	P 12	US_N_BS_Washington Post_8	national	USA

Figure 3.10 PD-Family Table using nominal labels

Additional information for teams

When working in a team, you can set up your project in the same way as recommended for single users. What may be different is the location of the project folder, depending on the nature of the project. Basically, there are two possibilities: to store it on a server that each team member can access; or, if access to a server is not always possible, team members can also store the project folder on their personal hard disks or external storage device. The one-folder setup is the optimal solution for all these scenarios.

In the following section, only the technical aspects of data management are discussed, such as the role and tasks of the project administrator and those of the team members. In addition, members of a team project need to discuss a number of further issues like how to develop the coding system, how to divide the work, how and when to inform the others about what one has done, how to share the analysis, etc. You will find further suggestions for team work throughout this book, directly linked to various topics like coding, writing memos and asking questions about the data.

Finding a project administrator

When working in a team, it is best to nominate one person to be the project administrator. If not everyone's skill is equal, choose the person with the greatest knowledge of ATLAS.ti and the highest degree of computer literacy. Even though you don't have to be a computer whizz to work with ATLAS.ti, anyone who does not know how to copy files, or has trouble converting doc files into rich text format, or does not know how to search for a file within the system, is not so well suited to the task. The job of the administrator is to set up the project, to distribute it to team members, to provide instructions for team members, and to collect the subprojects from time to time in order to merge them.

Creating user accounts

You may already have noticed in some of the above figures that my name is shown in the author field. If no other user account is created first, the superuser is the default login and all new entries are stamped with the author name 'Super'. When working in a team, it is clearly important to know who has done what, so not all entries should be stamped 'Super'. Creating a user account and logging in with a personal user name allows to trace the steps of the various team members. It is not a perfect system for every situation, but in most cases it is the best option. For example, modifications to an already existing object like a code are not automatically tracked. The author field only contains the name of the user who has created the object and not the name of the person who modified it.

User accounts are best created by each individual team member and not by the project administrator. Here is what you need to do:

- User information is stored in the program file directory. Therefore, in Vista and Windows 7, you need to start ATLAS.ti as an administrator, or you will not be able to store a newly created user account. Close ATLAS.ti and reopen it by right clicking on the Software icon instead of left clicking. Then choose the option: **Run as administrator**. A message will pop up asking you to allow this and then ATLAS.ti informs you that you run the software with administrative credentials.
- From the main menu, select EXTRAS / USER EDITOR. A window opens showing the three standard users: admin, guest and super.
- To create a new account, select EDIT / NEW USER. Four entry fields pop up, one after the other, asking you to enter an account name, a password, your last name and your first name.

You can enter a password or leave the field blank. You are not asked for a password unless you specify this in the user.ini file, since password protecting the user name is only asked for on rare occasions.

- Save the newly created user account by selecting FILE / SAVE from the User Editor window. A small window pops up informing you that the user base has been saved to disk.
- Close the User Editor.

Logging in:

- From the main menu select EXTRAS / LOGIN. Select your user account (Figure 3.11). Notice that you are not required to enter a password and that the default setting is 'Automatic Login'.

After logging in, you are greeted by the software. If you're working late or at weekends, however, the software may not be so friendly: I'll leave it to you to see what happens! ATLAS.ti will remember the setting and there is no need to log in every time. The automatic login can remain activated as long as the same user always works on the same computer. Only when different people use

Figure 3.11 Logging in using a personal user account

ATLAS.ti on the same computer at different times does this option need to be deactivated; in this case, the login window comes up each time you launch the software.

The server-based setup

Figure 3.12 illustrates the server-based team project setup. This is how it works:

- Marie, as project administrator, sets up the project using the one-folder (or HUPATH) setup. At this stage, she can log in as administrator so all new entries that she creates are authored by 'admin'. The name for the HU should contain the project name and also indicate that it is the Master HU.

Whether you actually call it Master or something else does not matter. What you need to know is that team members cannot work on one HU file simultaneously. Each person needs to work on a copy of the original 'Master' file. These copies need to be merged from time to time to create a new up-to-date Master file.

- The project administrator uploads the project folder to the server.
- All team members access the project folder on the server, create a copy of the Master file and rename it. A good naming convention is to add one's name or initials to the project name as shown in Figure 3.12.

The project folder on the server then contains all data files, the Master HU and the sub-HUs of the various team members as shown in Figure 3.13. I call them sub-HUs, as they do not remain pure copies of the original Master. Each team member now begins to work on a particular task and makes changes to his or her personal HU. The sum of all personal HUs results a few days later in a new Master HU which now contains the work of all team members.

- At an agreed time (e.g. every Friday at 4 pm), Marie accesses the project folder on the server and merges the four sub-HUs. Merging is explained at greater length in the addenda.

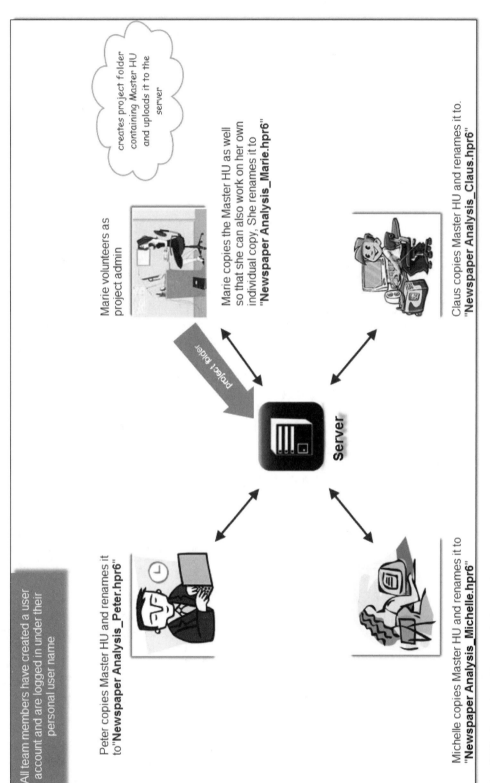

Figure 3.12 Server-based team project scenario

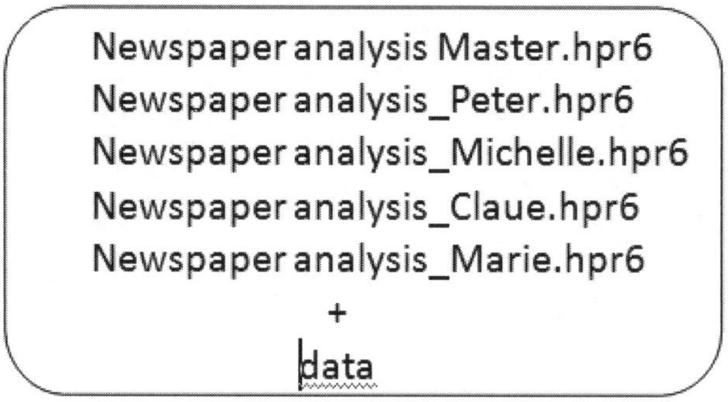

Newspaper analysis Master.hpr6

Newspaper analysis_Peter.hpr6

Newspaper analysis_Michelle.hpr6

Newspaper analysis_Claue.hpr6

Newspaper analysis_Marie.hpr6

+

data

Figure 3.13   Project folder before merging

The merged HU is still called Master, but this time the date of merging is added, so the project folder now contains only the new Master HU and the data (Figure 3.14). The old sub-HUs are deleted or moved to a backup folder.

- On Monday morning, all team members access the server again, create a copy of the new Master HU, rename it and continue to work.

Working with the server-based approach allows each team member to edit all primary documents when they see the need to make changes like correcting spelling mistakes, correcting transcripts or adding data (see addenda for further details). ATLAS.ti tracks all changes and all sub-HUs are updated; the codings are adjusted whenever a team member accesses a modified document. This is different in the more complex team scenario discussed next, where team members do not always have access to the same server.

   Note: Team members should not change the order of the primary documents in the P-Docs Manager. This creates problems for the project administrator when merging the sub-HUs. The administrator can reorder the documents in each HU, but this means additional work.

Complex team scenario involving various locations and computers

The initial tasks that need to be completed when the members of a team cannot or do not want to be server based all the time are the same. The scenario

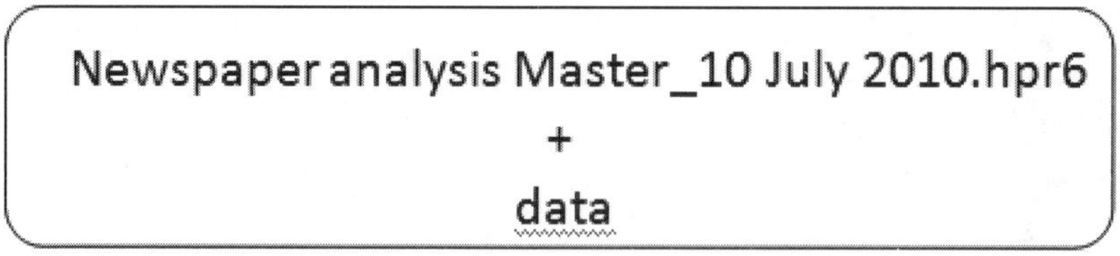

Newspaper analysis Master_10 July 2010.hpr6

+

data

Figure 3.14   Project folder after merging

depicted in Figure 3.15 describes teams working at different geographic locations, but it also applies to teams that work in the same institution. It is quite common today for someone to work in more than one place, like a university office and at home, or to work while traveling. When a team is spread out geographically, data exchange may not always be possible via a common server. In such cases, the server might be replaced by the Web, so data are exchanged via email or an online link is provided to download the data using a server somewhere. This is how to proceed:

- Marie has again volunteered to be the project administrator. She sets up the project using the one-folder setup. For this task she logs in as admin.
- She then makes the project folder available to the other team members via a server, an online link, a CD or DVD sent by regular mail, or – if the database is not too large – as a WinZip or copy bundle file via email.

The copy bundle file is a compressed version of the project folder and thus similar to a WinZip file when working with the one-folder setup. It is an option provided by ATLAS.ti and explained in more detail in the addenda.

- The team members log in under their respective user names.
- They download or copy the entire project folder to their personal computer or laptop. The location of the project folder does not matter, it can be stored anywhere.
- The team members rename the Master HU. There is no need to copy it as they already have copied the entire project folder. Let's take Michelle as an example. She has copied the project folder from the server to her desktop computer. She renames the Master HU to 'Newspaper Analysis_Michelle.hpr6' and begins to work. On Friday she decides that she wants to do some more work over the weekend and thus needs to transfer the project to her laptop.
- She copies the entire project folder to a memory stick and from there to her laptop.
- On Monday she continues to work in the office on her desktop computer. As the data are now stored on both computers, she only needs to take along the HU file. There is no need to overwrite the entire project folder with each transfer as long as the primary data source files are not modified.

You add an additional layer of complexity to this scenario when allowing for the data source files to be edited. The best solution is to leave this task to the project administrator, who can incorporate changes into a new Master HU and distribute the updated database to all team members, otherwise the process will require a lot of coordination and errors are likely to occur. Whatever the case may be, never modify an already coded document before reading either the chapter on editing primary documents in the manual or the addenda to this book. Editing is not difficult, but it is a crucial task. You do not want to end up with a project full of misaligned codes.

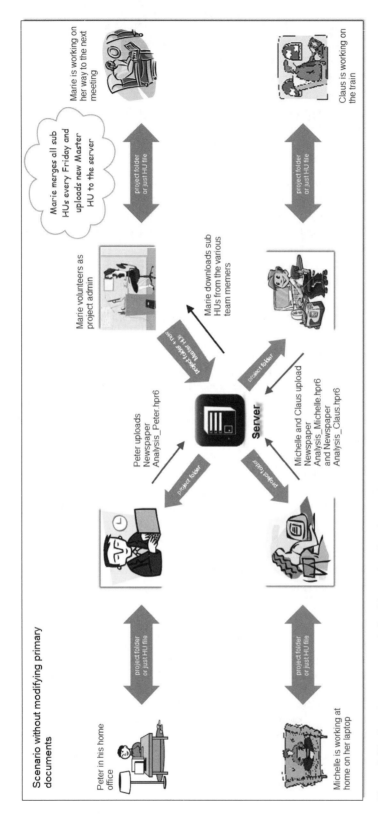

Figure 3.15 Complex team scenario involving various locations and computers

The team has agreed to combine the individual work carried out by each researcher after three weeks. This means sending all sub-HUs to Marie, the project administrator.

- When a server is available, each team member saves the sub-HU into the project folder located on the server. If this is not possible, the sub-HU files can be sent via email to Marie.
- Marie collects all sub-HUs in order to merge them. She can either add her own sub-HU to the three others on the server, or move the sub-HUs to her personal computer and merge them there.

One reason for merging the sub projects locally might be an unstable connection to the server; apart from that, ATLAS.ti does not mind where the merging takes place.

- When Marie merges the sub-HUs on her personal computer, she needs to save the new Master file to the project folder on the server. When the files are merged on the server directly, all old sub-HUs should be deleted or moved to a backup folder.
- When the new Master HU is on the server, Marie informs the other team members. In case a server is not available, she emails the new Master HU file to each team member. As all team members already have a complete copy of the data set, sending the new HU file is sufficient. The HU contains all codings, comments, memos, networks and all the newly created ATLAS.ti objects, and reflects the current status of the work in progress.
- The team continues to work until the next agreed 'merging day'.

Scenario 2: working with internal documents (for projects containing only text files)

Using version 6.2 or higher, it is possible to create internal documents. This means you no longer have to worry about document references and document locations. Your ATLAS.ti project consists of a single data file, the HU. This project setup can be used for smaller projects where the data material comprises text documents only. As this function was added to the software at the time of writing, it is difficult to know yet how small is small. I am currently working on a project that contains 40 interviews as internal documents. The total size of the documents outside ATLAS.ti is 5.3 MB. The HU file containing all documents plus the coding, etc. has a size of 730k. Thus, my best guess is that ATLAS.ti can easily handle projects containing up to 100 internal documents without slowing down too much.

This approach is also a good option for working with sensitive data material. When saving the HU, the data material is highly compressed and therefore unreadable outside ATLAS.ti. In addition, the HU can be password protected. This should make unauthorized access reasonably difficult.

This is how it works: you generate a new empty text document within ATLAS.ti and then you copy and paste into it the contents that you want to analyze:

- Open ATLAS.ti and select the main menu option **Documents / Assign / New Text Document**.
- Enter a name for the document into the window that opens.

The document is loaded in Edit Mode.

- Copy the text you want to analyze and paste it into the primary document.
- Protect the document by quitting Edit Mode. You will find the edit mode button in the second toolbar below the main menu on the left hand side. Click on the pen and select the option **Save and Leave Edit Mode**.

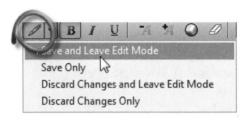

- Proceed in the same way with all other documents that you want to analyze.
- Save the HU file.

Make sure that you always create a backup copy of this file and store it in a safe location!

Scenario 3: project setup for transcripts and synchronized media files

Note: *You can download an example f4 transcript and audio file from the companion website to follow the instructions starting at the point marked with an asterisk (*).*

The advantage of this project setup is that the transcripts remain linked to their original audio or video files. Thus, you can select a quotation and play the associated audio or video segment (see Chapter 1, p. 28). Transcripts prepared in f4 are not assigned; they are in fact imported and are stored within the HU file as embedded documents. An alternative is to transcribe your data directly in ATLAS.ti instead of using f4. If you do so, you can create internal documents as explained above for scenario 2 and associate them with your audio or video files in the Association Editor (**A-Docs / Edit Associations**). Refer to the manual for more detailed instructions on how to transcribe data with ATLAS.ti.

The associated media files are not imported. This means that the ATLAS.ti project will contain a mix of internal and referenced documents. The internal documents are the transcripts and for the media file the one-folder setup can be used (see Figure 3.18 below).

By the way, f4 uses the same method of referencing as ATLAS.ti does. When using f4 to transcribe your data, store all audio files in one folder and, when saving the transcripts, save them in the same folder as the audio files. You can use this folder later as your ATLAS.ti project folder.

- Save all audio files in the same folder when downloading them from your recording device.
- Rename the audio files to something more meaningful than the default name given by your recording device.

My suggestion is that you use the same name that you later want to use for your primary documents (see: 'About "good" data file names' on p. 38). The reason for using the same name at this point is that f4 creates an association between the audio file and the transcript by way of the data file names. If you later change the names of the audio file or the transcript, this association will be lost. You can recreate the association by reloading both the audio file and transcript in f4, but that means unnecessary extra work.

- Prepare the transcripts in f4. When you save them, save them under the name that you want to use as the primary document name in ATLAS.ti.
- Store all transcripts together with the audio files in the same folder. You can use this folder as your ATLAS.ti project folder or leave it as backup and create a copy to use as your project folder. The latter makes sense if you begin your analysis before all interviews have been conducted and all transcripts finished. You can then successively copy and paste transcripts and associated audio files into the project folder once completed.
- Open ATLAS.ti and select **A-Docs / Import f4 Documents... .**
- A file loader window opens. Go to the location where your transcript and audio files are stored. Only the rtf transcripts will be shown. Select one or more transcripts and click on the button **Open**.

If the audio file is stored in the same folder, as recommended, the audio file is automatically assigned as primary document and the two documents are associated. Let's see what happens to the HU after importing an f4 document.

- Open the list for P-Docs. It shows the transcript and the audio file.

Figure 3.16 shows the transcript and the audio file of an interview (I) with me (Friese, w for female) as expert (Exp) in computer-assisted qualitative methodologies.

- Load the transcript. This loads the associations with the audio file as well so that we can take a look at them. Then open the Association Editor: **A-Docs / Edit Associations**.
- When you click on an association (Figure 3.17), the associated text segment is highlighted in the transcript. If it does not work, then the synchro mode is not activated. Press **F3** or select **A-Docs / Synchro Mode**.
- Press **Ctrl+P** to listen to the highlighted text in the transcript (or **A-Docs / Play Selected Text**).
- Save the project file: **File / Save** to the same folder as transcripts and audio files.
- As the transcripts were imported in the ATLAS.ti HU, you can remove them from the project folder so you end up with a folder that contains only the HU and the audio files (Figure 3.18).

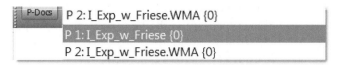

Figure 3.16 P-Docs drop-down list after importing an f4 transcript

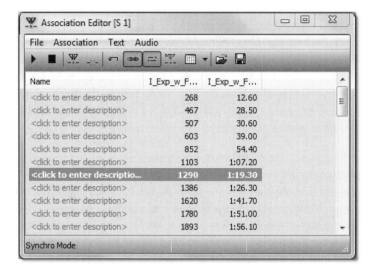

Figure 3.17 Association editor showing the links between the transcript and the audio file

Figure 3.18 Project folder when working with internal f4 documents and associated audio files

Scenario 4: documents and HU file need to remain at different locations

If it is not possible to add all data files to a common folder, then you need to set up the project with absolute path references. Using absolute path references means you must be careful when moving and renaming documents. There is nothing to worry about but it involves some extra work – and if it is not necessary to use this setup, I do not recommend it.

> By the way, working with a set of video files or other large databases stored on an external hard disk is not necessarily a reason to save the HU file in a different location. I recommend saving the HU file on the external device as well.

If it is unavoidable, here is a list of issues that you need to be aware of.

Location of the HU file

Think about an appropriate location to store the HU file. A good place might be the TextBank folder under the Scientific Software\ATLAS.ti folder under My Files.

Project transfer

The transfer of such a project to a different computer is not as straightforward as working with the one-folder setup. The situation on the target computer can differ considerably from the computer on which the project was created. You need to use the ATLAS.ti copy bundle function to transfer such a project (see addenda for further details).

If the original project references a drive that does not exist on the target computer, then transferring is still possible but you need to use the path mapping option.

Mapping paths

Select the main menu option DOCUMENTS / DATA SOURCE MANAGEMENT / EDIT PRIMARY-DOCUMENT MAPPINGS (Figure 3.19).

- Enter the previously valid path on the left side (From:) and click on ADD PATH.
- Enter the new path on the right hand side (To:). Click on ADD PATH to enter it as the target path.
- Click on APPLY & CLOSE.

Mapping path reference can also become an issue when storing data on external devices in combination with using absolute path references. You need to be aware of the fact that the drive letter may change depending on the computer it is connected to. It could be the D drive, but if the D drive is already in use the computer may use the E drive for the external device. This results in the HU not being able to load the documents as the references still point to the D drive. A similar situation arises if the server administration suddenly decides that the network drive is no longer a Z drive, but an H drive. The solution in such cases is to map the original path including subfolders as has been explained above.

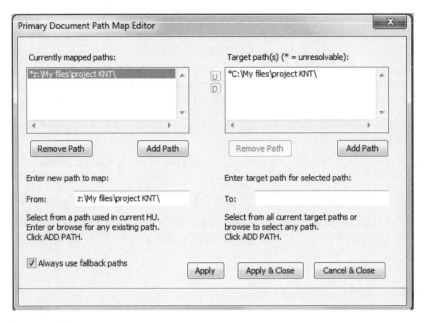

Figure 3.19 Mapping paths

Mapping, however, only applies to drive and folder names, not to single file names. If you need to make changes to file names, you need to proceed as follows.

Changing path references

If file names or locations are changed, you need to 'tell' the HU about the new details. This needs to be done manually for each file.

- To change a reference for a primary document, open the P-Docs Manager.
- Right click on the primary document for which you need to change the reference and select the option DATA SOURCE MANAGEMENT / CHANGE PATH.
- Correct the path information in the *window that comes up and click on the OK button.*

Summary

The ATLAS.ti way of handling documents offers flexibility and economy in handling large numbers of sizable documents and allows teams to work concurrently on shared data sources. However, you need to be aware of what it means to access documents via external references, as has been discussed in this chapter.

Before starting a new project, give some thought to the names and location of the documents and the HU. Choosing a proper location can make your work significantly easier, especially when it comes to team work. Maximum flexibility can be achieved by storing all associated documents in a common folder hierarchy.

When working on smaller projects like interview studies, it is also possible to work with internal documents and to make use of the associated document function where you can link transcripts with the original audio or video files. Setting up a project using absolute path references is not recommended unless the other options cannot be implemented.

In the context of setting up a project, you may want to consider: (1) adding comments to your primary documents, usually some kind of meta information; and (2) using document families as a way of organizing your project and adding its first structural element.

REVIEW QUESTIONS

1   How does ATLAS.ti handle documents?
2   Why is it important to know this?
3   Why does ATLAS.ti handle data in such a way?
4   How should you set up and organize your own project?

GLOSSARY OF TERMS

Document families: Document families in ATLAS.ti can be thought of as variables. Technically they are a group of documents. You can for instance group all female and male respondents, all teachers, all postmen, all engineers, all moms, all dads, all singles and all married, unmarried, or divorced respondents. You can group all documents by a certain month, year, author or source; all documents from company X into a family called Company X; all documents from companies in industry sector X to a family called Sector X; and so on. Families can be created at any time during the analytic process, then modified, renamed or deleted. Their purpose is to serve as a filter. Thus, you can restrict a search to a particular group of documents. This applies to text searches as well as code retrievals. Using the query tool, you can restrict searches by clicking on the scope button and selecting a primary document family as filter. Document families can also be filtered via the main menu option Documents/Filter → Families.

External document references: The basic data management concept in ATLAS.ti is that the project file, the HU, does not contain the actual files that you analyze. It only stores an external reference where the source file for each primary document can be found. This potentially allows you to work with large data sets or large data source files like videos.

HUPATH: HUPATH describes the easiest and most flexible project setup. It means that you store all documents to be analyzed and the ATLAS.ti project file, the HU, in one folder. If your project contains a lot of documents, you can create subfolders within the main project folder and then store the documents to be analyzed in those and the HU file on the top level in the main folder.

Internal documents: f4 transcripts are imported and referenced in the P-Docs Manager as: @embeded. Text files created via the option DOCUMENTS / ASSIGN / NEW

TEXT DOCUMENT also become internal documents and are also referenced as: @embedded. Both f4 documents and newly created text files become part of the HU file.

Master HU: Master HU is a term I invented for team projects. The project administrator begins by creating a first Master HU. This Master HU is distributed to team members. Team members add their initials to the file name and work on the part that is assigned to them. When they are done with their work, they send their (now) sub-HUs to the project administrator who merges them into a new Master HU, adds the date, then distributes the new Master HU back to the team members – and so on.

Merging: Merging means to combine the contents of various HUs into one HU. You can merge two HUs at a time. The HUs can contain either the same documents or different documents. In the first case, the documents are merged; in the second case they are added. The same applies to codes. The HUs can contain the same codes or different codes. If they contain the same codes, you merge them; if they contain different codes, you add them. If you have some codes the same as well as some different, you still use the option **Merge** otherwise all codes that have the same name will be duplicated. The merge option also allows you to merge only specified objects; for example, you can add only networks or memos and ignore the rest (see addenda).

Primary Document/P-Doc/PD: see Chapter 2.

Primary document comments: You can write a comment for each primary document. The recommendation is to write meta information about a document into the comment field. For interview transcripts these might be the interview protocols or interview postscripts. Information like age, gender, etc. is managed in primary document families, not the comment field. For other document types, you may use the comment field to specify the source of the document, the context of obtaining the information, a description of who published it, the target audience and so on.

Project administrator: When working in a team, I recommend that one person takes on the role of project administrator. The task of the project administrator is to set up the project, to distribute it to team members, to collect project files from team members and to merge projects.

User account: All newly created objects in ATLAS.ti are stamped with the user name. The default user is 'super'. If you want to see your own name instead of 'super' in the author field for each object, you need to create a user account (under the Extras menu) and log in using your personal account name. This is a nice but not essential option if working on your own, but a necessity if you work in a team. Based on the name in the author field, each team member can see who has done what.

Variables: see document families.

FOUR

Technical aspects of coding

In this chapter I will tell you all about the technicalities of coding, like the different ways of applying codes to text and multimedia data, modifying the length of a coded segment, renaming, deleting merging codes and writing definitions for codes. I will use the Schwarzenegger data to explain how to code text. You can use your own data set for these exercises as long as it is not yet coded. When showing you how to code other data file formats, I will use the Jack the Ripper sample data that you have already seen in Chapter 1. This data set includes all data file formats supported by ATLAS.ti.

For the exercises we will work with four test codes that we will simply label test 1, test 2, test 3 and test 4. Content does not matter at this point. The only exception is when I explain the use of in-vivo codes. Simply knowing how to create an in-vivo code (basically two clicks) does not help you to understand what are they used for, so I will provide a few examples.

As mentioned in the Introduction, there is more to coding than just the technical aspects. Questions like what a code actually is, apart from a label in a computer program, or how to build an efficient coding system, or how to code in a way that you can best utilize the options software offers apart from simple retrieval, are all discussed in Chapter 5.

Variants of coding

In ATLAS.ti you can often use a number of different routes to achieve the same result. Once you see that you can use any one of three options – the main menu, the context menu or the buttons on the toolbar – you can use whichever suits you best.

Open coding

You may have heard or read about open coding related to grounded theory. In GT, open coding refers to the process of 'breaking data apart and delineating concepts to stand for blocks of raw data. At the same time, one is qualifying those concepts in terms of their properties and dimensions' (Corbin and Strauss, 2008: 195). Thus, it refers to the extensive process of developing a coding system. In ATLAS.ti open coding simply means creating a new code. And this is how you do it:

- Open the Schwarzenegger project that we created as part of the project setup exercise in Chapter 3.
- Load one of the documents.
- Select a text segment with the mouse and right click on the highlighted area.
- Select the option **CODING / OPEN CODING** (Figure 4.1).

OR: Select CODES / CODING / OPEN CODING from the main menu.
OR: Select the open coding button from the vertical toolbar on the left-hand side of the screen.

- Then enter the code name 'test 1' in the field that pops up. Click on the OK button.
- Take a look at your screen. With one click, you have created four new entries (Figure 4.2)

You have created your first quotation and code. Each is displayed both textually (in the respective drop-down list) and graphically (in the margin area).

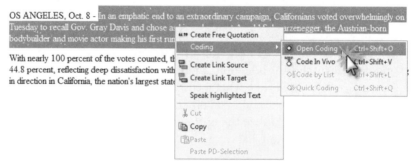

Figure 4.1 Selecting the open coding option via the context menu

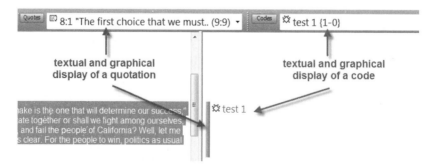

Figure 4.2 HU editor after setting a first code

The separation of quotation and code has a number of advantages. As they are independent objects, you can comment on each code and also on each quotation. Quotations cannot only be linked to codes, but also to each other and to memos. This is a prerequisite for the hyperlink function discussed in Chapter 7. It allows you to work directly at the data level without necessarily using codes.

Let's code three more segments using this method:

- Highlight a different text segment, right click, select the open coding option from the context menu and enter 'test 2' as code name.
- Code two more segments using 'test 3' and 'test 4' as codes. Overlap some of your codings and observe what happens in the margin area.

As you can see in Figure 4.3, overlapping codes are displayed in different colors in the margin area. These colors help you to distinguish which bar belongs to which code word. If you were to add even more layers, the next two layers would be displayed in violet and blue. After that, silver is used again. The colors do not contain any information about the different code levels in the sense of higher or lower ranked categories. When you delete a quotation, the colors may also change. It is possible to set your own colors for codes, but not for the bars marking the length of a quotation. How to personalize code colors, how to display them in the margin, and for what purpose this can be used, are detailed in Chapter 5.

Next, before showing you more variants of coding, I would like to explain how quotations and codes are referenced and what the entries in the drop-down lists mean.

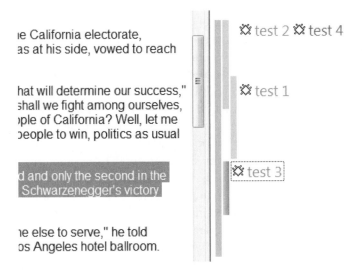

Figure 4.3   Meanings of colored bars in the margin

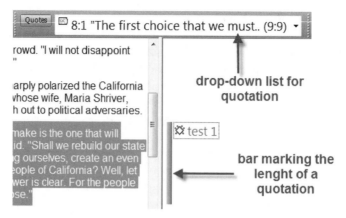

Figure 4.4 How quotations are referenced

Quotation references

The bars in the margin mark the length of the quotation graphically. The entry in the quotation field shows a textual reference for the quotation. It consists of the following elements: ID, name, start and end position.

ID: The quotation ID is composed of the number of its P-Doc and a second number indicating when the quotation was created (Figure 4.4). The ID 8:1 means that the quotation is from P-Doc 8 and is the first one that was created in this document. The reason for the chronological numbering is to do with the fact that you will not necessarily code a document from the first line to the last. You will jump between passages and modify or delete some quotations during the coding process. A linear numeration would have to be updated with every single quotation that is inserted, which would take up unnecessary computational capacity. Sorting the quotations by their start position, for example, offers a clear linear view of your quotes. Recently an option was added to change the chronological numbering to a sequential order if need be **(Quotations / Miscellaneous / Renumber all to Docflow)**. This can be useful for example when coding open-ended questions from survey data and you want to keep the cases in synch with the cases in the SPSS file.

Name: The name shows the first 30 characters of a textual quotation. This is the default setting which can be changed under **Extras / Preferences / General Preferences.** Quotations based on image, audio or video files show the file name. The name of a quotation can be renamed. This is a useful option for image, audio and video quotations, as we will see below.

Start and end positions: The figures in brackets after the quotation name show the location (start and end position) in the document. For textual quotations, the reference given is to the paragraph numbers within which the coded segment occurs: (9:9) thus means that the quotation starts and ends in paragraph 9. Do you remember what I said in Chapter 2, when I discussed good practice rules for preparing transcripts? The suggestion was to break larger speech units into smaller paragraphs because of the way ATLAS.ti references quotations. The reason why paragraphs instead of line numbers are used as reference points is because, in digital environments, the width of a document is not set. You can move the windows splitter to the right or left, adjusting the width of the document to your computer screen. Paragraph numbers are not affected by this, whereas line numbers are.

For image files, the rectangular area marked as the quotation is referenced. Audio quotes use a time reference, and for video quotations you can choose between time or frame numbers.

References for PDF quotations consist of: page number and number of characters on the page for start and end positions. In case the document contains columns, the column number is provided as well.

The quotation ID in combination with the start and end positions can be used when citing quotations in a report. For example:

'The first choice that we must make is the one that will determine our success,' he said. 'Shall we rebuild our state together or shall we fight among ourselves, create an even deeper division, and fail the people of California? Well, let me tell you something: the answer is clear. For the people to win, politics as usual must lose.' (P8:1; 9:9)

The reference allows the reader of a report to trace the quote and to find it either in the original digital material or in a printed version of the coded data.

There is one more issue where quotation references can serve a useful function. Remember that I suggested (in Chapter 3) naming documents according to analytical criteria whenever applicable? Assume that for an in-depth analysis of newspaper reports on the Schwarzenegger election we had selected 600 articles instead of just 12, and that we had thought of some meaningful data file names. The beginnings of the names are shown in Table 4.1. When assigning these files to ATLAS.ti, they appear in alphabetic order and in the order of the criteria included in the name.

This way of ordering the documents adds a bit more information to the quotation ID than it would otherwise have done. The first thing you see when retrieving quotations is the quotation ID. Let's assume that a retrieval results in quotations showing only numbers lower than 300. Then we would know – without having to enter anything further – that the quotations come from German newspapers. Or if the IDs show numbers below 75, you know that all quotations come from German local broadsheet papers. Numbers between 21 and 40 indicate that these are all quotations from the newspaper HAZ.

Taking a less complex case, let's assume that you have interviewed 20 women and 20 men and you use their first names or pseudonyms as data file names. This could mean that P1 is Anne, P2 is Bert, P3 Chris, P4 Dana, and so on. It is much easier to label all transcripts of your female interviewees

Table 4.1 Examples for analytically meaningful file names

File name prefix	PD numbering	Meaning of the prefix
G	P-Docs: 1–300	Germany
Adding further detail		
G_L	P-Docs: 1–150	Germany: local
G_N	P-Docs: 151–300	Germany: national
Adding further detail		
G_L_BS	P-Docs: 1–75	Germany: local: broadsheet
G_L_T	P-Docs: 76–150	Germany: local: tabloid
G_N_BS	P-Docs: 151–225	Germany: national: broadsheet
G_N_T	P-Docs: 226–300	Germany: national: tabloid
Adding further detail		
G_L_BS_BZ	P-Docs: 1–20	Germany: local: broadsheet: Berliner Zeitung
G_L_BS_HAZ	P-Docs: 21–40	Germany: local: broadsheet: HAZ
G_L_BS_tz M	P-Docs: 41–55	Germany: local: broadsheet: tz München
G_L_BS_WB	P-Docs: 56–75	Germany: local: broadsheet: Westfalen Blatt

P1 to P20, and all those of male interviewees P21 to P40, than to remember that P1, P4, P7, P12, P13, P19 and so on represent females and the rest males. This is another benefit of using good data file names in combination with the way ATLAS.ti references quotations, and it's well worth doing.

Code reference

The entered code word is written next to the quotation bar in the margin. You can recognize codes by the yellow diamond symbol. The entry in the drop-down list reads: test 1 {1-0} (Figure 4.5). I explained the meaning of the numbers behind the code in Chapter 1: the first number shows the frequency (how often the code has been applied) and the second number the density (how many other codes this code is linked to). Hence the code test 1 has been used only once so far and it is not yet linked to any other code. The density remains 0 for the purposes of this book until we reach Chapter 7, where the network view function is discussed.

Coding by list

At the beginning of the coding process, it is normal to generate a lot of new codes. But after a while you will find similarities and repetitions in the data and want to apply codes that already exist. Your sample project should currently contain four codes. If you want to reuse them:

- Mark a text segment, right click on the highlighted text and select **CODING / CODE BY LIST** from the context menu.
- A window opens. It contains a list of all code words created so far. Select one or more codes and confirm your selection by pressing the Enter key or click on **OK**.

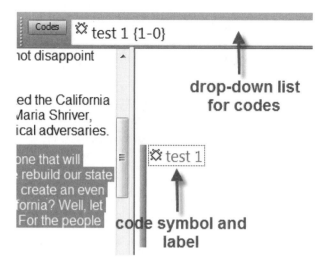

Figure 4.5 How codes are referenced

It is quite common that more than one code is used for coding a data segment. The segment might contain ambiguous information or different layers of meaning. You may want to code for content and also for context, use of language or aspects of time. It is difficult and also not very efficient to incorporate a variety of aspects into a single code name and it should not be done (see Chapter 5 for more information). You can later rely on the computer to find all kinds of combinations for you.

Coding via drag and drop

I personally do not find the coding by list option very convenient. After selecting a code the list is closed, and for the next coding action you have to open it again. The easiest way is to code from the Code Manager via drag and drop.

- Open the Code Manager and change the view to **single column** view (VIEW / SINGLE COLUMN) if not already activated.
- Highlight a text passage and select a code from the Code Manager. Hold down the left mouse button, drag the code over the windows splitter and drop it on the other side (Figure 4.6).

There is no need to drop the code into the highlighted area. It just has to be dropped somewhere on the left-hand side as shown in Figure 4.6. Whatever is highlighted gets coded. Intuitively one often drags the code on top of the highlighted data segment. If you spend a long time coding, this gets very tiring on your eyes and requires more and more concentration, and the constant twisting action of your wrist in trying to hit the highlighted area may even strain the muscles. The software does not require you to do this. Thus, be

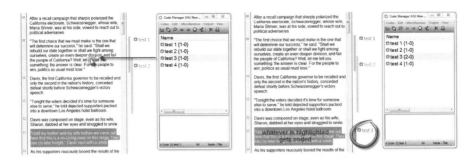

Figure 4.6 Drag and drop coding

gentle on yourself. In the latest version of 6.2 (6.2.27), you also find a coding button in the toolbar of the Code Manager. This is especially useful, if you want to code a highlighted data passage with multiple codes: Select the codes and then click on the coding button instead of using drag & drop.

Changing a code

If you want to change a code (perhaps because you have changed your mind, found a more fitting code, used a code by accident or want to develop subcategories) then the easiest way is also to use drag and drop. This time, however, you cannot drop the code just anywhere; you have to drop it exactly on top of the one that you want to replace.

- Let's assume we want to replace the gold test 2 code in Figure 4.6 with **test 4**. Click on the 'test 4' code in the Code Manager, hold down the left mouse button, drag the code to the 'test 2' code in the margin area and drop it. *Voilà* – the code is changed.

Modifying the length of a quotation

Modifying the length of a quotation is also quite a common procedure. Maybe you discover that a chosen segment is too large or that you forgot something and need to extend the length of a quotation. Both ways of modifying are possible.

- Activate the quotation that you want to modify (e.g. with a click on the code word in the margin). The bar and the code word will be framed by a dotted line. The currently activated quotation is also displayed in the quotation drop-down list.

To enlarge a segment   Highlight an extended area by simply overwriting the existing one. Then click on the button **Revise quotation size** in the vertical toolbar (see left).

To decrease the size of a segment   As you cannot select a segment within an already highlighted area, you first need to 'erase' the highlighting by clicking above or below it. When nothing else is highlighted you can select the smaller area that you want. Then click on the button **Revise quotation size** in the vertical toolbar.

Unlinking a code

Just as you can erase a pencil mark in the margin of a paper document, you can 'erase' a code in the margin area on screen as well. The digital equivalent is called **unlinking**. It is mostly used when a segment is coded with more than one code.

- To unlink a code, right click on the code in the margin area and click on the option **UNLINK**.

When you unlink a code from a segment that only has one code, the bar remains in the margin. If you want to 'erase' both the code and the quotation, you need to proceed as explained below. (See also Figure 4.7, which shows the difference between unlinking and removing.)

Removing a coded segment

- Mark the coded segment to be removed (e.g. by clicking on the code in the margin).
- Move your pointer over the highlighted quotation and select **DELETE** from the context menu.
- A message pops up asking you to confirm that this quotation and associated links should be deleted. Click **OK**.

Note that removing a coded segment does not delete the text or other data material that you have coded. The quotation is an object stored in the HU file. You can think of all objects stored in the HU as a layer on top of your data material. The HU only accesses the data via a reference and loads it into the HU editor. The data themselves are not touched.

The only exception is for text and rtf files, when you enter Edit Mode. Then you access the data on the computer disk and all changes you make within Edit Mode are also reflected inside the source file. The edit option is explained in more detail in the addenda.

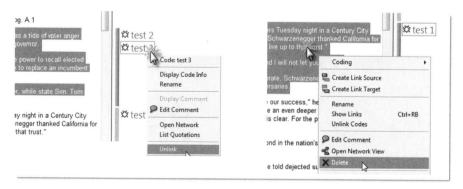

Figure 4.7 Differences between unlinking and removing a code

Writing comments for coded segments

If you notice something interesting while coding and you want to write it down, use the quotation comment field for it. A lot of ATLAS.ti novices attach a memo instead of using the comment field. Memos, however, are more than mere comments (see Chapter 6). As the word 'comment' indicates, it is a short note, one or two sentences long. Comments are attached directly to data segments; memos do not have to be attached to anything, or can be attached to more than one data segment. Memos can therefore be used to develop more informed ideas at a higher level of your analysis. If you use memos as comments early on you'll end up in a mess, producing an additional body of data next to the primary data that you want to analyze – and you may well get completely lost.

Thus, when you want to comment on a data segment:

- Right click on the highlighted quotation and select the option **Edit Comment** from the context menu (Figure 4.8).

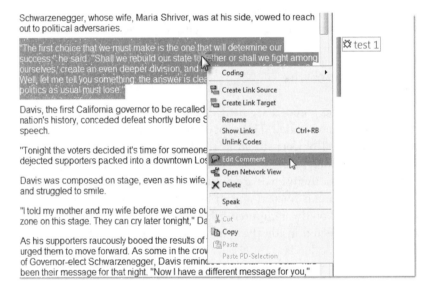

Figure 4.8   Commenting on a quotation

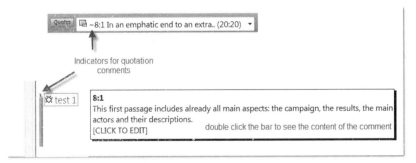

Figure 4.9   Visibility of quotation comments

- An editor pops up. Write a comment on the selected data segment.
- Save your comment by clicking on the accept button and close the editor.

Quotation comments are visible in the bar in the margin area (Figure 4.9) and by the tilde (~) sign in front of the quotation name in the quotations list.

Coding with in-vivo codes

The term 'in-vivo code', like open coding, is also often associated with grounded theory (GT). As we have already learned, open coding in ATLAS.ti does not mean the same thing as in GT. However, in-vivo codes in ATLAS.ti can be used as suggested by GT. In-vivo codes are 'concepts using the actual words of research participants rather than being named by the analyst' (Corbin and Strauss, 2008: 65).

Technically this means that when you highlight a text segment, the segment itself is used as a code name. In-vivo codes are especially useful at the beginning of the coding process when collecting ideas. As it is quick and easy to create them, this is what they are often used for in computer-assisted analysis. This first collection of ideas mostly takes place at the descriptive level. Description, according to Corbin and Strauss (2008), is the basis for more abstract interpretation of data and it does embody concepts, at least implicitly. Proper concept building, however, needs to happen at some point of the analysis. It does not make much sense to collect 200 in-vivo codes without developing them further. You just end up with a very long code list.

When in-vivo codes are used as a quick device for collecting things that you notice in the data, with progressive analysis they should be replaced by merging some and renaming others in more abstract terms (see below for how this works). I have seen projects gone mad – the champion being a project with over 16,000 codes. I will tell you in Chapter 5 why this is not a good idea and what has gone wrong if you end up with thousands of codes. For now, as a rule of thumb, remember that a project should only have between 120 and 300 codes. There are projects that have fewer codes and others that have more, but 16,000 is definitely too much.

Now let's turn to the technical practicalities again. The maximum length of an in-vivo code is 40 characters. If you want more, you need to modify the length of the quotation in a second step as described above.

- Mark a text passage of 40 characters maximum. Right click and select the option **CODING / CODE IN VIVO** from the context menu.

You can also highlight a text passage and drag it into the Code Manager. Then the limit of 40 characters does not apply. However, a code of 100 or so characters is even further away from being a proper code in an analytical sense. In addition, you just clutter up the margin and cannot see the full name of the code anyway because it is too long.

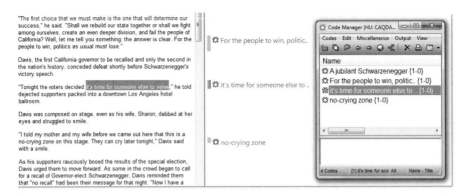

Figure 4.10 Coding in vivo

Figure 4.10 shows an example based on the Schwarzenegger project where some text segments are collected in the form of in-vivo codes. The ideas that I collected had to do with why voters were unhappy with Gray Davis as governor and why they wanted to recall him.

After collecting some more instances and reviewing them, I could think of better and shorter names as code labels. These first ideas could, for example, be developed further into a category called 'Reasons for Davis's defeat', with subcategories like lack of trust/poor performance/scapegoat for economic downturn, etc.

Further coding-related options provided by the Code Manager

There are a number of other options in the Code Manager, which you can access via the menu and toolbar or the context menus. For instance, you can create new codes, and rename, delete or merge codes.

Creating a new code

You can also create a new code in the Code Manager instead of using the open coding option.

- Click on the 'Create a new item' button that we came across when creating P-Doc families. Or select **CODES / CREATE FEE CODE** from the Code Manager menu.
- Enter a code name and click on OK.

Frequency and density are both zero as this code is not yet linked to anything.

Renaming codes

The renaming option is a global option. This means that renaming a code word in the Code Manager affects all coded segments that use this code.

- Mark a code word in the Code Manager, right click and select **RENAME** from the context menu.

OR: Use the **'in-place'** way of renaming entries that you may know from working with the Windows file manager.

- Select a code word with the left mouse button and then – separately – left click it again. The entry changes as shown in Figure 4.11. You can modify the name simply by overwriting it.

Coloring codes

If you want to color your codes:

- Select a code in the Code Manager and click on the rainbow-colored circle in the toolbar.
- To make code colors visible in the margin, right click on a white space in the margin area and select the option **USE OBJECT COLORS**.

In order to still be able see which code label belongs to which quotation bar, a small bar in the same color as the quotation bar is shown in front of the code label (Figure 4.12). The code label shows the user-defined color.

Figure 4.11 In-place editing

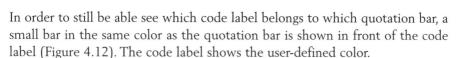

Figure 4.12 Display of code colors in the margin area (see companion website for color image)

Deleting codes (and other objects)

The delete option also has global effects, at least within the boundaries of the HU. That means that deleting a code removes it from the entire HU and from everywhere in your primary documents, code families or network views – anywhere it was used. So please use this option very carefully, especially as there is no undo option in ATLAS.ti. Actually, there is one under the Extras menu, but most of the time it won't help you. It can only undo simple things like the modification of a name.

There is a safeguard when using the delete option. You need to confirm a delete action before it is executed. You just have to read the message that pops up when selecting DELETE anywhere in the program. But as I know very well, we don't always read what the computer tells us. We click on **OK** and then it is too late.

Because there is no undo option in ATLAS.ti, I can only urge you to click on the save button in the main toolbar or use the hotkey CTRL+S now and then, every 20 minutes or whenever you think of it. Another safeguard against data loss and undoing mistakes is to make a project backup in the form of a copy bundle file that I discuss in the addenda.

Having said this, of course, there are times when we want to delete codes. And this is how. Select the code word in the Code Manager, right click and select DELETE from the context menu. You can also click on the delete button in the toolbar of the Code Manager (e.g. when you selected more than one code to delete).

- A message pops up: 'These items are linked to code "[*code name*]": [x] quotations. Continue with deletion?' Confirm by clicking on **YES**.
- After you click on **YES**, another message pops up asking you whether the linked quotations should also be deleted (Figure 4.13).
- Don't take too much pity on the orphaned quotations. If you don't need them any longer, click on **YES** and delete them as well.

Figure 4.13   Completing the deletion process

Merging codes

The merge codes function can be used to combine two or more codes with each other. This is a common procedure when you begin to clean up your code list after initial coding, or when you work in a team and merge subprojects. You may realize that there are two codes that have different names but they essentially mean the same thing. Thus, the contents of the two codes, the coded quotations, can be combined under one code name.

- Begin with the code whose name you want to keep. Select, for example, the code 'test 1'.
- Right-click and select **MERGE CODES** from the context menu.

- A small window pops up listing all other available codes. Select one or more codes (e.g., 'test 4') from this list and click the OK button. To select more than one code, the usual Windows selection procedure can be used.

- Now one more window pops up, telling you that the selected codes have been merged into the target code. A comment leaving an audit trail of the merge process will only be entered if the codes already had a comment before merging. All existing comments will be kept.

As you can see in Figure 4.14, before merging, the code 'test 1' coded two quotations and 'test 4' one quotation. After merging, 'test 1' contains (2+1) three quotations. However, the numbers do not always add up like this; for instance, it wouldn't be the case if both codes had previously coded the same quotation.

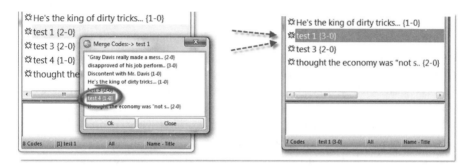

Figure 4.14   The process of merging codes

As the message in ATLAS.ti tells you, if the codes have not yet been defined you won't be able to see later that the codes were merged unless you enter a comment manually. You can do this if it is important to leave an audit trail to trace your steps. Another option is to enter a comment on the codes before merging. Figure 4.14 shows an example of this. If you merge codes early on in an analytic process it will most likely not be necessary to leave an audit trail, as the code labels are often still exploratory and there are no set definitions yet.

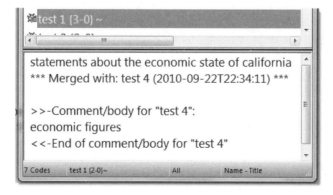

Figure 4.15   Combined comments after merging leaving an audit trail

Writing code definitions

Comments can be written into the white field below the windows splitter, as we have seen in Chapters 1 and 3. When entering a comment (for codes this is in most cases a definition, a coding rule and possibly a sample quotation) the commented object is marked by a tilde (~). See also Figure 4.14.

- Try it out: write a comment for one of your codes. When you are finished, click on another code: the definition is saved and you will see the tilde after the code. If you close the window immediately after writing the definition, a message pops up asking you whether you want to save the comment.

Writing code definitions is analytically speaking a very important process (see also Fielding and Lee, 1998: 94ff.). When I look at team projects, code definitions are never missing as it seems self-explanatory that in teams one has to write down what a particular code means. This is not the case when analysts work alone. They typically think that writing code definitions is not necessary, since they think they know what their codes mean. I can tell you that this is not always the case and that you cannot just take it for granted. What happens if you are ill and cannot work at your project for some time, or if you go on vacation, fly to a meeting, or have other commitments that keep you away from your analysis? Returning to your data, you sit down, click on a code and ask yourself, 'What is this code doing here? What was I thinking of when I created it?' You try to remind yourself by browsing through the quotations and perhaps you begin to remember – but if only you had written a code definition at the time, or at least some comments; so you see, it does help to put some information into the code comment field.

There are other benefits as well. Coding is a process and your thoughts about the data will evolve. The meaning you attached to a code word at the beginning of an analysis may change over time. There is nothing unusual about that. If there is no definition for the code, you may not notice the subtle changes over time and in the end the code may contain quotations that in fact no longer fit under a common label. ATLAS.ti makes it easy for you to track changing meanings or associations, since you see the code definition right in front of you in the Code Manager as you use it.

Furthermore, going through all of your codes and defining them helps the analytic thought process. It forces you to draw clear-cut boundaries between codes. If you realize there are overlapping meanings, you can either merge the codes or make them more distinctive. Code definitions also add transparency to your analysis. They are necessary for a third person to understand and follow your analytic ideas. Try it out, even if it means some extra work. I promise you'll see that it is worth doing.

Coding other media types

Now I will explain differences in handling other file formats. The differences mostly relate to selecting data segments. There are a few additional issues to pay attention to when it comes to creating output. Other than that, the different data file formats are smoothly integrated into all functions of the software. When you click on a code that codes data in different formats, all quotations are listed and you can browse through them one by one. Text quotations are displayed in context on the left hand side, audio or video quotations are played, the coded image quotation is highlighted within the image file, and Google Earth is loaded to show a geographic location that you have coded.

When you want to output coded segments, you need to be aware that the output will be in rich text. In Version 7, the rtf output will also include the area of a picture you have coded. For all other data sources, only the quotation reference is provided. You can create more meaningful outputs by making extensive use of the option to rename quotations and to write comments.

As the Schwarzenegger project only contains text and image files, for the following exercises I will use the Jack the Ripper quick tour data which you can access vie the help menu.

- Load the stage 1 project by selecting **HELP / QUICK TOUR / LOAD "JACK THE RIPPER STAGE 1"** from the main menu.

Coding a PDF document

- Load P5 by selecting it from the P-Docs drop-down list.

Check your version number of ATLAS.ti. If your version number is lower than 6.2, I recommend updating. It is a maintenance update and thus free of charge. It is worthwhile because in the new version the handling of PDF files is greatly improved and other features are available too.

Coding a PDF document is essentially the same as coding *.rtf, *doc or *.txt files. Selecting a text segment in PDF documents, however, requires a bit of practice. If you place the cursor too far to the left of the text, you will select only a rectangular graphical image instead of the actual text segment.

- To select a string of text, place the cursor directly to the left of the first letter.
- Use any of the coding techniques described above (e.g. open coding or coding via drag and drop from the Code Manager).
- Try coding a few text passages in the PDF file.
- Now experiment with selecting a graphical image in the PDF file: select and code the picture of the victim Mary-Ann Nichols.

Coding an image document

- Load an image document (e.g. P20), select a rectangular area and proceed to code it as has been described for text segments (Figure 4.16).
- To change the display type, right click on the image quotation and select the option Selection-Display Type / Inverted Area.

Figure 4.16   Coded image file using the inverted display for quotations

Coding audio and video files

I will now describe the procedure for coding video files as it applies to version 5 and 6 of ATLAS.ti. At the end of this section you find a preview of how audio and video files are handled and coded in Version 7. It would be unusual to code audio files directly without a transcript, but these instructions apply to working with audio files as well as video. Coding both audio and video files involves two steps, not just the one we have seen when coding text and image data. First a quotation needs to be created, and only then can we link a code to it.

- Load P7, the short video showing the location of the Chapman murder.
- In addition to the Code Manager, open the Quotation Manager. Resize the two windows, so they fit next to each other. Move the timeline to a convenient position and expand it so it covers the full width of the screen (Figure 4.17).

Currently the timeline cannot be scrolled. Thus, the entire video somehow needs to fit onto the timeline. Therefore I recommend not using films longer

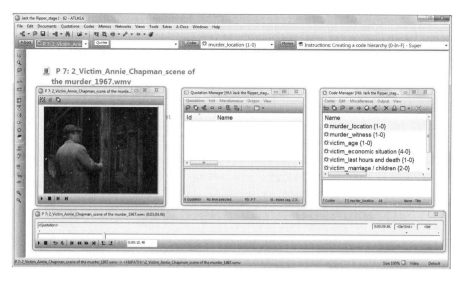

Figure 4.17 Preparing the screen for coding a video file

than 20 minutes. If they are longer, split them into smaller files. Otherwise, the visual presentation of the quotations becomes very tiny and difficult to set.

When I work with video files, I usually set a filter to the currently selected document so that the Quotation Manager only shows the quotes for the video I am working on.

- From the main menu, select **QUOTATIONS / FILTER / SELECTED PD**. The drop-down list and manager show a pale yellow color, indicating that a filter is set.
- To create a quotation, move the cursor to a start position on the timeline. Click on the button **MARK SELECTION START** (see Figure 4.18).
- Position the cursor at the end point of the quotation. Click on the button **MARK SELECTION END**.
- Then click on the button **CREATE QUOTATION**.

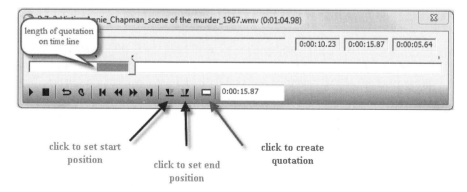

Figure 4.18 Creating a video quotation

A new quotation is listed in the Quotation Manager with the ID 7:1. The default name for audio and video quotations is the document name. Each quotation can, however, be renamed (right click on a quote and select the option RENAME).

Coding an audio or video quotation

- To code the video quotation, **drag and drop** a code from the Code Manager onto the quotation in the Quotation Manager (or vice versa). You can also right click on the quotation in the Quotation Manager and select the other options discussed above from the coding menu.

When applying a code, the quotation count behind the code name increases by one. This is all you can see, as there is no margin area yet.

Reviewing audio and video quotations

With the current version, you can only review video quotations via the Quotation Manager or after retrieving them via their codes:

- Double click on a code in the Code Manager.

OR:

- Right click on the white background. There you will find the option SHOW LINKS.

Unlinking codes

- To unlink a code from a video quotation, you also have to right click on the white background. Then select the option UNLINK CODES.

Modifying the length of a video quotation

- To modify a quotation boundary, activate a quotation in the Quotation Manager. Then reset either the start or end position. You can use the right and left arrows on your keyboard to adjust the length of a quotation by frames. To modify the length, use CTRL+CREATE QUOTATION.

Resetting the filter

- To reset the set filter, select the main menu option EXTRAS / RESET ALL FILTERS.

Describing video quotations to improve outputs

As mentioned above, the name of a video quote is its data file name. In most cases this is not very useful, at least not for analytical purposes. I suggest two options: renaming the quotations and adding comments.

Making use of quotation names

- In the process of creating video quotations, rename them so they can serve as titles for your video segments. To do so, right click on the quotation name in the Quotation Manager and select the option RENAME.
- If 30 characters are not enough for quotation names, you can extend the number. From the main menu, select EXTRAS / PREFERENCES / GENERAL PREFERENCES / TAB: GENERAL. At the bottom right, you will find the option List name size for quotes. Increase it to the desired number of characters; 75 characters are probably enough for short titles.

In Figure 4.19 you can see an output of the quotes set in P7, coded by a newly created code labeled 'Location of murders'. To create the output, I selected OUTPUT / QUOTATION LIST FOR SELECTED CODE(S) in the Code Manager. As there is no textual content, the list option is sufficient.

You can see the titles I have entered for each video quotation by renaming the default name. The brackets at the beginning of each line (<>) indicate that the quotations are linked to other quotations via hyperlinks (see Chapter 7). The numbers after the title show the position in the document in the form of frame numbers. The first number indicates the start position; the second number in square brackets provides information on the length of a quotation.

- If you want to change between frame and time settings for quotation references, right click on the bottom right-hand side of the timeline and select **Choose TIME FORMAT** (FIGURE 4.20). Then a small window pops up showing you the various options available.

---

8 quotation(s) for code: LOCATION OF MURDERS

<>7:1 Hanbury Street 29 in 1967 (0 [459])
>7:2 the two entrances (209 [97])
<7:3 The swinging door (704 [111])
~<>7:5 The swinging door and wooden fence (1154 [297])
>7:7 Place where Chapman was found (1506 [125])
~<7:8 Comment about Hanbury Street in 1967 (1850 [97])
<7:10 Look into the Yard where Chapman was ki. (704 [427])

Figure 4.19 Quotation list output showing video titles

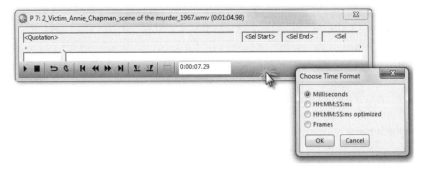

Figure 4.20 Changing the time format for video quotations

Making use of quotation comments

In addition to using quotation names for titles, you can add a description for each video quotation in the comment field. When you output quotations and there is at least one comment, ATLAS.ti asks you whether comments should be

---

7:1 Hanbury Street 29 in 1967 (0.00 [15.32])
>7:2 the two entrances (6.96 [3.24])
<7:3 The swinging door (23.50 [3.70])
~<>7:5 The swinging door and wooden fence (38.50 [9.91])

Comment:

This is Jack the Ripper territory. The old people-here-even remember some of his murders

View in 1988

Backyard of 29 Hanbury Street.
It was in the backyard of 29 Hanbury Street that the body of the second of the victims of Jack the Ripper, Annie Chapman, was discovered by John Davies an elderly resident of the building. Her body was found in the gap between the steps and the fence.

>7:7 Place where Chapman was found (50.25 [4.16])
~<7:8 Comment about Hanbury Street in 1967 (1:01.73 [3.25])

Comment:

These streets were exactly the same as they were at that time...

<7:10 Look into the yard where Chapman was ki.. (23.50 [14.24])

Figure 4.21 Quotation list output including comments

included in the output. To create the output shown in Figure 4.21, I used the quotation list for selected code(s) option again, and I confirmed the option to include comments in the output. This time I changed the time format to 'hours: minutes:seconds:milliseconds optimized'. For example, the reference for quotation 7:2 means that the quotation starts at 6 seconds and 96 milliseconds and lasts for 3 seconds and 24 milliseconds.

Associating a transcription

I would not spend months transcribing a video file as some people do. I recommend beginning your analytic work directly on the video file. All the information is self-contained and I do not see the point of repeating some of it in transcript form unless you need a very detailed transcript (e.g. for sequential analysis). But then you would probably not be working with ATLAS.ti.

Thus, my suggestion is to assign your video files to ATLAS.ti and begin your analytic work. Assign an internal text file for each video file and associate these with the video files via the A-Docs function.

To associate the text and video document:

- Open the P-Docs Manager.
- Open the Association Editor. Select **A-Docs / Edit Association** from the main menu.
- Drag the two files, one after each other, next to the name column in the Association Editor as shown in Figure 4.22.

If you come across something in your video file that you feel is important to fully transcribe, use the built-in transcription function and type the text into the associated text file. You will find some instructions on how to transcribe with ATLAS.ti at the end of primary document P14: "Transcript: The Ripper Revealed" in the Jack the Ripple sample file, or take a look at the manual.

If you transcribe selected parts of the video, you should then code the text transcript and not the video itself. Via the association links you can access the video at any time and at the correct entry points without having to search for frame references and the like. You can use the Association Editor to navigate through the links, or you can use the key combination Crtl+P to play the linked video segment.

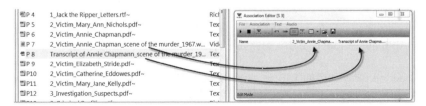

Figure 4.22   Associating video file and transcript

The future of coding video and audio files

There are some changes to come in version 7 regarding the way audio and video data are handled in ATLAS.ti. From what I have seen, they will be a great improvement and will make working with these media forms much easier and better. The handling of audio and video files will become very similar to handling text. Loaded audio and video files will also display a margin area with the timeline running vertically from top to bottom. The video will play on the left-hand side in the same place where text and image files are currently also displayed. You can highlight a video segment and code it just as you highlight a text segment with your mouse, by simply selecting an area on the timeline. The code is displayed on the right-hand side in the margin area and you see preview images along the timeline. Furthermore, the plan is to add an rtf output option that includes the preview images for the start and end positions of the video quotations, and possibly play list for selected video quotations by code. This is very exciting news and will offer new opportunities for working with audio and video files.

Figure 4.23 shows a screenshot of the current alpha version.

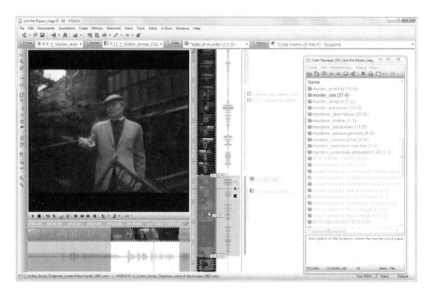

Figure 4.23 Preview of coding video clafa in version 7

Coding a Google Earth document

Before you can assign or load a Google Earth (GE) document in ATLAS.ti, you need to install Google Earth on your computer.

- Load the GE document P15 or assign a new GE document by selecting **Documents** / **Assign** / **New GoogleEarth PD**. Loading the document may take a while, depending on the speed of your Internet connection.

- When working with GE documents, try reducing the main workspace size to leave some space to the right or left for other ATLAS.ti windows.
- The managers for quotations and codes should still be open. Position them to the right of the GE editor, for example stacked on top of each other. Now we are ready to 'fly' to a specific location and set ATLAS.ti tags.
- Let's fly to New York City. In the 'Fly To' field, type the following location: 'New York City'.
- To set a quotation, zoom into the map and look for an interesting place. Double click on a specific point on the map that is not already set as a tag. Then select **Quotations / Create Free Quotation** either from the main menu or from the Quotation Manager menu. You can also click on the respective button in the vertical toolbar (see right).

The following new entry will appear immediately in the Quotation Manager:

Just as with audio and video quotations, the file name becomes the quotation's name. The geographic reference is visible in brackets.

- Now change the name of this quotation to something more meaningful.

In order to view the ATLAS.ti tag and the new name in the GE Editor, the document must be reloaded:

- Hold down the Shift key and click on the P-Docs button. *Voilà* – the new quotation name will appear (Figure 4.24).

The ATLAS.ti tag can be displayed at various heights. In Figure 4.24 it floats 175 m above the ground. You can set this under Extras / General Preferences / Google Earth Preferences.

Figure 4.24 ATLAS.ti tag and quotation name in Google Earth

- A new entry is also added to the **Places** section of the GE Editor in the lower left pane.
- To code this new GE quotation, drag and drop a code from the Code Manager onto the quotation in the Quotation Manager (as before for video quotations).

You can also create a quotation and code it directly:

- Select a point on the map by double clicking on it. Then select Codes / Coding / Open Coding or Code by List, depending on whether you would like to enter a new code or assign an existing code. Alternatively, you can use the vertical toolbar buttons for coding.

Summary

If you have worked through this chapter thoroughly you should now know the procedures of coding with ATLAS.ti. That is:

- The various options which ATLAS.ti offers for coding.
- How coded segments and code words can be modified.
- How codes can be renamed, merged or deleted.
- How to define code words and what this is good for.
- How to code data formats other than text and what kind of issues there are to consider.

Below you will find a list of review questions to test your knowledge of the technical aspects of coding. You can practice a bit more when you do the suggested coding exercise in Chapter 5. Then you should feel quite secure in handling the technical aspects of coding. What comes next, the methodological aspects, probably needs more practice and time to learn. In Chapter 5, I want to share with you what I have learned in nearly 20 years of working with CAQDAS so that you can take a few shortcuts and speed up the learning process.

REVIEW QUESTIONS

1   Which coding options does ATLAS.ti offer?
2   What is meant by open coding in ATLAS.ti?
3   What are in-vivo codes and what can they be used for?
4   Explain the quotation references in the Quotation Manager when it is set to single column view: what do the numbers before and after the quotations mean?
5   Regarding the way quotations are referenced, how does this relate to good data file names and what is the advantage of it?
6   Explain the code references in the Code Manager when it is set to single column view: what do the numbers after the codes mean?

7   Why is it important to write code definitions?
8   What in particular do you need to know when coding PDF files and non-textual data files like image, audio and video files?

Code: Keywords that are generally linked to quotations, but don't have to be. You can also create free codes. When you link free codes to a number of different codes, then they are called abstract codes.

Code comment: Technically, the code comment field fulfills the same function as the quotation comment field. While coding you can add some notes to this field, and thoughts and questions that occur during the process of first-stage coding. If it becomes clear over time and with further analysis that something should be coded, a code definition should be entered, maybe a coding rule and an sample quotation.

Code reference: The code reference consists of the so-called groundedness and density of a code. The groundedness provides the frequency of how often a code has been applied; the density shows the number of links to other codes.

In-vivo coding: For the computer this means that the highlighted characters are used as the code name. In a computer-assisted analysis, in most cases, it does not make a lot of sense to have code words that are the same as the text they code. Generally a bit of context is needed and this requires extending the quotation beyond the characters used as in-vivo code.

Open coding: The open coding option in ATLAS.ti is unrelated to the process of open coding in grounded theory. It simply means to create a new code.

Quotations: Marked data segments that have a clearly defined start and end point. Often quotations are coded, but they don't have to be. You can also create so-called free quotations. Free or coded quotations can be used as source or target to link data segments to each other. Linked quotations are called hyperlinks (see Chapter 7).

Quotation comment: Technically, the quotation comment field acts as an editor for written text. Potentially, a comment can be added to each quotation. To avoid drowning in too much data, your comments (i.e. short notes) should be written in the comment fields rather than using an ATLAS.ti memo for them. Memos are the place to write down more extensive thoughts and ideas that you elaborate on over an extended period of time (see Chapter 6).

Quotation reference: The quotation reference is made up of an ID, a name and the position of the quotation in the document. The ID consists of the primary document number that it belongs to and a number that indicates the sequence of when it was created. The quotation name is based on either the first 30 characters of a text quotation or the name of the primary document. This automatically generated name can be modified. If the default number of characters is not sufficient, they can be increased under Extras / Preferences / General Preferences. The location where a quotation can be found within a primary document is indicated after the name. Depending on the document type, different references are used:

References for rtf or doc(x) quotations: paragraph numbers for start and end positions.

Reference for a PDF document: page number and number of characters on the page for start and end positions. In case the document contains columns, the column number is provided as well.

References for audio and video quotations: hours, minutes, seconds and milliseconds. If desired, references for video segments can also be provided in the form of start and end frames.

References for Google Earth (GE) quotations: the geographical coordinates for latitude and longitude (e.g. 51°30'49. 21"N, 0°4'41. 38"W) as provided by GE.

FIVE

Embarking on a journey – coding the data material

In Chapter 4, you learned how to handle codes on the technical level. To the software, a code is simply a code, and what you do with it, how you name it and whether you have codes on different levels are not its concern. A code might be a basic description, an indicator, a main category or a subcategory, or a placeholder modifying a link in a network view. In addition to regular codes, the software offers code families and supercodes. Technically speaking, a code family is a group of codes and a supercode is a saved query. There are no actual rules about these functions; they are all at your disposal, and the software does not tell you how to use them, just like a tool box. The tool box contains everything you might need to build a table from a pile of wood. If you have no knowledge or experience, you might – eventually – build something that looks like a table, but you won't feel so clever if it falls over when you use it. It is much better to let someone give you instructions. In this chapter I am that someone, standing next to you with suggestions and rules of thumb on how to work with codes and all related issues. I have been through the process of trial and error myself and, 15 years ago, I was coding and approaching analysis very differently from how I do today. In the following, I would like to share with you what I have learned over the years. Remember the data landscape that I

Figure 5.1 Looking at data like a landscape to be explored

showed you in the Introduction? I have pasted the image of it here again to prepare you for the journey that now lies ahead of you. And before the journey begins, I would like to call for one last preparatory meeting.

The NCT model of qualitative data analysis

Thanks for stopping by. The aim of this meeting is to tell you what to expect from this journey, the challenges that lie ahead and the tasks awaiting you. The model underlying the method is originally based on a paper by Seidel (1998). The model was first presented to me in 1992 and since then I have developed it further, adapting it for computer-assisted analysis procedures. The three basic components of the model are noticing things, collecting things and thinking about things (i.e. NCT; see Figure 5.2). The three thin arrows indicate that the process of analysis can be linear – starting with noticing interesting things in the data, collecting these things and thinking about them, and then coming up with insightful results. This direct sequential process is, however, rather rare. More often, analysis means moving back and forth between noticing, collecting and thinking, as shown by the heavy arrows in the middle of the figure.

First, I would like to explain the three components in more detail. Although there is a large range of analytic practices in qualitative research, the three components of noticing, collecting and thinking can be regarded as basic elements common to all of them. For example, if you take a look at the book by Creswell (1998), you will find these three elements in each of the five research traditions described. Let's take a closer look at them now.

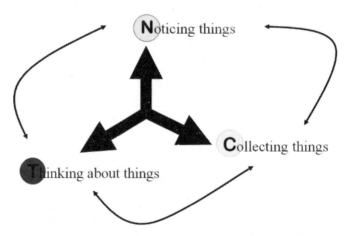

Figure 5.2 The NCT model of qualitative data analysis adapted from Seidel (1998)

Noticing things

Noticing refers to the process of finding interesting things in the data when reading through transcripts, field notes, documents or newspaper articles; when viewing video material or images; or when listening to audio files. In order to capture these, the researcher may write down notes, mark the segments or attach preliminary codes. Codes may be derived inductively or deductively. At this point, the level of a code does not play a role. Codes may be descriptive or already conceptual. The important point is to mark those things that are interesting in the data and to name them.

Collecting things

Reading further, you will very likely notice a few things which are similar to some you have noticed before. They may even fit under the same code name. If a similar issue does not quite fit under the same heading as the first issue you noticed, you can simply rename the code to subsume the two. Even if the term is not yet the perfect code label, it does not matter. You can continue to collect more similar data segments and later, when you review them, it will be easier to think of better and more fitting code words to cover the substance of the material you have collected. The intellectual work that needs to be done at this stage is the same as has been described in the past for manual ways of coding. As Strauss and Corbin wrote in 1998:

> As the researcher moves along with analysis, each incident in the data is compared with other incidents for similarities and differences. Incidents found to be conceptually similar are grouped together under a higher-level descriptive concept. (p. 73)

Differently from grounded theory, the NCT analysis does not prescribe any particular way of coding. The initial process of collecting, i.e. coding, can be manifold depending on the underlying research questions, research aim and overall methodology you are using. To name just a few of the various procedures that you will find in the literature:

- descriptive or topic coding (Miles and Huberman, 1994; Saldaña, 2003; Wolcott, 1994)
- process coding (Bodgan and Biklen, 2007; Charmaz, 2002; Corbin and Strauss, 2008)
- initial or open coding (Charmaz, 2006; Corbin and Strauss, 2008; Glaser, 1978)
- emotion coding (Golemann, 1995; Prus, 1996)
- values coding (Gable and Wolf, 1993; LeCompte and Preissle, 1993)
- narrative coding (Cortazzi, 1993, Riessman, 2008)
- provisional coding (Dey, 1993; Miles and Hubermann, 1994).

The NCT method of analysis encompasses all methods of coding and suggests computer-assisted procedures for how to deal with them. Researchers may choose to follow just one of the suggested procedures or combine them. The things you collect in your data may include themes, emotions and values at the same time. You may approach the process with a deductive framework in mind, as used in provisional coding, or you may develop codes inductively, as suggested by initial or open coding, or use a mix of deductively and inductively developed codes. Some researchers develop 40 codes, others a few hundred or even a few thousand.

The NCT method of analysis provides answers for what to do with your codes within a software environment. Often there is a lack of methodological understanding of what a code is. The software does not explain it; it just offers functions to create new codes, to delete, to rename or to merge them. The metaphor of collecting helps novice researchers to understand better that a properly developed code is more than just a descriptive label for a data segment and that it does not make sense to attach a new label to everything one notices. Developing too many codes is clearly an adverse effect of using software – no one would ever come close to 1000 or more codes when using old-style paper and pencil techniques – and too many codes lead to a dead end when using software to analyze your date. There might be exceptions, but in most cases this hinders further analysis.

In order to understand this better, I would like to do a virtual jigsaw puzzle (Figure 5.3) with you (see also Seidel and Kelle, 1995). Imagine that you and your fellow traveling companions are sitting with me, your guide, at a table in a rest house. I open up a box filled with 1000 jigsaw pieces; I dump them on the table and spread them out, making sure that all the pieces are picture side up. It's your turn now. You have to solve the puzzle. How do you go about it?

Figure 5.3 Playing a puzzle

Most people would answer that either I begin with the corners and the edges, or I sort by colors or shapes. Let's begin with the corner and edges. Why do you think that most people begin like that?

These pieces are easy to recognize since they have at least one straight edge. When it comes to analyzing a project in ATLAS.ti, I likewise recommend you begin with what is easiest.

The easiest option for setting up a project, as explained in Chapter 3, is to create a project folder and add all the documents to it that you want to analyze. In addition I recommended you make use of already known characteristics,

Figure 5.4 Starting to lay the frame

incorporating them into the file names for easy sorting and ordering of the documents within the HU. If applicable, document groups like male, female, location, age, etc. can also be created during the project setup stage. By setting up the project in this way, literally speaking, we have framed it (Figure 5.4).

Once the frame is ready, we need to take a closer look at what is inside. Following the second suggestion, this means sorting the pieces of the puzzle by colors and shapes (Figure 5.5). The sample puzzle here depicts a castle, with a forest around it and a lake in the upper right-hand corner (I know this as I have seen the lid of the box!). In terms of your research projects, what is equivalent to the lid of the box?

That's right – your research questions. However, they only guide your research, they do not show a predetermined result as the picture on a puzzle box does. Some puzzles are more similar to what we do as qualitative researchers, the

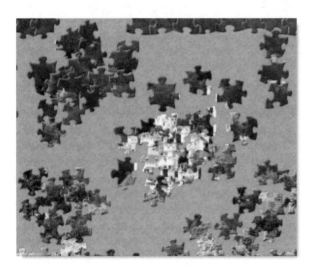

Figure 5.5 Sorting pieces by colors and shapes

so-called WASGIJ puzzles (that's 'jigsaw' backwards). The finished puzzle does not correspond to the picture on the box. The solver needs to assume the role of one of the people on the cover and the solution is the motive as seen from the perspective of this person. However, he or she does not know which of the perspectives must be taken. Only the puzzle itself provides the answer. That makes the task more difficult – but who said that qualitative research is easy?

There are inevitably some puzzles with no picture on the box. They are comparable to a project where it is difficult to find existing literature or previous research on the subject matter. Thus, you may have a hard time developing detailed research questions based on previous knowledge and the only option you have is to go into the field and start collecting data. Like a puzzle with no premade solution, such a project is proportionately more difficult than one which is guided by research questions, so I would leave it to more experienced researchers. For smaller classroom projects or for a short-term thesis, select a research question that can be clearly outlined so it can serve as your guide. When you conduct an interview study and develop an interview guideline, the questions can be used to look for themes in the data. This is similar to collecting all the pieces in the sample puzzle that look like parts of a castle, a lake or a forest.

To remind you of the three basic steps of the NCT model, collecting during the phase of qualitative data analysis means coding. Thus, our initial ideas for coding can be derived from our research questions, from theories, from the literature or from the interview guideline. Ideas for coding in the grounded theory sense can also emerge from the data, but this is not so easy for a beginning researcher, as Kelle and Kluge (2010) note: 'novices in the field of social research have a particularly tough time following recommendations like "let theoretical concepts emerge from your data material". For them, such attempts will likely result in drowning in data material for months' (p. 19).

Staying with the puzzle analogy, a few additions need to be made. The puzzle is already broken down into pieces. In computer-assisted analysis, we actually need to create the pieces. In ATLAS.ti these are quotations. You can work with so-called free quotations without labeling them, as some users do, but the pieces are easier to recognize if you give them names. In ATLAS.ti these names are codes. There is no visual differentiation between different levels of codes, whether they are already codes in a methodological sense or just a description of a data segment. One could indicate this in the code definition, but often at the beginning of the coding process the development is still very open. Most codes are preliminary. Thus, I would not spend too much time initially contemplating whether a code is already a code or just a piece of the puzzle. It is more important to collect ideas and to develop them into proper concepts and categories over time. You will find a glossary at the end of this chapter where the various terms like codes, concepts or categories are defined.

The 'right' length for quotations

As with other aspects of qualitative research, there are no set regulations, only rules of thumb. Consider the likelihood that you will not always work in the context of your data. You will create paper output from time to time, some more than others. This is user specific. The paper output only contains the quotation, not the surrounding context. A quotation should be long enough for you to understand its meaning without the context. If you know the data very well, quotations can probably be shorter. Three words might be enough to remind you of everything else that is going on in the data. When you work in a team and the labor of coding is divided, you are less familiar with all of the data and so quotations need to be longer. There could, for example, be a rule that quotations should be at least the length of a full sentence.

Quotation length also relates to the chosen analytic approach. Conversation analysts tend to code very short data fragments of only a few words. Therefore, the answer needs to be: It depends …

In order for you to test whether the quotations are the correct length for your first coding experience, I will explain two ways of creating an output of quotations for a specific code:

- Open the Code Manager and select a code.
- From the Code Manager's menu select **Output / Quotations** for the selected code(s).
- Select **Editor** as the output destination.
- Read through the quotations and decide whether you have chosen the right length.

The other way is provided via the query tool. The output only contains the text of the quotations and their references and needs fewer pages:

- Open the query tool via **Tools / Query Tool.**
- Select a code from the list at the bottom left of the window. Double click on it.
- The results are shown in the pane at bottom right (Figure 5.6). Above this pane, you will see an output button in the form of a printer symbol. Click on the output button and select the option **Full Content – No Meta**. A window will open: accept the default settings.
- Next, select **Editor** as the output destination.

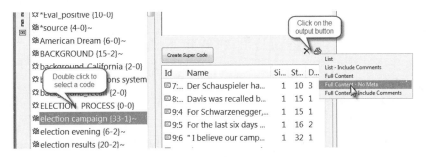

Figure 5.6 Creating output without meta information

Another question that is frequently asked is what to do when the same thing is mentioned several times in a longer paragraph. Can quotations be 'interrupted' or should the entire paragraph be coded, or every segment separately?

As there is no option for collecting different data segments to form one quotation, I recommend coding each instance separately. If you code the entire paragraph you cannot focus on the issue of interest, as there will be too much other information around it when retrieving the quotations later. Coding only the first occurrence and ignoring the rest is not a solution either, because this will not reflect the data adequately. If the duplications include different nuances, and thus are not mere repetitions, this is a good reason to code them. When there is no new information, you can simply code the first instance, create quotations from the repeated instances and link them to the first one via hyperlinks. That way you do not lose anything. Everything that you do not code or mark is forgotten after a while. You are not likely to look at it ever again. An example is shown in Figure 5.7. For more information about hyperlinks and how to create them, see Chapter 7.

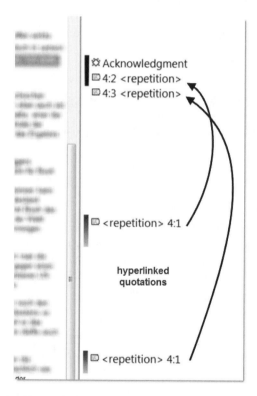

Figure 5.7 What to do with repeated occurrences

The 'right' number of codes

Initially, codes might be nothing more than individual named pieces of the complete puzzle. A project containing 2000 or more codes only presents the first stage of the analysis: that of breaking up the data into pieces by noticing interesting things in them. Collecting has so far only occurred very rarely. This can easily be seen by looking at the code frequencies in the Code Manager. When a project contains a large number of codes, the code frequency is usually low for most of them.

You don't need to worry if this is so in a few cases. Perhaps it is because there aren't enough data yet, or it is just one aspect of an otherwise larger elaborated category. But if most of your codes show a very low frequency then there is still some work to be done, and the development of the coding system is not yet finished. A general rule is that a developed project should show a healthy balance between the total number of codes and the frequency of each one.

After the first coding exercise you can try to evaluate yourself. Are you a person who uses more abstract terms as code labels, and thus likely to generate fewer codes containing a lot of quotations, or are you the type who works very closely at the data level creating a large number of descriptive codes, each only containing a few quotations? Or are you somewhere in between?

I have not conducted a randomized quantitative survey on coders and coding styles, but from experience and knowing that most things in this world are evenly distributed, most coders will be somewhere in the middle, using a mix of abstract and descriptive codes, while a few will be at the extremes, creating either just a few abstract codes or a lot of descriptive codes.

The puzzle analogy assumes that we begin with abstract codes. It is a model and models tend to simplify this world so we can better understand it. Keep this in mind when we continue to discuss the next steps in solving the puzzle.

So far we have put together the frame and we have collected those pieces that look as if they are related, like castle or lake pieces, into separate piles. The next step is to take a closer look at one of the piles, let's say the castle. Naturally, one now looks again for related pieces like parts of the roof, the towers, the windows, or the battlements. Now we are creating subcategories; these are the properties of the castle (Figure 5.8).

Figure 5.8 Creating subcategories of the main category castle

By the way, you are already very skilled at constructing subcategories. You do it every day and you learned the technique a long time ago when discovering the world as a child. You may have first realized that a certain animal is a dog and then probably used the word 'dog' for all the different kinds of dogs. Later you learned that they are beagles, boxers, golden retrievers, poodles or mongrels. Developing subcategories for your data is not much different.

Let's assume you have collected lots of quotations under a common label; the next step is to look through them, as I did with the castle pieces. After reading or looking at a few quotations, you will quickly notice where the commonalities are. This is easier now than it used to be when coding a document from start to finish. The software allows you to take a focused look at only a selection of the data.

After your first day on the trail, after you have already collected a few things that we can use as examples, I have planned a feedback session and some more skills training. Then I will show you how the development of subcategories works technically. Further, I will explain what to do with descriptive codes and how to move them to a more abstract level.

To finish solving the puzzle, we need to put together the other main themes in the same way as we did with the castle pieces. The last step is to see how it all fits together. This brings us to the thinking part.

Thinking about things

We need to use our brains from the very beginning of the analytic process, even though I have left the thinking aspect of the model until last. We need to think when noticing things, when coming up with good names for codes, or when developing subcategories. We need to do some more thinking when it comes to finding patterns and relations in the data. This mostly takes place after coding when asking, 'How do the various parts of the puzzle fit together? How can we integrate the various aspects of the findings in order to develop a comprehensive picture of the phenomenon studied?' At this later stage we need different ATLAS.ti tools like the **query tool** (see Chapter 6) or the **co-occurrence explorer**. When we begin to see how it might all fit together, we can use the **network view** function to visualize these ideas and to explore them further (see Chapter 7). According to Konopásek (2007), ATLAS.ti is especially suited to making the thinking part of qualitative data analysis visible.

Projecting the NCT model onto computer-assisted qualitative data analysis

When looking at the three basic aspects of computer-assisted analysis – preparing data and creating a project file, coding the data, and using the software to sort and structure them with the aim of discovering patterns and relations – the NCT model can be projected as shown in Figure 5.9.

It would be great to be able to move in a straight line from the data to noticing, then to collecting, and finally to thinking and discovering wonderful new insights. Unfortunately, it is not as simple as that. Let's take a look at the possible variations in conducting a qualitative data analysis.

Variations of the three notes: noticing, collecting, thinking

One variant is the **sequential** process where you move directly from A to B to C as described above. Unless you have a very structured and simple project like the analysis of an open-ended survey question, then this will seldom be possible.

More likely is a **recursive** process where you move back and forth between noticing and collecting, for instance when developing subcategories. You may also want to go back to noticing and recoding after already having discovered some relations and created networks. The visualization gives you a different angle on the data: it may be used to talk about your ideas with others and then you may notice you have overlooked something and you need to go back, rethink and recode. You may also decide that you need to collect some more data and thus, after further collecting, you begin with noticing again.

A third variation is a **holistic** approach. If you get to a point where you cannot see the wood for the trees or the sheer number of pieces of the puzzle is overwhelming, or if you feel you simply cannot sit in front of a computer

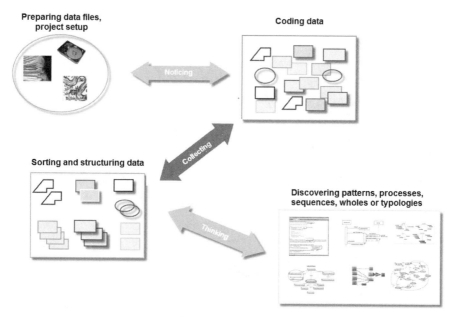

Figure 5.9   A simple projection of the NCT model

screen any longer, then it is time to take a look at the whole again. Take a print-out of one or more transcripts. In summer, look for a nice place outside; in winter, find a cozy spot in front of the fire. Have something to eat and drink and then spend some time reading through your data from beginning to end in a sequential order, reminding yourself of the interview situation or other contexts. Do the same with videos or other types of data you may have. There is no need to sit in front of the computer all the time. Reading the data via a different medium, such as on good old-fashioned paper, is likely to provide further insights. It may help you to see how it all fits together and how the results that you have so far can be integrated.

To sum up, real-life qualitative data analysis looks as shown in Figure 5.10: a bit messy but fascinating and exciting. Did you note the new element in Figure 5.10, the report? Usually there are deadlines for submitting a research report or your thesis or a paper. Thus, in addition to noticing, collecting and thinking, you need to do some writing. While writing, a lot more thinking occurs. The memo function in ATLAS.ti greatly supports you in this. When used appropriately, it provides you with the building blocks for your results section.

You are likely to use memos throughout the entire process of analysis, but they play a major role when it comes to writing and producing a report. We need to talk some more about memos in an analytical sense and memos as a technical function in ATLAS.ti. I often come across projects where the memo

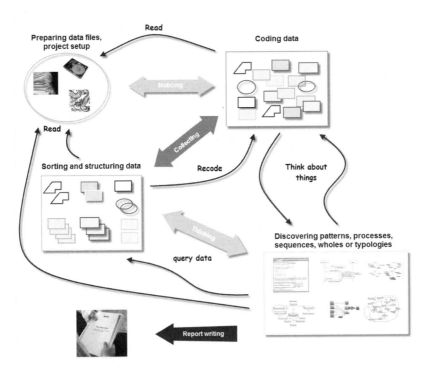

Figure 5.10   The process of computer-aided qualitative data analysis

function is used very little or not at all, as users either have no idea what to do with it or misuse memos as comments and drown in a large number of what aren't really memos at all. You will learn more about the memo function and how to use it in Chapter 6.

I hope that you are ready now and raring to embark on the journey. Remember the NCT model: if you get lost, it will remind you of the tasks that need to be done. The first day will be easy going – just keep an open mind, notice as many things as you can and collect them via coding. We will meet up again after this first day for a feedback session. Thus, there is nothing to worry about; we'll take it step by step.

The journey begins: noticing things and collecting them

Finally, the first day of the expedition has arrived. Here are some final instructions:

- Open the Schwarzenegger sample project.
- Read through a couple of the newspaper articles (or all of them) to get a feeling for the data.
- When you start noticing things in the data (Figure 5.11), begin to collect them by assigning them a code. Don't think too much about a perfect code label, just write whatever comes to mind and continue. You can always rename the codes later.

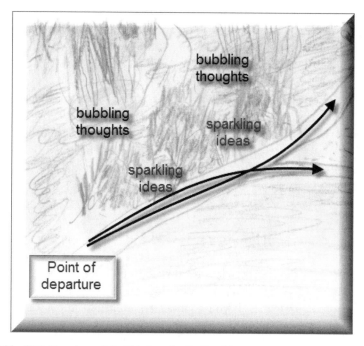

Figure 5.11 First day out – noticing things and collecting things

In case you already wondered, here is the **research question**: That Arnold Schwarzenegger won the election on 8 October 2003 is an objective fact. How is this fact portrayed in the media? Do all newspapers report the same-thing? In what way do they report the event? What similarities and differences can you find?

If you feel that it is important to read through all of the articles first and to write down notes on a piece of paper before you create codes in ATLAS.ti, then this is a suitable way to proceed. If, after reading a few of the articles, you already have some ideas for codes, then go straight ahead and start coding in ATLAS.ti. This is fine as well. Do whatever feels most natural to you.

- Continue with this exercise for at least 45–60 minutes. You may create up to 20 codes within this time or only six or seven, depending on your style of coding.
- If you have questions regarding how to structure your list of codes and how to organize them, don't worry about it now. We will discuss that in our next feedback session. I want you to keep your mind open and notice as many things as possible without putting them into little boxes too soon. Remember, this is only your first day of coding.

Feedback session: what did you find?

How did it go? Was it fun? How did you cope with the technical aspects of coding in ATLAS.ti: creating codes, modifying quotations, renaming codes, etc.? Please write down any thoughts and questions that arose during your first day of the journey before you read on.

I cannot ask you to show me your list of codes, but I have some lists created by four other coders who have already done this exercise based on the German/English data set (Table 5.1). The English-only data set (including only American newspaper articles) may result in slightly different codes.

You can see from Table 5.1 that there is considerable overlap, even though the four coders coded the data independently and at different locations. I have not counted the number of people who have coded these data, probably a few hundred by now. The results always look very similar. Therefore I allow myself to conclude (even though not scientifically proven) that qualitative research is not as subjective as it is often accused of being.

How to add more structure to your exploration

In order to generate sufficient ideas for developing a coding system, an hour or less is not enough. You need to plan more time for it. There are no set rules, but I can offer a few guidelines. If you conduct an interview study, select three to five interviews depending on their length. If you analyze newspaper data, as in the sample study, you will probably need 20 to 30 articles. Begin by coding the data as we did on the first day of our journey: keep it very open, just collecting

Table 5.1 Ideas collected by four coders

Coder 1	Coder 2	Coder 3	Coder 4
American Dream	Accusation of sexual misconduct	Arnie's best sayings	Emotions
Austria	Bush	Bush	Election results
Bush	California	California	California
California	Campaign pledges	Democrats	Description of person
Car taxes	Election campaign	Campaign pledges	Economic framework
Democrats	Emotional reaction on election results	Election victory	Hollywood career
Economic situation	Gray Davis	Electoral statistics	Media
Election	Landslide victory	Information about person	Policy framework
Election poll	New elections?	Republicans	Private life
Election results	Personal description of Schwarzenegger	Rival candidate	Voter opinion
Election victory	Political position of Schwarzenegger	Sexual allegations	
Energy crisis	Reasons for recalling Davis	Supporter	
Financial gap	Reasons for voting Schwarzenegger		
Five-point plan	Turnout		
Gray Davis	Wife		
Hollywood star			
Majority			
Maria Shriver			
New comer			
Republicans			
Schwarzenegger			
Sexual misconduct			
Turnout			
Unemployment insurance			
Unemployment rate			
Voting behavior			

some ideas. At first you will generate lots of new codes; in time you will reuse more and more of the codes that you already have and you won't need to create new ones. You will have reached your first saturation point. In technical terms, you will drag and drop existing codes from the Code Manager onto the data segments.

As soon as you reach this point – when no new codes are being added and you only use drag and drop coding – it is time to review your coding system. If you do it at a much later stage it will take more work, because then you'll have to go through all documents again to apply newly developed subcategories and recheck all other codings.

Let's assume you have taken your first round of coding up to this point. Those coders who naturally develop a mix of descriptive and abstract codes will probably end up with approximately 100 codes, depending on the project. Smaller student projects may contain around 50 to 70 codes. Generally, the cleaning up and restructuring of a first code list is done within the software. When you do it on paper, you need to apply the changes inside ATLAS.ti in a second step.

Figure 5.12 provides the visual equivalent of the various elements that were noticed in our data landscape on the first day of the excursion.

If you have noticed a lot of things – let's say you already have 200 or 300 codes – your codes are probably very descriptive. Coders of this type often find it very difficult to let go of their codes by merging and sorting them, for fear of losing something. I can assure you that this is not going to happen. Instead of labeling almost every quotation and making a code out of it, after restructuring you will end up with a single code containing maybe 10 quotations in their original form. This is much better than one which basically just paraphrases the original data.

The need to push codes from a descriptive to a conceptual, more abstract level was just as relevant to manual ways of coding. Corbin and Strauss (2008) wrote:

> One of the mistakes beginning analysts make is to fail to differentiate between levels of concepts. They don't start early in the analytic process differentiating lower-level explanatory concepts from the larger ideas or higher-level concepts that seem to unite them. … If an analyst does not begin to differentiate at this early stage of analysis, he or she is likely to end up with pages and pages of concepts and no idea how they fit together. (p. 165)

This still applies to a computer-assisted analysis, even if the computer can handle 5000 or more codes. But this won't help you with your analysis. You'll just end up in what I call the code swamp. If you are a person that likes to work close to the text, at least at first, then it might be easier for you to print out the

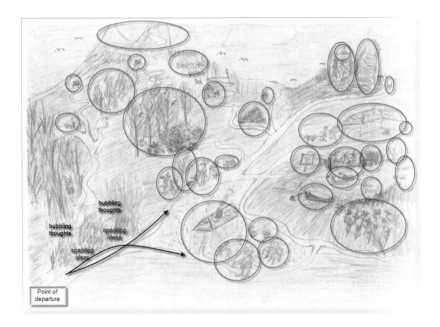

Figure 5.12   After the first day of collecting

list of codes so you are forced to think on a more abstract level away from the data on a piece of paper. And this is how you do it:

- Open the Code Manager and select OUTPUT / CODE LIST. Send the output to an editor. In ATLAS.ti all of these will be rich text editors. You can make changes to the text: delete it, save it, print it or copy and paste it into a Word document.

I will demonstrate how to clean up and structure a code list within ATLAS.ti, using the codes collected by the four coders in Table 5.1. If you are working in a team, you can proceed likewise. The first step is to merge all codes with the same name or meaning. Then you begin to sort and resort the codes. On the one hand, you look for codes that are similar and might fit together under a more abstract category name. On the other hand, you try to identify very broad codes that may already be at the category level. Those need to be broken down into smaller subcodes.

As I have not yet explained merging, I will simply add the four code lists in a rich text editor and then import the combined code list into a new project. Thus, I am restructuring the codes based on their labels without checking back with the data themselves. If you go through this process in a team, I recommend merging the subprojects so that access to the data is given.

Sometimes two coders may have chosen the same or similar labels, but they mean different things. In that case it is necessary to see the data that were coded. Remember to work with user accounts when working in a team, so you can see who has done what (see 'Creating user accounts' on p. 49). If you are on your own, then you are working in the context of the data anyway. I recommend doing the sorting and restructuring only on paper if you are the type of analyst who generates lots of descriptive codes and has a hard time thinking of more abstract code labels.

For sorting and ordering the Schwarzenegger data codes, I proceeded as follows. I merged all duplicate codes. This reduced the list to 53 codes. Next, I merged all codes that use a different label but appear to have the same meaning, like 'accusation of sexual misconduct' and 'sexual allegations'. The list is now cleaned up and I can move on, adding more conceptual structure to the list. Codes like Maria Shriver or Hollywood do not tell us much apart from the fact that the name or word is likely to be mentioned in the coded data segment. These codes have to be either renamed or subsumed under other codes. When looking at the codes we have, Maria Shriver and Hollywood relate to other codes that describe Arnold Schwarzenegger in different ways: a description of him as a person or as a political newcomer or of his past, offering some biographical detail. As it appears, developing a category for Arnold Schwarzenegger seems to be a good idea. This way I can sort all these aspects into different subcategories.

How can this be achieved in ATLAS.ti? The code list in ATLAS.ti is linear and by default sorted in alphabetic order; therefore we need to play with the name in order to add some structure to the list. I usually add prefixes to the name followed by an underscore. Instead of the underscore, you can also use a different character like a column. What is important is that you clearly separate the prefix indicating the main category from the subcategory name. This way all subcategories are automatically sorted under the main category name.

For the main category name, I use capital letters. This is a habit I developed when using version 5, when code names could not be colored. In version 6 that became possible, but I still like the capital letters for the main category name, to indicate the start of a new category. Sometimes you will need to play around with the prefixes so that the codes are in fact in the order that you want them, with the main category name on top. Therefore I added the characters SCHW_ in front of the name SCHWARZENEGGER:

SCH_SCHWARZENEGGER
Schw_biography origin
Schw_biography professional
Schw_description as person
Schw_political new comer
Schw_political position
Schw_private life

Another category I created from the above collection of ideas is 'Political Program':

POL PROGRAM
pol program_energy crisis
pol program_five-point plan
pol program_reducing financial gap
pol programm_car taxes
pol programm_unemployment insurance
pol programm_unemployment reduction

The categories as proposed here have a provisional character as they are based on very little open coding. With additional coding, they are likely to be developed further. I like Saldaña's idea of first-cycle and second-cycle coding. The idea of the cycle fits the nature of the NCT model where we have seen that qualitative analysis is cyclical rather than linear. First-cycle coding, according to Saldaña (2009), refers to those processes that happen during the initial coding (p. 45). In NCT analysis these are the ideas we have noticed and collected on our first day of the journey as shown in Table 5.1. Second-cycle coding is the next step. Its main goal is 'to develop a sense of categorical, thematic, conceptual, and/or theoretical organization from your array of first cycle codes' (Saldaña, 2009: 149). The process of second-cycle coding refers to classifying, prioritizing, integrating, synthesizing, abstracting and conceptualizing. In NCT analysis, Saldaña's notion of second-cycle coding means adding more structure to the code list. This is still part of what I call **first-stage coding**. In second-stage coding, you apply the developed codes to the remaining data material.

Describing coding as a process that consists of at least two stages is common to a number of authors (see, e.g. Kuckartz, 1995; Kuckartz, 2005; Charmaz,

2006, Fielding and Lee, 1998, Lewins and Silver, 2007; Bazeley, 2007; Bazeley and Richards; 2000; Kuş Saillard, 2011). From my experience, telling software users that it is a good idea to develop codes into categories and subcategories makes sense to them as they will already have read about it in the literature. The problem is the translation of this process into mouse clicks and the technicalities of it in a software environment. Even if they know the technical aspects of coding, the users still find it difficult to apply these skills. It is actually not difficult, but neither is it self-explanatory. If you find yourself struggling, I invite you below to another skills training day offering three training sessions.

Figure 5.13 shows how the first-cycle codes from the four coders were sorted and reordered during second-cycle coding. There are a few codes that could not be classified into a category, since it was too early to make a decision.

Figure 5.13 Sorted and structured code list

The code 'American Dream', for instance, may turn into a category of its own at some point. If you take a look at the subcategories of 'Political program', you may notice that they are still very close to the data. Reviewing more data material is likely to allow for formulating more conceptual labels. Other categories still need to be filled, such as the background information category, or the emotions or future outlook category. There is probably also more to come in terms of reactions from other individuals, groups, official representatives of other countries, etc.

Another way of sorting a code list is with the help of numbers and special characters. The sort order is as follows: special characters, numbers and letters. Sorting by numbers has the advantage that you can determine the sequence of your categories. The code list in Figure 5.14 describes a merger and acquisition process and questions regarding organizational fit come before the final results. As the label 'final results' begins with an f, it would come before the category 'organizational fit'. In addition to the number, letters were inserted indicating the major theme, like J for Justice and C for Controllability. The characters a, b, c were used when it became necessary to develop more subcategories for an already existing subcode. Continuing the number scheme would have otherwise ended up in long chain of numbers. Inserting letters also

1_EXOGENOUS VARIABLES
11_OP_ Organisational Fit

2_ INTEGRATION PROCESS
21_J_Organisationale Justice
211_J_distributive
212_J_procedurale
212a_J_evaluation of the process
212b_J_time span
212c_J_ working conditions
213_J_interpersonal

22_C_Perceived Controllability
221_C_explicability
222_C_transparancy

3_EMOTIONAL RESULTS

4_FINALE RESULTS

Figure 5.14 Sorting a code list by numbers and letters

avoids changing the sequence of numbers all the time when inserting new categories or subcategories.

Thoughts on inter-coder reliability

As you can see from the list of codes in Table 5.1, the four different coders dealing with the same research question did not come up with four completely different coding ideas. There are some differences but considerable overlap as well. As the saying goes, four eyes see more than two. Thus, the combined coding scheme of all four is probably better than one developed by just one person, but they won't be completely different. As Strauss and Corbin (1998) point out: 'The data themselves do not lie' (p. 45). If we try to apply our personal view to the reality of data, we are likely to find out that it does not work and that we have a hard time relating in a meaningful way. Different coders may detect different aspects, but if they stay true to the data, it will be difficult to draw merely subjective conclusions originating from the persona of the researcher who conducted the study. In addition, there are of course a number of other aspects to consider in order to ensure the validity of a qualitative research project. You can find these in almost any book on qualitative research methods (see, e.g., Charmaz, 2006; Denzin and Lincoln, 2000; Seale, 1999).

When it comes to the issue of inter-coder reliability, I am not an advocate for calculating a value that determines the degree of agreement between two or more coders. It can easily be done with the help of computers. When working with ATLAS.ti, you can upload data coded by different coders to the free Web-based software CAT (the Coding Analysis Toolkit).[1] The result is a figure between 0 and 1 and it will tell you how good the level of agreement is between two or more coders. This is suitable for studies with a large database where only few codes are used, when for instance analyzing public comments on issues like climate change, the Gulf coast oil spill, etc. CAT itself, or its sibling PCAT, are probably the best tools for such an analysis anyway.

When using ATLAS.ti, I am not greatly interested in the actual figure indicating the degree of agreement. Rather, I would take a closer look at the content of those segments where the two coders do not agree and have them talk about it. It may be simply that they mean the same thing but used a different code, in which case the code definition is not yet clear enough. If they disagree on the actual content, then they have to find a compromise on how to handle such segments in the future: they might agree to apply one of their two codes or one that is more suitable, on a higher level or with a different label. In the end, there should be no differences in their coding and 'convergent validity' will have been achieved (in case you are looking for some terms for your methodology section).

If you have the opportunity to ask a second person to code one or two of your documents after you have developed a coding system and added code definitions, it is very valuable. For me, however, this has more to do with increasing the validity of a coding scheme than being an issue of reliability.

---

1 The Coding Analysis Toolkit (CAT) is available at: http://www.qdap.pitt.edu/cat.htm, or via the ATLAS.ti main menu HELP / MORE RESOURCES / THE CODING ANALYSIS TOOLKIT.

More on code word labels

We have seen above that you can create a classification system to distinguish between different kinds of codes in the code list. A code word label should not be too long, however, even though ATLAS.ti does not dictate a maximum number of characters. The margin offers only limited space and the Code Manager, which is usually used for coding, should be no wider than necessary. Because of this, you should accustom yourself to use significant abbreviations and to write a longer and more detailed definition in the comment field of the Code Manager instead of creating long code word labels.

Do I need to code everything?

This is a typical student question. After asking whether they need to transcribe everything, the next question is, 'Do we need to code everything?' The crystal clear answer is again *yes* – with a few exceptions.

Some authors propose procedures like focused coding, where you only focus on a specific aspect of the data and leave out everything else. This might be okay when coding already existing documents or data that were not written or produced for the purpose of your own research. But when you collect your own data, why go through all that effort only to analyze half of it? Seemingly unimportant parts of an interview may turn out to be very relevant when you look at them more closely. At first, it may seem no more than a polite gesture when an interviewee asks whether you want some more coffee. Examining the text more closely, it may turn out that the interviewee was trying to avoid answering your question and looking for an opportunity to digress from the topic or gain time to think of an answer. You cannot know this initially and therefore I don't think it wise to transcribe an interview only partly or code it only selectively. If you do not know from the outset whether a passage is important or not, you can invent a code name that reflects this – such as 'not sure yet' or 'maybe important' or 'review later'. These codes mean that you will not completely forget about these passages. Anything not coded has no chance of being reviewed later on, and if these seemingly unimportant passages turn out to be helpful in understanding what is going on in your data, then this outweighs the little extra work required.

In contrast, some methodological approaches require researchers to look only at certain aspects of the data, for example in phenomenological research. Phenomenologists are only interested in how something is experienced and not in any of the interpretations the research participant may provide. They therefore may code only those parts that are relevant for a phenomenological assessment. Coding the entire data corpus, however, will allow the same or other researchers to look at other aspects of the data to complement the findings.

Skills training day

In Figure 5.15 we can see how the charting of the landscape is taking shape. Flowers of the same kind are identified along with different types of animals, different aspects of the forest, the benches, various elements of the houses, the people and the various destinations.

This is basically the same as I did with the codes of the four coders. I identified everything that describes Arnold Schwarzenegger in some way, his political program or the election campaign. You already know the ATLAS.ti tools and functions that you can use to structure your coding system in the same way – but as a novice it may not be obvious how to use them. Therefore, I have organized this skills training day where I will show you:

- how to create subcategories from a larger group of quotations that you have collected;
- how to build a main category from small pieces of data that are still coded on a descriptive level.

I have prepared a special project that you can download from the companion website (www.quarc.de/qualitative-analysis-with-atlasti.html) as practice material. The project contains some codes that contain a lot of quotation and need more finely grained development, and others that are descriptive and still very close to the data. They demand more conceptualization.

Skills Training 1: developing subcategories

The goal in developing subcategories is to achieve a good description of heterogeneity and variance in the data material. In principle, two approaches are

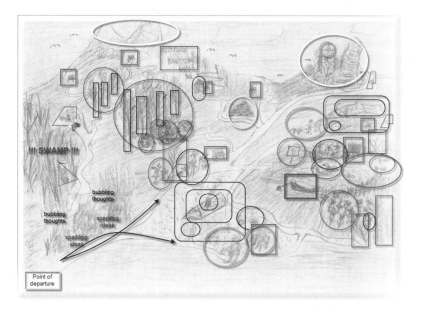

Figure 5.15 Structured landscape

possible: subcategories can be developed based on previous knowledge (i.e., known aspects from theoretical literature), or founded empirically on the basis of the data material. In the following I will explain the empirically based approach.

- Load the Schwarzenegger project for Skills Training 1.
- Open the Code Manager and take a look at the list of three codes. Three aspects have been coded for this exercise: BACKGROUND, ELECTION CAMPAIGN, POLITICAL PROGRAM.

Here the codes are described:

BACKGROUND: background information provided on the state of California, the political system, the recall and past events (23 quotations).
ELECTION CAMPAIGN: all reports on the election campaign (32 quotations).
POLITICAL PROGRAM: all aspects related to the political program of Arnold Schwarzenegger and his plans for the state of California when he is elected as governor (21 quotations).

The three codes in capital letters are equivalent to the castle pieces of the jig-saw puzzle. They contain a loose collection of data segments relating to back-ground information, the election campaign or the political program of Arnold Schwarzenegger. No attempt has yet been made to separate these various aspects. When you begin to code, you may not know which aspects are salient and provide good reasons for forming a group of their own, so it is easier to collect the various aspects under a main theme first instead of wondering where a data segment might belong and how to name it. You will see when doing the exercise that it is much easier to develop suitable code labels when reading through 20 or 30 examples of similar quotations.

- Choose one of the three codes in capital letters (BACKGROUND, ELECTION CAMPAIGN or POLITICAL PROGRAM).
- Double click on the code and read through the quotations. Your task is to develop sub-categories based on the major theme.

The NCT model comes into play here again:

- After reading through a few quotations, you are likely to notice quotations that refer to the same aspect and others that describe another facet of the main theme. When you are at this point, start collecting these aspects. Usually I write them down on a piece of paper and run a tally. Figure 5.16 shows my notes on the category 'Political Program'.

Looking at the extracted terms helps to conceptualize them further. Abortion rights and gay rights can be brought together under the heading 'human rights'. Emotional appeals, vague promises and general change could be summarized under 'non-specific pledges'; tax issues can be integrated into

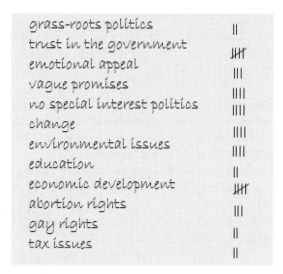

grass-roots politics	II
trust in the government	JHT
emotional appeal	III
vague promises	IIII
no special interest politics	IIII
change	IIII
environmental issues	IIII
education	II
economic development	JHT
abortion rights	III
gay rights	II
tax issues	II

Figure 5.16   Noticing and collecting in the process of developing subcategories

economic development, and so on. The aim is to look at the bandwidths of issues mentioned and to come up with a label that best describes the most similar ones.

After you have decided which subcategories you want to use, you need to enter them into ATALS.ti and then recode the data. In order for the subcodes to show up under the main code, you need to use a prefix:

Pol program_grass roots politics
Pol program_trust in the gov.
Pol program_non-specific pledes
Pol program_economic development
Pol program_human rights
Pol program_education

You can manually create these subcodes in the Code Manager, or you can use an option in the Memo Manager to add a list of codes. I want to show you the latter option as it is also useful to know when working with an already known list of codes:

Importing a list of existing codes

- Open the Memo Manager. You should know by now how to do so.
- Create a new memo by clicking on the button for creating a new item.
- The Memo Editor opens. Change the default title in the Memo Manager to **code list**.
- Type the list of subcodes into this memo, one code per line.
- Save the memo by clicking on the button with the check mark and close it.
- Highlight the newly created memo 'code list' and select from the menu **MISCELLANEOUS / CREATE CODES FROM SELECTED MEMO**. A window pops up telling you that x number of codes have been imported.

You can reuse the code list memo when developing other subcategories. It is not meant to document your analytic steps in any way. You do this in your research diary. Consider the code list memo as a little helper that makes your life a bit easier.

- Go back to the Code Manager and see whether you can find the new codes in the list. If you followed the above example, the subcodes should appear above the main category code. This means that we need to change the name of the main category code to P_POLITICAL PROGRAM. Then click on **F5** to resort the list.
- The main category code is green. To colour the subcodes as well, highlight them and click on the colour wheel in the toolbar. Select a colour and click on **OK**.

All quotations are still contained in the main category code. The next step is to distribute them to the subcodes (Figure 5.17).

- Double click on the main category code P_POLITICAL PROGRAM and select the first quotation.
- Read it and decide into which subcategory you want to move it. Select the appropriate subcode in the Code Manager and drag it onto the main code in the margin area, thus replacing it.

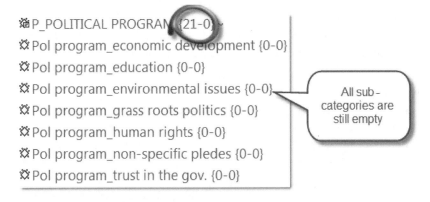

Figure 5.17 Main category code with subcodes

There is no need to leave the main category code attached to the segment. It just clutters up the margin. It is easy to collect the quotations in one main category via a code family later. For now the aim is to empty the main category code and fill the subcategories with content (Figure 5.18). You may need to adjust the length of some quotations or create new ones. If you come across a quotation that you find difficult to sort into any of the existing subcategories, code it to the main category. The important thing is that you do not force your data into a subcategory just because it exists. Regard the developed subcategories as preliminary; they may change. Over time you may think of better names, or even decide that a subcategory is not suitable after all and you need to

Figure 5.18 Subcategories filled with content

intergrate it somewhere else. You have only coded a very few documents up to this point and this is most likely not the final version of your code list. But you can already work with it and when coding more documents you can sort data segments right away into the developed subcategories. It is not very efficient to loosely code all of your data material now and have to go through the above process of developing subcategories later. It is best to begin quite early with this. As mentioned earlier, a good time to do this is the first saturation point when you mainly apply existing codes via drag and drop from the Code Manager.

Skills Training 2: searching for a common denominator – building categories from the bottom up

- Load the Schwarzenegger project for Skills Training 2.

This project contains 42 codes related to addressing and describing Schwarzenegger. These codes were created in vivo and thus are very close to the data. The length of the quotations was extended in order to include a bit more contextual information. For this exercise, I want you to take a closer look at the 42 codes. The aim is to learn how to move analysis from a descriptive to a conceptual level.

Most of the codes just reflect single pieces of the jigsaw making up the person of Arnold Schwarzenegger. There are already a few larger groups like the names Mr. Schwarzenegger, Arnold Schwarzenegger or just Schwarzenegger or Arnold. For the moment, let's focus on the codes with lower frequencies and to see whether you notice any similarities and can do some more collecting. If we leave it as it is, there is the danger of ending up in the code swamp (Figure 5.19).

What often happens at this stage is that analysts use code families to collect their descriptive codes. The codes are not renamed, they stay as they are in the

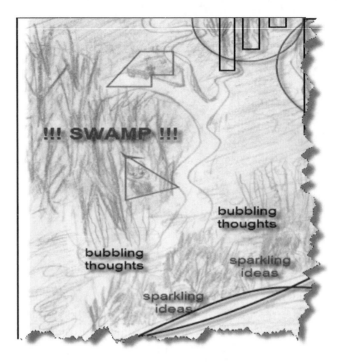

Figure 5.19   Avoiding the code swamp I

Code Manager and the abstract code names end up in a different window, namely the Code Family Manager. This is not a good idea. It leads to endlessly long code lists that are of no use in querying the data in the next phase of the analysis; it creates problems when visualizing your findings with the help of the Network View Manager; and it makes it impossible to explain your coding scheme to a third person. Read more about it during the 'intermezzo' in Chapter 6.

Applying the NCT process once again

The codes describing Arnold Schwarzenegger in various ways may look like real codes at first glance but they are not yet proper codes in a methodological sense. They just represent things I noticed in the data and in order not to lose them I gave them a name. Now I can use the software to retrieve the things I noticed about the different ways Arnold Schwarzenegger has been described and to think some more about them. The aim is to find some commonalities within this conglomeration of terms and to add some order to it. This is what I suggest you do:

- Open the Code Manager.
- Think of some abstract terms that allow you to summarize the various description of Arnold Schwarzenegger. For example, there are numerous codes referring to his professional

background as a body builder or actor. We can subsume these codes under the more conceptual label **biography_professional**.

- Click on one of these codes like 'a blockbuster recall'. Right click and select the option **RENAME**. Rename the code to 'biography_professional'.
- Now we need to merge all other codes into this code: right click again and select the option **MERGE CODES**. A window pops up listing all codes currently filtered.
- Select all codes that refer to Arnold Schwarzenegger's professional past by holding down the **Ctrl**-key. I found a total of four codes and 13 instances that were merged into the new code 'biography_professional' (Figure 5.20).
- Continue with this process. Collect what you think is similar and can be subsumed under a common code label. Suggestions are:

Biography_personal
Biography_origin
Official title
Political orientation_moderate republican
Political orientation_democratic positions
Political novice
Characteristics attributed by author
Characteristics attributed by voters

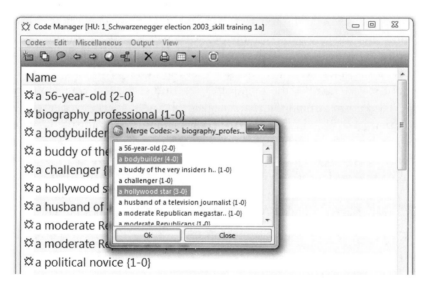

Figure 5.20 Building a conceptual code from the button up

As these code labels would still appear all over the place in the alphabetic code list, we need to add a prefix to all of these labels, so that they are united under a common heading. I have chosen the prefix Schw_ and the category name SCHW_SCHWARZENEGGER and listed all the codes in Figure 5.21. This category shows the heterogeneity in the descriptions of Arnold Schwarzenegger and now only contains nine codes.

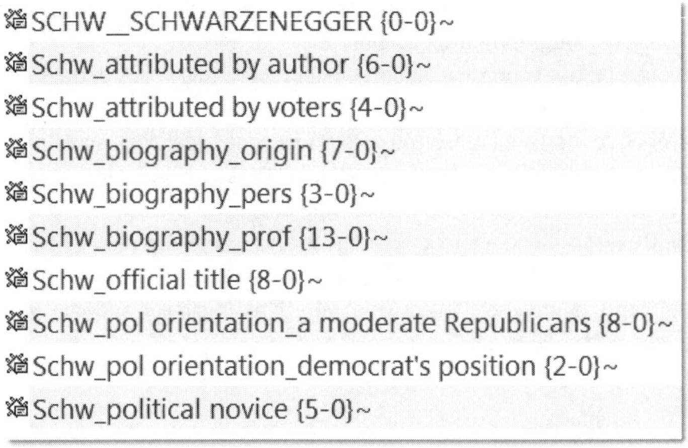

SCHW__SCHWARZENEGGER {0-0}~
Schw_attributed by author {6-0}~
Schw_attributed by voters {4-0}~
Schw_biography_origin {7-0}~
Schw_biography_pers {3-0}~
Schw_biography_prof {13-0}~
Schw_official title {8-0}~
Schw_pol orientation_a moderate Republicans {8-0}~
Schw_pol orientation_democrat's position {2-0}~
Schw_political novice {5-0}~

Figure 5.21 Describing Schwarzenegger conceptually

The 61 coded data segments and 38 codes are now subsumed under 9 code labels and 56 quotations. The reduced number of quotations means that some of the descriptive codes coded the same data segment. If you want to read the original text behind them, double click on any one of the conceptual codes and ATLAS.ti will lead you directly to the original text passage. Nothing is lost. If you hold onto the collection of individual data pieces instead, you are likely to end up in the code swamp. The symptoms are a very long code list (over 400 or more codes) and very low frequencies for most codes.

As you may remember, the total list of descriptive codes contains four more codes. These are: Arnold Schwarzenegger (10), Mr. Schwarzenegger (28), Schwarzenegger (32) and Arnold (9). Each of these codes already contains a larger number of quotations as indicated by the number in parantheses. Hence we don't need to aggregate these codes further. Moreover, we can use them to ask different questions like, 'Which of the names is used in what kind of context? When is Arnold Schwarzenegger addressed by his full name, more formally as Mr or like a friend as Arnold?' A fitting category name could be FORM OF ADDRESS:

> FORM OF ADDRESS
> Form of address_Arnold
> Form of address_Arnold Schwarzenegger
> Form of address_Mr Schwarzenegger
> Form of address_Schwarzenegger

Reconsidering the other codes we already have, it might be more suitable for the code Sch_official title to be moved into the new category FORM OF ADDRESS:

- You do this by renaming the code 'Sch_official title' as 'form of address_official title'. To re-sort the list, press the F5 button.

To examine the FORM OF ADDRESS category:

- Read through the quotations where Arnold Schwarzenegger is addressed in different ways. Can you find any interesting patterns?
- If you notice that certain ways of addressing him occur in specific contexts, take the analysis a step further and continue to develop the FORM OF ADDRESS category.

A possible result might be that you no longer need this category. Maybe the full name is always used in the context of reporting on the election result. Then it might be more suitable to turn it into a subcategory of election results. Another analytic focus could be the use of language. Then you could develop a 'Use of Language' category and possibly the form of address codes would fit there too. The point I want to make here is that a first reordering and re-sorting may not immediately result in the final version of your coding scheme. Analysis is an ongoing process and as long as it continues, your code labels may change and their positions may shift.

Skills training 3: rules for hierarchical coding schemes

In Skills Training 2, we learned what to do in order to avoid the code swamp. There is another dangerous track that leads us to the swamp if we are not careful. You may wander onto this track when one code is made up of two or more content layers. Taking a look at the Schwarzenegger project, there are codes related to the various people involved, like Mr. Davis, Mr. Schwarzenegger, Mr. Bush, etc. Depending on the author, these persons may be evaluated positively, negatively or neutrally. The election results or the various campaign strategies may also be evaluated in different ways. If you were to add the type of evaluation behind each code name, then you would create an unnecessary long code list. It would look like this:

Person_ Davis_negative
Person_ Davis_neutral
Person_ Davis_positive

Person_ Schwarzenegger_negative
Person_ Schwarzenegger_neutral
Person_ Schwarzenegger_positive

Person_ Bush_negative
Person_ Bush _neutral
Person_ Bush _positive

Election results_neutral
Election results_negative
Election results_positive

Do you see what is happening? The evaluation is added to each code label it applies to, thus extending the code list unnecessarily. What needs to be done is to extract the second content layer from the code and create a new

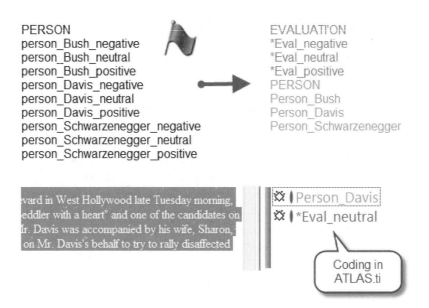

Figure 5.22   Coding for different content layers

main category code with subcodes that describe variability, like the type of evaluation or other subcategories. In this case, we want a main category code 'Evaluation' containing the subcategories positive, negative and neutral. You can make use of the capabilities of the software later to find all desired combinations, like all positive portrayals of Davis to compare to all positive depictions of Schwarzenegger. Figure 5.22 shows how to deal with codes that occur repeatedly.

When you notice repetitive coding, imagine a park ranger standing at the side of the track brandishing a red flag. It's a warning that you're heading for the swamp. Don't continue on this route. Instead, delete the repetitions at the end of the code word labels and create a new category for the codes that indicates a different layer of content. To separate theme codes from those adding a further description like an evaluation or a measurement of some sort, I suggest marking all these kinds of codes with an asterisk (*) or a hash sign (#). This way they will show at the top of the code list and be easy to find.

To avoid the code swamp, apply two (or more) codes to the same data segment, one code from each content layer (see also Richards and Richards, 1995; Araujo, 1995).

Advantages of well-sorted and structured code lists

There are a number of advantages when you organize your code list in the way presented in the previous skills training sessions. It not only helps you to find

Figure 5.23 Avoiding the code swamp II

your way around better, but also adds transparency to the research process and others can follow what you have done more easily. It also adds methodological rigor. It is when you begin to bring some order to your list that you realize what might be a good candidate for a category; it points to those codes that are in need of differentiation and it helps you to identify those codes that are not yet on the conceptual level, being too close to the data and offering no more than just a summary of a data segment (see also Fielding and Lee, 1998: 92ff.; Charmaz, 2006: Chapter 3; Saldaña, 2009).

Sorting and structuring your codes also prepares for the next level of the analysis where you begin to look for relations and patterns in the data with the ultimate aim of integrating all findings to tell a coherent story. Similar to statistical research, if you only ask questions with yes and no answers you'll end up with variables on the lowest level. This means that you cannot take the analysis much beyond the descriptive level, cross-tabulations and chi-square tests being the most sophisticated analytical procedures you can run. This is comparable to a code list that consists of a bunch of codes whose analytical level remains undetermined. An example of such a code list is shown in Figure 5.24. The

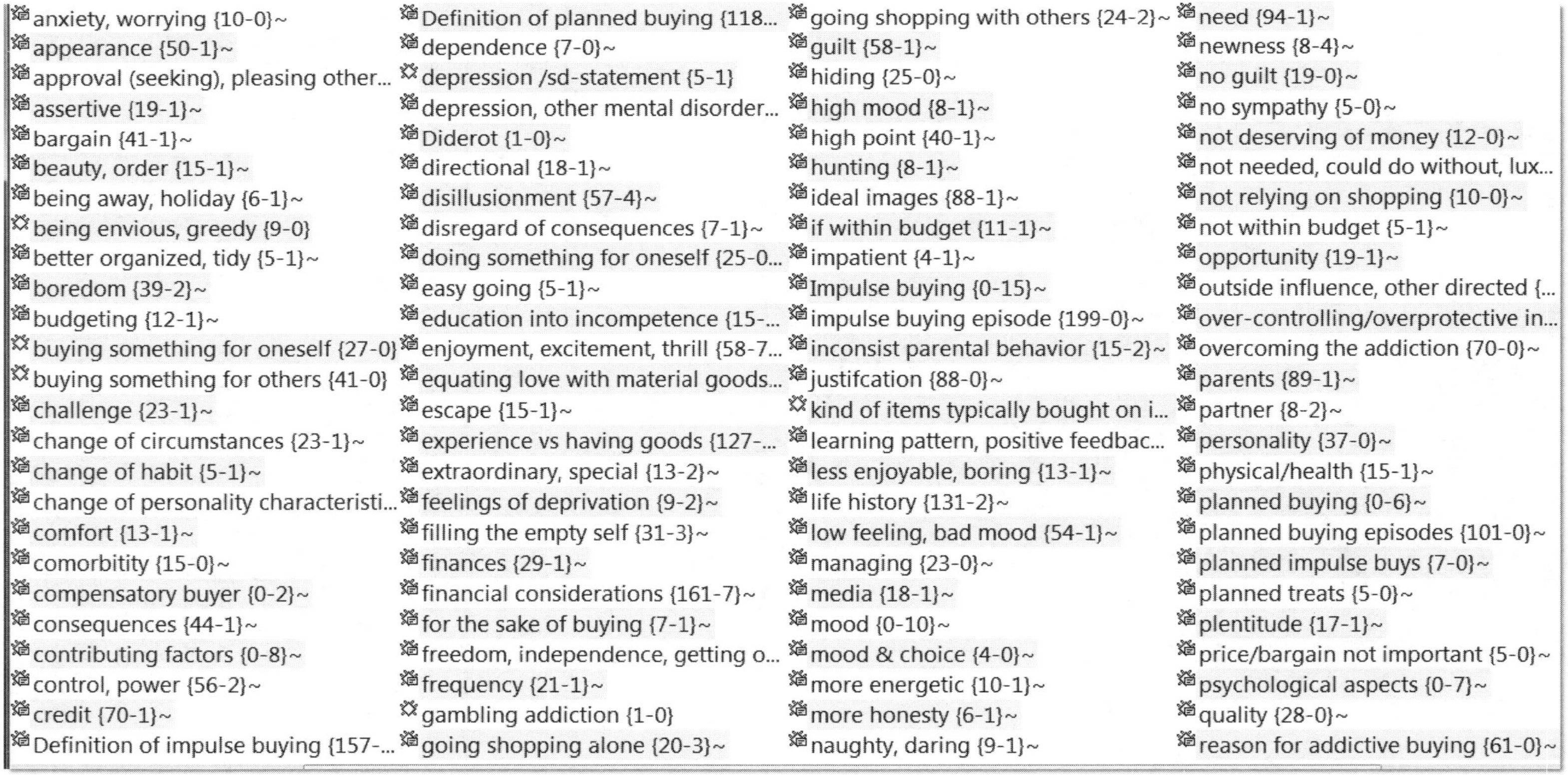

- anxiety, worrying {10-0}~
- appearance {50-1}~
- approval (seeking), pleasing other...
- assertive {19-1}~
- bargain {41-1}~
- beauty, order {15-1}~
- being away, holiday {6-1}~
- being envious, greedy {9-0}
- better organized, tidy {5-1}~
- boredom {39-2}~
- budgeting {12-1}~
- buying something for oneself {27-0}
- buying something for others {41-0}
- challenge {23-1}~
- change of circumstances {23-1}~
- change of habit {5-1}~
- change of personality characteristi...
- comfort {13-1}~
- comorbidity {15-0}~
- compensatory buyer {0-2}~
- consequences {44-1}~
- contributing factors {0-8}~
- control, power {56-2}~
- credit {70-1}~
- Definition of impulse buying {157-...
- Definition of planned buying {118...
- dependence {7-0}~
- depression /sd-statement {5-1}
- depression, other mental disorder...
- Diderot {1-0}~
- directional {18-1}~
- disillusionment {57-4}~
- disregard of consequences {7-1}~
- doing something for oneself {25-0...
- easy going {5-1}~
- education into incompetence {15-...
- enjoyment, excitement, thrill {58-7...
- equating love with material goods...
- escape {15-1}~
- experience vs having goods {127-...
- extraordinary, special {5-1}~
- feelings of deprivation {9-2}~
- filling the empty self {31-3}~
- finances {29-1}~
- financial considerations {161-7}~
- for the sake of buying {7-1}~
- freedom, independence, getting o...
- frequency {21-1}~
- gambling addiction {1-0}
- going shopping alone {20-3}~
- going shopping with others {24-2}~
- guilt {58-1}~
- hiding {25-0}~
- high mood {8-1}~
- high point {40-1}~
- hunting {8-1}~
- ideal images {88-1}~
- if within budget {11-1}~
- impatient {4-1}~
- Impulse buying {0-15}~
- impulse buying episode {199-0}~
- inconsist parental behavior {15-2}~
- justifcation {88-0}~
- kind of items typically bought on i...
- learning pattern, positive feedbac...
- less enjoyable, boring {13-1}~
- life history {131-2}~
- low feeling, bad mood {54-1}~
- managing {23-0}~
- media {18-1}~
- mood {0-10}~
- mood & choice {4-0}~
- more energetic {10-1}~
- more honesty {6-1}~
- naughty, daring {9-1}~
- need {94-1}~
- newness {8-4}~
- no guilt {19-0}~
- no sympathy {5-0}~
- not deserving of money {12-0}~
- not needed, could do without, lux...
- not relying on shopping {10-0}~
- not within budget {5-1}~
- opportunity {19-1}~
- outside influence, other directed {...
- over-controlling/overprotective in...
- overcoming the addiction {70-0}~
- parents {89-1}~
- partner {8-2}~
- personality {37-0}~
- physical/health {15-1}~
- planned buying {0-6}~
- planned buying episodes {101-0}~
- planned impulse buys {7-0}~
- planned treats {5-0}~
- plentitude {17-1}~
- price/bargain not important {5-0}~
- psychological aspects {0-7}~
- quality {28-0}~
- reason for addictive buying {61-0}~

Figure 5.24 A fully developed code list should *not* look like this one

total number of codes is not too bad: 168 for the entire project. Thus, the problem is not that too many codes have been applied to only a few data segments each. Rather, the list contains both: there are codes with low frequencies and those with very high frequencies of over 150 quotations. What is missing is the development of subcategories on the one hand and the aggregation of codes under a common denominator on the other (i.e. the processes you learned about in skills training 1 and 2).

I am allowed to criticize this code list as it is my own, developed in 1999 for my dissertation research. Learning doesn't stop even after you get your PhD! From an analytic point of view, I did develop the ideas collected in the code list further. For example, I differentiated the code 'Definition of impulse buying' which contains 157 quotations, but this is not visible in the code list. For this particular code, I used the network view function.

The study was on impulse buying and in the interview study I identified three groups of shoppers:

1 Utilitarian buyers: those who do not like to go shopping at all.
2 Compensatory buyers: those that don't mind going shopping and sometimes also shop for emotional reasons.
3 Addicted buyers: those who go shopping mostly for emotional reasons.

I asked all of them for their own personal definition of impulse buying. This is what is shown in the network views by type of consumer. On the right-hand side are codes that I derived from the literature, as others before me had already studied impulse buying. In addition, the consumers' definition included psychological aspects and financial considerations. For illustration purposes, I only show two of the network views here (Figures 5.25 and 5.26). You will see that not all of the codes are relevant to each subgroup. The code 'reminder impulse buying' derived from the literature did not apply to addicted shoppers. For them the psychological aspects took up a major part of their definitions. Financial considerations were mentioned along the lines of 'well, it's on the credit card', and thus were more or less disregarded.

In the network views, the analytical work that I have done becomes visible. However, for other codes it is hidden in the written-up results (Friese, 2000).

Today I would differentiate the code 'Definition of impulse buying' in three subcategories, further divided into the various facets. I would probably also work on the code labels a bit more, possibly merging codes like 'something extraordinary' and 'something unexpected'. But for this I would need to take a look at the data material again. Just using what I see today in the network views, I suggest the following structure:

D_DEFINITION IMPULSE BUYING
Def imp_f_disregard of consequences
Def imp_f_not within budget
Def imp_f_within budget
Def imp_psy_for the sake of buying

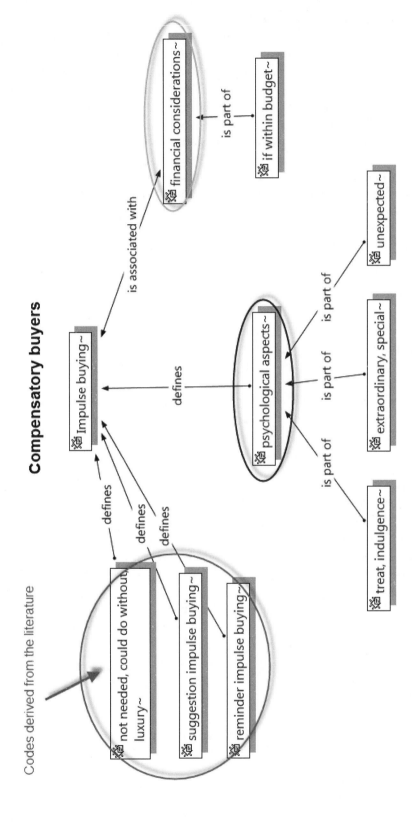

Figure 5.25 Differentiation for the code 'Definition of impulse buying' for compensatory shoppers

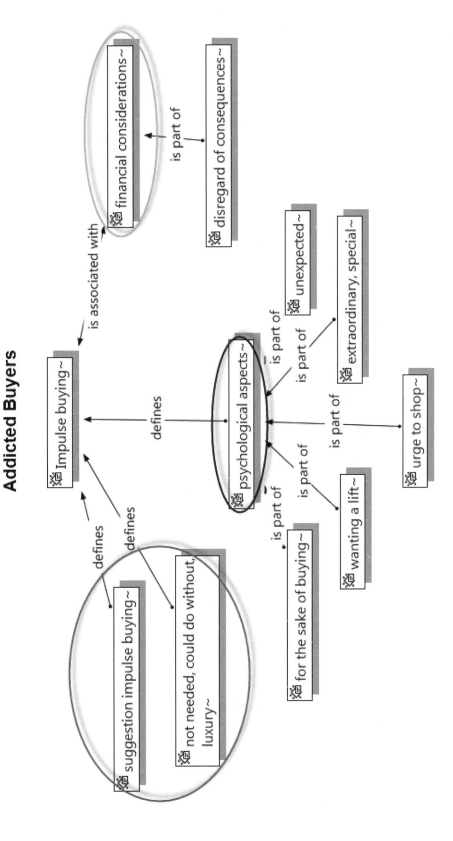

Figure 5.26 Differentiation for the code 'Definition of impulse buying' for compensatory shoppers

Def imp_psy_s.th. extraordinary
Def imp_psy_treat
Def imp_psy_unexpected
Def imp_psy_urge to shop
Def imp_psy_wanting a lift
Def imp_th_non needed_luxury
Def imp_th_reminder impulse buying
Def imp_th_suggestion impulse buying

Such a code list adds more transparency to the research and is easy to explain to another person. After more than 10 years since doing this research, it would take some time to go through the data again in order to retrace my own steps. Had I taken it a bit further and developed the codes into proper categories and subcategories at the time, it would be much easier for me now, or you as the reader, or another third person, to see what was in the data. It would have helped me to follow my own analytic steps and remind myself how I derived my results.

This is one advantage and, from a methodological point of view, an important one. What I have done above with the code list from my dissertation research is of course too late and should not be done just for the sake of transparency at the end of your research project. As I have advised, begin with the sorting and structuring quite early, after the first saturation point when coding your data. Then, during second-stage coding, apply the structured code list to the rest or to the newly incoming data. This allows you to confirm or deny the developed categories and subcategories and it suggests possible missing data and aspects to look for.

Suppose you analyze a total of 20 documents. After coding five documents, you begin to add more structure to your coding system. Then you continue to code. If you need to change a lot, then you know that the coding system needs to be developed further. If you only need to make a few modifications, that is if you don't find many new things of interest or only a few new subcategories, then this is a reassurance that your coding system fits the data well and justification for having developed a valid code system. An obvious precondition is that you need to stay alert to new, as yet unlabeled phenomena in the data and that you do not force the developed coding system onto the data.

Moving on

We are now midway through the journey. The first days (I hope) have been very exciting for you as you discovered lots of interesting things. After the first excitement, some duller days may follow as you continue applying your codes, plowing through the data material. When using manual methods, analysts may not have reviewed all of their material again after developing new codes, applying them consistently to all data. Now that we use software, you are more likely to do this. This allows us, for example, to pick out some numbers and see how frequently a code is applied across different data files. This is only useful if you know that all the codes have been applied to all the data, and it also means that coding at certain stages of the analysis might become a bit tedious – but there is a reward. Well-coded data are likely to reveal interesting insights when querying them. The journey is varied and there is still much to enjoy and to discover if you keep going.

Equipped with these new skills, you will be sent on your way again to continue exploring your data landscape. However, I recommend that you stop at the next skills training session on memos as soon as possible. Note taking and writing a diary is an important part of your equipment and there are some specifics you need to know regarding the ATLAS.ti tool you are using to facilitate your journey.

▰▰▰ 'OPEN BOOK' ASSESSMENT AFTER COMPLETING SKILLS TRAINING 1–3 ▰▰▰

After working through this chapter, you should be able to answer the following questions:

1 How do you navigate through the list of codes in the Code Manager (technically speaking)?
2 How do you generate ideas for codes?
3 Which function do you need to use to import an already existing list of codes?
4 What makes a good code label?
5 Are there any rules regarding the length of a coded segment?
6 What options do you have to structure the list of codes in the ATLAS.ti Code Manager?
7 What are code families useful for?
8 How would you go about developing categories?
9 How would you go about developing subcategories?
10 How can the code swamp be avoided?

▰▰▰ TEST YOUR UNDERSTANDING OF COMPUTER-ASSISTED NCT ANALYSIS ▰▰▰

1 Explain the NCT model and how it can guide the process of developing a code system.
2 Collecting is an important aspect of the NCT model. What role does it play in the process of developing a code system and why is it important?
3 After reading this chapter and putting it into practice, can you describe how to apply the process of noticing, collecting and thinking when working on your own data set?
4 How is solving a jigsaw puzzle similar to qualitative data analysis?
5 How is qualitative data analysis different from solving a jigsaw puzzle?
6 What is a WASGIJ puzzle and what can be learned from it regarding qualitative data analysis?
7 What are the advantages of a well-sorted and structured code list?

Categories and subcategories: The aim of developing a coding system is to organize the data into main categories and subcategories. Main categories at the end of coding are likely to contain no data. They provide a common label for the subcategories united underneath. Depending on your way of coding, you may at first collect data segments within main category codes. This is likely when using a deductive framework. Then subcategories are built based on the items within this main category container by reviewing them, looking for items that are similar and uniting them under a common subcategory label until all items from the main container have found a place in one of the subcontainers.

When beginning with descriptive-level codes, main category codes are developed via the process of conceptualizing, comparing and contrasting data segments and descriptive code labels, looking for things that are similar and developing new code labels that allow for these segments to be collected under a common name. During this process it is likely that main categories and subcategories are developed at the same time.

Categories can contain more than one level of subcategories, if the main aspect can be subdivided further within the same meaning context. Subcategories should, however, not be built up of different types of aspects like reflecting content, an evaluation or a time. A category that contains three or more levels of subcategories should be closely reviewed to check whether in reality it contains different content layers that may be better coded in different categories.

Code definitions: A code definition describes the meaning of a code and how it has been or should be applied to the data. It can contain a coding rule and an example of a typical data segment coded with this code.

Writing code definitions helps to improve the methodological rigor of a study. It forces the researcher to think about the meaning of a code in comparison to other codes. It may turn out that the code system contains codes with different labels but more or less the same meaning. These can then be merged under one common label, which is now also easier to define. Writing definitions also helps to develop codes that are clearly distinct from each other so that they can be applied unambiguously.

Codes as methodological device: You turn codes into methodological devices by adding an appropriate label. Here the process of collecting becomes very important. You need to compare and contrast data segments and think of suitable names for data segments that are similar. Thinking of a common name under which similar data segments can be collected is likely to enable the researcher to move away from the descriptive to a conceptual – and over time to a theoretical – level. During this process the researcher begins to develop categories and subcategories.

Codes as technical device: Technically speaking, a code is a device that can be attached to a data segment as a label. At the beginning of an analysis, this is a useful first step in gaining an understanding of the data. With progressive analysis, however, codes need to be turned into a methodological device. For this, the human interpreter is needed. Software cannot distinguish between different meanings and levels of codes. It can handle 50 as well as 5000 codes without telling you whether they make sense or not. There is no computer function that can bring order and logic into your collection of codes.

Coding system: A well-developed coding system describes the data material in all its facets. It shows the main aspects in the data in the form of categories and the variations within a main category in the form of subcategories. The coding system can reflect different types of main aspects depending on the research questions and the aim of the study. These can be the pure content of the data, the layout, the language used, aspects of time, different speakers or actors, evaluations, level of importance, degree of expression, etc.

As a rough guide, computer-assisted coding systems contain on average about 100–250 codes and 15–30 main categories.

Collecting: The first codes that are created may just be descriptive labels. These need to be conceptualized with further coding. The aim is to collect similar data segments under a common code label and not to give each data segment a name.

Conceptualizing: Conceptualizing refers to the process of (1) moving from descriptive-level codes to conceptual-level codes, and (2) developing subcategory labels based on data segments collected within too large a container. Conceptual-level codes unite data segments with similar content; they fulfill the criteria of being a properly sized container where all those things are collected that have something in common and that are in some ways different from others.

Method of computer-assisted NCT analysis: The recurrent components of the methods are noticing things, collecting things and thinking about things. They occur during the process of initial first-stage coding, are repeated when structuring the code list into higher and lower order categories, and play a role again in second-stage coding and also during the further analytic process. Then noticing, collecting and thinking shifts to collecting ideas, interpretations and gaining insights. For a detailed description of the method, see Chapter 8.

Noticing: Noticing refers to the process of reading or looking through your data (like an explorer walking through an unknown landscape) with the aim of describing the territory in as much detail as possible. The explorer takes out his or her notebook and starts writing down notes or drawing sketches. The qualitative researcher as explorer begins to mark and label segments, creating quotations and adding first codes.

Further reading

Araujo, Luis (1995). Designing and refining hierarchical coding frames, in Udo Kelle (ed.), *Computer-Aided Qualitative Data Analysis*. London: Sage. Chapter 7.

Bong, Sharon A. (2002, May). Debunking myths in qualitative data analysis [44 paragraphs]. Forum Qualitative Sozialforschung/Forum: Qualitative Social Research [Online Journal], 3(2). Available at: www.qualitative-research.net/fqs-texte/2-02/2-02bong-e.htm.

Breuer, Franz (2009). *Reflexive Grounded Theory: Ein Einführung in die Forschungspraxis*. Wiesbaden: VS Verlag.

Charmaz, Kathy (2006). *Constructing Grounded Theory: A Practical Guide Through Qualitative Analysis*. London: Sage.

Dey, Ian (1993). *Qualitative Data Analysis: A User-friendly Guide for Social Scientists*. London: Routledge.

Gibbs, Graham (2007). *Analysing Qualitative Data (Qualitative Research Kit)*. London: Sage.

Kelle, Udo (2004). Computer-assisted qualitative data analysis, in C. Seale et al. (eds.), *Qualitative Research Practice*. London: Sage. pp. 473–89.

Kelle, Udo und Kluge, Susann (2010). *Vom Einzelfall zum Typus: Fallvergleich und Fallkontrastierung in der qualitativen Sozialforschung*. Wiesbaden: VS Verlag.

Kluge, Susann (2000, January). Empirically grounded construction of types and typologies in qualitative social research [20 paragraphs]. Forum Qualitative Sozialforschung/Forum: Qualitative Social Research [Online Journal], 1(1). Available at: www.qualitative-research.net/fqs-texte/1-00/1-00kluge-e.htm.

Lewins, Ann and Silver, Christine (2007). *Using Software in Qualitative Research: A Step-by-step Guide*. London: Sage. Chapter 7.

Miles, Matthew B. and Huberman, Michael (1994). *Qualitative Data Analysis* (2nd edn).Thousand Oaks, CA: Sage.

Richards, Tom and Richards, Lyn (1995). Using hierarchical categories in qualitative data analysis, in Udo Kelle (ed.), *Computer-Aided Qualitative Data Analysis*. London: Sage.

Saldaña, Jonny (2009). *The Coding Manual for Qualitative Researchers*. London: Sage.

Seidel, John (1998). Qualitative data analysis. www.qualisresearch.com.

Seidel, John and Kelle, Udo (1995). Different functions of coding in the analysis of textual data, in Udo Kelle (ed.), *Computer-Aided Qualitative Data Analysis*. London: Sage. Chapter 4.

SIX

Further steps in the data analysis process

Coding is a necessary step for describing what's in the data. But you can go beyond description and develop your analysis further. In this chapter you will learn how to work with comments and memos in ATLAS.ti and how to query your data, in order to find answers to your research questions. I have decided to put both aspects in this chapter because, when doing qualitative data analysis, they belong together. You are not just writing notes or simply querying your data. The two need to go together so you can move forward with the analysis. A lot of the analysis happens as you write, not by clicking on some buttons and outputting some results. You need to look at what the software retrieves, read through it and write it up in your own words in order to gain an understanding of what is happening in the data. Most of the time insights need to be worked at and are not revealed to you immediately by looking at the results. Simply seeing that there are, say, 10 quotations is not enough; numbers are sometimes useful, they hint that there might be something interesting there, but the important step is to take a closer look and to see what's behind them.

As you can see in Figure 6.1, I included lots of benches in the data landscape that we are exploring. The benches signal points of reflection on our journey as an important part of data analysis. Reflection is important throughout the entire research process. Before even beginning a project, researchers should reflect on their personal position on the issue that they plan to examine.

We need to be aware of bias and how we as researchers might impose our own views on the data. Thus it may seem odd to be introducing the memo function first in Chapter 6 after I have already shown you how to build up a coding system. Memos also play a role in earlier steps of the analysis, but as I mentioned before, it's best to take things one step a time. I did not want to put you off by explaining too many things at once.

Introducing the memo function

ATLAS.ti's 'benches for reflection' in the data landscape are its comment fields and the memos. We have already looked at three of the comment fields: those for primary documents (see Chapter 3) and those for quotations and

Figure 6.1 Benches of reflection

for codes (see Chapter 4). As a reminder, it was explained that the P-Docs comment field is useful for adding meta information to a document like an interview protocol, which contains reflective notes on the interview situation and its circumstances. Quotation comments are useful for writing notes on a particular data segment. And code comments were described as being very useful in clarifying what is meant by a particular code. It is a place for writing down a code definition or a coding rule, forcing you to reflect more closely on its meaning. In addition to this, ATLAS.ti offers memos as a place for writing.

Memos are an object class of their own. This should already hint that memos are different from comments (see also Konopásek, 2007). However, I have no idea why, but memos are highly underutilized in ATLAS.ti. Users often treat them like a comment function and discover after a while that this isn't very successful; or else they don't use memos at all. This is not to say that many analysts don't write memos, they probably do – but using a word processor rather than directly in ATLAS.ti. The disadvantage if you do that is that you are away from the data and you cannot link a Word document to a segment in your data. Within ATLAS.ti, you can. In 1998, Fielding and Lee reported that CAQDAS users having difficulties with the idea of writing memos within the software and after coding abandoned the package they were using and completed the analysis manually. More than 10 years later this still appears to be an issue. As writing memos is an essential step in qualitative data analysis, as pointed out by the authors quoted below, I would like to make some suggestions on how to utilize memos within ATLAS.ti and the kind of advantages they offer, as compared to writing notes on a piece of paper or in a word processor:

> Memos and diagrams are more than just repositories of thoughts. They are working and living documents. When an analyst sits down to write a memo or do a diagram, a certain degree of analysis occurs. The very act of writing memos and doing diagrams forces the analyst to think about the data. And it is in thinking that analysis occurs. (Corbin and Strauss, 2008: 118)

> Writing is thinking. It is natural to believe that you need to be clear in your mind what you are trying to express first before you can write it down. However, most of the time, the opposite is true. You may think you have a clear idea, but it is only when you write it down that you can be certain that you do (or sadly, sometimes, that you do not). (Gibbs, 2005)

The quotes allude to the fact that memos are different from comments or short scribbled notes in the margin. They represent analytic work in progress and you can use some of the writing later as building blocks for your research report. In this chapter I will show you how to use the memo function in ATLAS.ti.

As this is a book on software usage, I am not going to give a definitive class on how to actually write memos. This is explained at great length in the third edition of *Basics of Qualitative Research* by Corbin and Strauss (2008) or in the book by Charmaz (2006). I will teach you about possible types of memos and how to set up analytical memos in ATLAS.ti in a way that makes your research transparent and helps you engage with your data, and to enter into an internal dialogue, advancing your analytical thoughts and ways of thinking. Thus, the focus of the chapter is on the thinking aspect of the NCT model of computer-assisted qualitative data analysis. Engaging with your data also means querying them and therefore you will also learn about different methods of data retrieval. At some point in your analysis, you will also want to diagram your thoughts; that will be discussed at greater length in Chapter 7, where you will learn how to do so using the ATLAS.ti network view function.

Skills training 4: some technicalities of memo writing

You are hopefully joining me for this training session before all of your data have been coded. If you have already used the memo function for writing comments, my suggestion is to copy your text into the comment field of the respective data segment and then delete the memos. But you may be asking, 'What should I use memos for if not for commenting on the data?'

You can create 'free' stand-alone memos; that is they need not be attached to any object, or they can be linked to quotations, codes or other memos. Let's start by providing some examples for stand-alone memos. The technical aspects of how to create them are described below.

Examples of stand-alone memos

Research diary

If you are writing a thesis or dissertation, or working on a student or a scientific research project, it is important that you document the analytic process. This is best done in a research diary. You can do this in a Word document, but using an ATLAS.ti memo has some advantages. After an analysis session in ATLAS.ti, you can immediately write down what you have done and timestamp it without having to open another program. It becomes part of your evolving project and can later be submitted together with your project data and your analytic work in ATLAS.ti (e.g. in the form of an html or xml document). Supervisors can follow your analytic steps and for teachers it is useful when grading a project. But there is more to it than just adding transparency; research diaries are useful reminders for the analyst too. It is difficult to keep everything in mind when a project continues over months or even years. The research diary can be reviewed, for example, when it comes to writing the method chapter for a thesis or a paper publication.

Team memos   When you work in a team, all the members can add a team memo to their subprojects. In the team memo you can write down things that you want to discuss at the next team meeting. Put all the team memos together and you already have your agenda for the next meeting. I would advise against merging team memos, as this will only works once. If you merge a second time, the previous entries will be merged again and you will end up with duplications. This also applies to all other memos that use the same title. Therefore, during a merge process, it is best to add rather than to merge memos (read more about merging in the addenda).

Idea memo   If you have a great idea but no time to follow it up right away, write it down before it is lost. However, do not write a memo for every single idea you have! Collect all the good ideas in one memo that you might entitle 'Great ideas to follow up'.

To-do memo   Similar to the idea memo, you can have a memo that contains a to-do list for the next work session or a plan for the next week or analysis period.

Code memo   While your coding scheme is evolving, you may come across a code that needs further attention or a definition that you are not happy with yet. This can be written down in a code memo and, when you have the time, you can deal with all such issues. The code memo therefore collects all ideas and things to do that relate to your coding system. You can of course also add coding-related issues to your general to-do memo.

Code list We have already used this kind of memo for developing subcategories in Chapter 5. It is not a memo in a methodological sense; it is just a technical device to import a list of previously prepared codes (see Chapter 5, 'Importing a list of existing codes', p. 115).

Creating stand-alone memos

Let's create a research diary:

- Open the Memo Manager and click on the button for creating a new entry.
- The memo editor opens. Note that an automatic title has already been entered into the title field. Overwrite that title with 'Research Diary'.

Before we create a second memo, I will show you how to change the default settings to prevent ATLAS.ti from automatically entering a title. It is quite common for users to leave the default title (current date) and then end up with numerous memos that just show the date. This does not give any indication of the content of the memo and facilitates misusing memos as comments.

- To the right of the memo editor, you will see the type field. It shows the current default type, probably 'memo'. You can (1) leave it as it is, as the purpose of the research diary is to help you to memorize the steps of the analytic process; or (2) overwrite it if you don't like it. Another fitting type might be 'method'. Any new type that you enter here can be used also for other memos within the same HU.

Looking at the memo settings, I will show you where to enter global types that will be valid for any HU you are going to work with.

- Click on the down arrow to see the other two default types: 'Commentary' and 'Theory'. As already explained, I do not think that memos serve well as comments. ATLAS.ti already offers enough places to write those. We can get rid of this type in the memo settings a bit later.
- It is a good idea to enter at least the date before writing a new entry into the research diary. You do not need to do this manually. Just select **Ctrl+D** or **Insert / Insert Date / Time** from the menu.
- Write a short entry into your research diary (Figure 6.2) and save the memo by clicking on the accept button.
- Close the editor. You will see that the text you have written into the memo editor also shows up in the lower part of the Memo Manager, the text editor pane. You can also continue to write the memo there, but it is less comfortable and you have fewer editing options.
- To open the memo editor again, click on the editor button in the toolbar.
- If you continue to write the diary after your next work session, remember to press **Ctrl+D** to insert the date and time in front of the new entry.

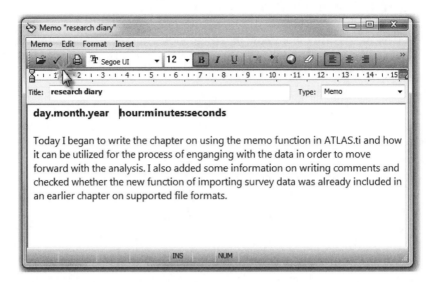

Figure 6.2 Creating a free memo

Changing memo settings

As already mentioned, the default memo settings are problematic in a methodological sense. A memo needs a proper title to serve an analytical purpose; therefore the automatic title setting should be changed. The setting window also allows for defining further memo types.

Let's have a look:

- Open the window for General Preferences: **EXTRAS / PREFERENCES / GENERAL PREFERENCES** or click on the preference button in the main toolbar, the wrench icon.
- Select the **MEMOS** tab.
- Click on the prompt for title option (Figure 6.3). This automatically deactivates the auto title option. When creating the next memo, you are prompted to enter a title before the memo editor opens.
- On the right-hand side of the window you will see the global memo types. Select an already existing type that you do not want to keep and click on **REMOVE**.
- To add a new memo type, overwrite an entry in the top field and click on **ADD** (e.g. enter the new memo type 'analysis'). We will need it a bit later.
- Select one type as **default type** (e.g. the newly created analysis type). Whenever a new memo is created, this will be used: therefore, the default should be the most frequently used memo type in your project.

The purpose of memo types is to sort and filter memos. They also add transparency to your analysis. You are free to create any memo type that seems suitable for your analysis. Keep in mind their purpose – sorting and filtering.

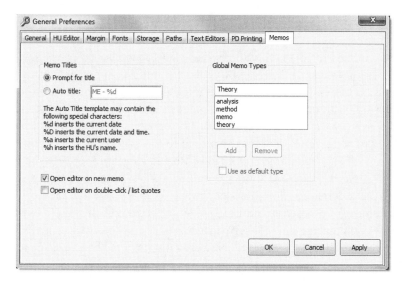

Figure 6.3 Memo settings window

Thus, three to five memo types are probably sufficient. In addition to the type '**memo**', which serves a classic reminder function like the above-mentioned stand-alone memos (things to do, topics to be discussed with team members, or any unresolved matters like ideas or questions), here are a few more ideas:

Use the type '**analysis**' for all memos based on research ideas and research questions. These are the kinds of memos that become more elaborate and longer during the course of the analysis and can serve as the building blocks for your report.

Use the type '**theory/literature**' for memos that contain excerpts from the literature that you are using for your research (see below on connected memos).

There are two more options in the preference window that I have not yet explained:

The option **Open editor on new memo** means that an editor window is opened every time you create a new memo. Deactivate this option if you prefer to write in the text editor pane in the Memo Manager instead.

The option **Open editor on double-click / list quotes** allows you to switch between two settings. If activated, the editor opens when double clicking on a memo title in the Memo Manager. If deactivated, the Memo Manager works in the same way as the Code Manager – that is, when double clicking on a memo that is linked to quotations, the list of quotations is shown. I recommend deactivating this option because you can always open the memo editor by clicking on the editor button in the toolbar; there is no alternative function to open the list of quotations.

- Click on **APPLY** and close the preference window.

Linked memos

Memos can be linked to quotations like codes, but also to codes and other memos. In the Memo Manager, you will also find a column for groundedness and density. Groundedness counts the number of links to quotations; density counts the links to other codes and memos. When linking memos to quotations, the idea is to connect a memo to the data segments that illustrate what you write in it. The direction is from the memo to the quotation and not the other way around. Thus, the memo should exist first, having a proper title and a type. Then you link it to one or more quotations. When you do it the other way around, that is, create a quotation and code it and then attach a memo, you are using memos as comments, and I explained in Chapter 4 that there is a better place for commenting on data segments.

Below, I introduce two kinds of connected memos. Feel free to come up with further ideas for connected memos that suit your project. What is important to remember is that memos are more than comments, in terms of both length and content. A connected memo could be linked to just one quotation, but more likely you will find several data segments that reflect your analytic writing in the memo. There are some parallels to building up an efficient coding scheme. We have seen that creating 1000 codes that only code a few quotations each is not a good idea. This is an indication that the codes have not yet reached a conceptual level. If you create lots of memos containing only one or two sentences and linked to one quotation each, then these are only comments and not conceptual ideas. Memos, like codes, are containers (Figure 6.4): code containers collect quotations, memo containers collect ideas. Below I present some ideas on what kinds of content connected memos can be used.

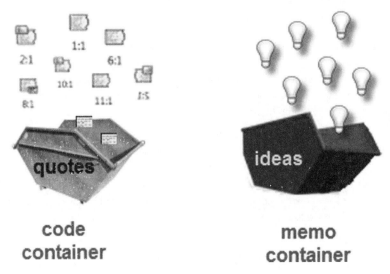

code
container

memo
container

Figure 6.4 Codes and memos are like container

Theory or literature memos

This type can be used to add information from secondary sources to the project, such as excerpts from the relevant literature, main theoretical concepts, etc. These memos partly serve as reminders; instead of having to switch programs or look through a stack of papers to remind you of important theoretical concepts and their definitions, they are right there within your ATLAS.ti project. Additionally, these memos can be used to collect empirical evidence for theories proposed in the literature. When you come across a data segment that ties in with ideas proposed in the literature by other authors, you can connect the respective memo to this data segment.

Technically, you attach a memo to a quotation just like you attach a code: by dragging and dropping a memo from the Memo Manager to the quotation. If working with PDF files, you need to drag the memo onto the quotation bar in the margin. If working with audio, video and Google Earth files, drag it to the relevant entry in the Quotation Manager. This process is described in more detail below.

Research question memos

At first I called these 'analytic memos', but I changed the name since a number of other authors use that term in a different way from what I am suggesting here. Originally, the idea of the analytic memo was developed by Glaser and Strauss (1967) to assist with the development of codes and conceptual ideas during the process of coding. Previously, this was done in the form of writing notes in the margin of the transcript (see also Fielding and Lee, 1998; Lewins and Silver, 2007). Based on this tradition, Charmaz (2006) and also Saldaña (2009) described all memos as analytical. Based on the examples provided above, you have seen that memos in a software environment can facilitate the technical handling of certain procedures or for project management purposes.

Research question memos are also analytic. I describe them as places where you develop the interpretation of your data step by step. You can set them up early in the process of analysis, but systematic writing and development of these memos occur after coding. Thus, I suggest that you concentrate on coding the data first. Then a new phase and different process of analysis begins.

If you are familiar with quantitative research procedures, it may help to compare the two levels of analysis with descriptive and inductive statistics. The equivalent of descriptive statistics in computer-assisted analysis is the development of the coding system. When set up as explained in the previous chapter, the coding system provides an overview of what is in the data. The codes on the category level can be regarded as equivalent to the variables in a survey; the subcategories indicate the variations within the code, similar to the characteristic values of a variable.

Once we are finished with coding, we can describe the data. Perhaps we can already see a few patterns there. We then can take the analysis a step further by querying the data. After coding, it is a matter of a few mouse clicks – and knowing where to click – to dig deeper into the data material and to ask further questions. The tools employed at this stage are the query tool, the co-occurrence explorer and the **Codes-Primary-Documents-Table**. The latter two tools are similar to cross-tabulating or creating a correlation matrix in statistical analysis. All of these are explained further on in this chapter. The aim of these tools is to help you find relations and patterns in the data. Thus, in qualitative research too, there are various levels of analysis. The second level is about asking questions and finding relations. This is the phase where research question memos begin to play a major role in the analytic process.

Differently from statistical analysis, the most important part of the results provided by these tools is the data behind them and not the numbers. You do need to read through, review or listen to those data and then write down your thoughts in a research question memo. These can be various things like description, interpretation or ideas for further questions and queries. You can find a more theory-oriented discussion on hypothesis examination using the various tools and operators which the software provides in Kelle (1995: part III).

Very likely you will not come up with models and highly integrated conceptual ideas from the very start. Thus, whatever you write in your research question memos does not have to be perfect and ready to be published. At some point you will get there, but to begin with your research question memos may simply contain descriptions and summaries of your data. Depending on your research approach and level of methodological knowledge, you may decide not to develop your research question memos further. A thorough description may be all that you want and need. If you take the analysis a step further, some of the descriptive memos may serve as building blocks for more abstract and theoretically rich memos (see also Bazeley and Richards, 2000: part 6).

Hence, working with research question memos and the various tools for querying data is similar in process to inductive statistics. I call it conceptual-level work as compared to the descriptive work of developing the coding system. Before everyone jumps on me and complains that analytic steps cannot be as clear cut as I claim, I confess I am simplifying for the sake of novices who are trying to learn method and software at the same time. With more experience, you can begin to vary the sequence. However, the suggested order is not completely arbitrary: the first step is always to develop some codes and to build up a coding system. Without that, you cannot query the data. You may begin to collect ideas in research question memos as you code, but more extensive writing occurs after all the data have been coded and you start to use the analysis tools which the software provides. In order to see the benefits of it, you have to try it. If you use this book for teaching, you are likely to hear from your students that a lot of things happen when they enter this second phase of the analysis. It is now that they begin to see how the various codes relate to each other; they develop and test new questions and they may find answers that they did not expect to find. I would not exactly call it magic, rather the added value of approaching analysis in a systematic way utilizing the options available.

Creating research question memos

After this long introduction, let's do some practical work and learn the rest by actually doing it. In qualitative research, we generally do not start with hypotheses but in most cases we have some research questions. When using an inductive approach, researchers develop questions and hypotheses along the way. If you begin your project with some research questions in mind, you can create research question memos very early on in the analytic process, adjust and modify them, and add some more with progressive analysis.

I have developed a few research questions for the Schwarzenegger project that we will use in the following to explore the data landscape and to learn more about querying data and writing research question memos.

- RQ1: What kind of information is transmitted via the headlines? What kind of style is used?
  - o Do the journalists use direct speech in headlines?
  - o Which topics are chosen to attract readers to the article?

- RQ2: What is reported about Arnold Schwarzenegger's political program? Are there differences between German and American newspapers?
- RQ3: How is Schwarzenegger presented in the images?
- RQ4: Which contents are reported in American vs. German newspapers? Are there differences?
- RQ5: In what contexts is direct speech used? Why? With what kind of effect?

RQ stands for 'research question'.

- Open the Memo Manager (if it is not still open) and create a new memo.
- As we have changed the settings, you are now prompted to enter a title. Enter the title 'RQ1: Headline contents'.
- Change the memo type to 'analysis'.
- Type the full research question into the editor (Figure 6.5).

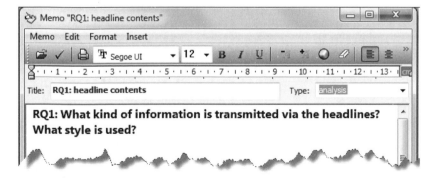

Figure 6.5   First steps in creating a research question memo

Next, we need to think about how to find an answer to this question. The formulation of the question is too broad. Therefore two subquestions have already been formulated.

- Enter the first subquestion in the memo editor: 'Did the journalists use direct speech in headlines?'

In order to find an answer, we need to use the query tool. How to click a query in ATLAS.ti is something you do not know yet. First I want to finish explaining the sequence of preparing a research question memo, then I will introduce the tools that you need when asking questions. We will go through all the research questions, searching for answers and writing research question memos (see 'Skills training 5').

A research question memo should cover the following points, as shown in Figure 6.6 (the lighter text is for instructional purposes only and normally it should not be included). It is important that a research question memo:

- has a proper title that tells you what it is all about;
- can be identified as an analytic memo by its type;
- begins with a well-written research question, possibly followed by subquestions;
- includes the query (!);
- contains an answer to the query – when you work on a memo over a prolonged period of time, you can also insert the date and time to mark your progress;
- contains your answer and interpretation;
- is linked to quotations that illustrate the points you are making in the memo and supports your analytic thoughts.

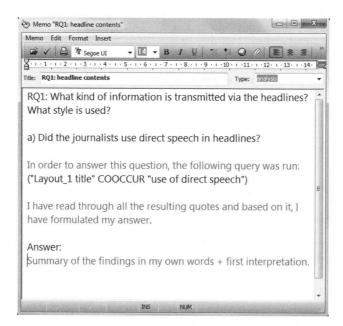

Figure 6.6 Contents of a research question memo

Thus, we still need to do a few things:

- Think of the kind of query that we need to run and add it to the memo in the form of written words, then save the memo by clicking on the accept button.
- Run the query.
- Look through the results, read and review them.
- Link the memo to 'good' quotes.
- Reflect on the results and write an answer.

In your first research question memos, the answers will probably be descriptive. But in time they will become more abstract as you get ideas for further questions, add new research question memos and basically take it one step further at a time, gaining more and more understanding, exploring more and more details of your data landscape and starting to see relations between them. But we are not there yet; so, as I said, for the moment I need to make it seem more rigid and sequential than it actually is. Noticing how things are linked in your data means you will want to get the notepad out to draw diagrams and your first models. In ATLAS.ti, this means creating network views. I have to ask you to be patient. You will learn all about drawing models and visualizing relations and patterns in the next chapter.

Linking a memo to a quotation

I haven't yet shown you how to link a memo to a quotation. Let's pretend that you have run a query and you have come across an interesting quotation:

- Minimize the memo editor. Highlight one quotation in the text by clicking on a code in the margin area. **Then drag and drop** the memo from the Memo Manager across the windows splitter to the left side of the HU editor (Figure 6.7).
- For this exercise, attach the memo to at least two quotations.
- Take a look at the Memo Manager. The count for **groundedness** has gone up.
- Double click on the memo entry. As in the Code Manager, a window pops up showing you all quotations linked to this memo (Figure 6.8).
- When you click on the quotations, they are highlighted in context and you can see where the memo is attached.

Figure 6.7   Linking a memo to a quotation

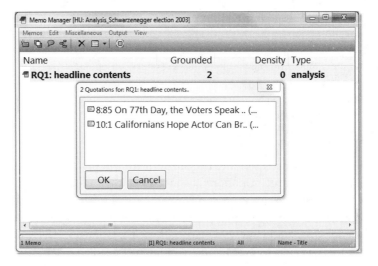

Figure 6.8 Reviewing the quotations linked to a memo

Creating output

That, however, is not the end of the story. What we want to do next is to output the memo, including the quotations. When you set up your research question memos as described, the output can be used as a building block for your research report.

- Select your research question 1 memo and then the option **Output / Selected Memo with Quotations**.
- Choose **Editor** as the output destination.

The memo output includes everything you need to write the results chapter of your research report or paper (Figure 6.9). It also adds transparency to your analysis. If someone asks how you derived your results, you can show your research question memos. If necessary, you can rerun the query. I have seen many memos that contained a lot of good interpretation, but when I asked the analysts how they came up with the ideas, they could not remember. It just takes a minute or two to spell out the query, and the return for this effort is manifold. It adds a lot to your analysis in terms of trustworthiness, credibility, transparency and dependability – in other words, the quality criteria by which good qualitative research is recognized (see, e.g., Seale, 1999).

Quoting data segments in reports

I am often asked how to reference a quote from an ATLAS.ti project. My suggestion is to use the quotation ID plus the location in the document:

'On 77th Day, the Voters Speak Loudly Against Davis's Record' (8:2, 12:12)

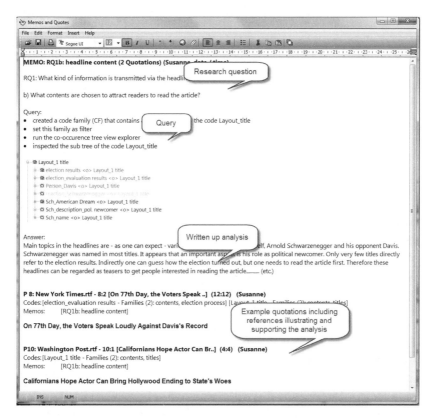

Figure 6.9 Research question memo as building block for a research report

You need to explain the references once, for example in a footnote. The coded documents where the quotation can be found in the data can be included in a paper or digital attachment to a report, thesis or dissertation. A Web-based publication such as an html document is also possible. Most choose the PDF output of the coded documents.

To create a PDF output of your coded documents:

- Select **Documents / Output / Print with Margin**.

As soon as you select the print with margin option, the screen view changes so you can see what the output looks like on paper or in a PDF file. Everything on the page is within the white area; everything off the page is shown in the gray area. You may need to adjust some settings to fit everything on the page and to create the output you want:

- If some codes fall off the page on the right hand side, I suggest that you set the page layout to landscape: **File / Printer Setup**.

- You can also adjust the windows splitter (move it to the right or left) and change the font for the codes (right click in the margin, select the option **Set Font**) to create the view you want.
- If you want to create a PDF file, a PDF writer needs to be installed on your computer. Nowadays you can find free versions online. When creating the output, the printer dialogue opens. Choose the PDF writer as your printer. Then the document will not actually be printed but saved as a PDF file.

Summary of skills training 4

This was quite a long but important session, as writing and reflection is an integral part of qualitative data analysis. I am certain that most ATLAS.ti users I have met over the years do write 'memos' somewhere, but seldom have I seen it done directly in ATLAS.ti. I don't think that this is a fault of the software design. It is more a matter of the software not 'telling' the user how the function works. It also involves some methodological awareness: knowing what memo writing is all about and that it is indeed an important part of the analysis. It is probably not by accident that Juliet Corbin includes a lot about memo writing in the 3rd edition of *Basics of Qualitative Research*; she wants to show readers how it can be done. In a talk at the CAQD 2008 Conference about the book, she linked the poor quality of many of today's qualitative research projects to a failure to use memos. Along the same lines, Birks (2008) devotes an entire journal article to memo writing, criticizing the limited exploration of its value in most qualitative methodologies. In turn, I just checked all my books on qualitative data analysis; nowhere did I find an extensive coverage of memo writing. The focus is usually on the data themselves and how best to prepare, structure and code them.

Learning how to write good memos is experiential. Reading about it and seeing examples of how it can be done is one part, but you need to do it yourself and practice it. In the first part of this chapter I provided you with some ideas for stand-alone memos to accompany the research process, such as the research diary, to-do memos or idea memos. Then there are the connected memos linked to your data. These might contain important bits and pieces from the theoretical framework you are using or from analytic memos.

My suggestion is to create one memo for each research question. Broader questions need to be divided into subtopics and it is probably best to create a memo for each subtopic. As we have done for codes, use letters and special characters to create abbreviations in order to structure and organize the list of memos, like:

RQ1: title

RQ2: title

RQ3: title

:

.

Or:

RQ1a: titlle

RQ1b: title

RQ1c: title

RQ2a: title

:

.

Special characters like an asterisk (*) are useful when you want to place certain memos at the top of the list, like your research diary. Depending on your project design, you may know the research questions from the start. If this is the case, I suggest adding these as memos when you start setting up. This will allow you to write reflections and first ideas about a certain topic in the proper container immediately, during the process of coding. As you develop more research questions and hypotheses along the way, add more research question memos.

After the data material has been coded, research question memos help you approach the data analysis in a systematic way, by formulating precise queries for each individual question. The crucial point is that the memos are thematically related to contents and data segments, instead of being spread out in bits and pieces all over the place.

'Open book' assessment after completing skills training 4

If you want to test your knowledge on memos and how to use them in ATLAS.ti, go through the following review questions and write down an answer for each one:

1 What is a memo and what are memos used for in qualitative data analysis?
2 What is the difference between a memo and a comment in ATLAS.ti? Why is it important to know this difference?
3 ATLAS.ti offers the option to create different memo types. What types will you need for your project and why? What can you use them for?
4 What kind of information should a research question memo contain in order to add transparency to your research?
5 Thinking about your own research project, what kind of memos would be useful to you and why?

Positioning and further directions for the onward journey

Ideally you have begun to explore your data landscape and you have developed some ideas, marked those things that are interesting and collected similar items in code containers. Maybe you have already added a bit of structure to the developing code system. As you now know what memos are and what to use them for, integrate them into your analysis and continue your coding work until all data are coded.

The next step is to query the data in a systematic way by going through the research questions and thinking about how to find an answer for each question in the data. ATLAS.ti offers several options to query the data. Thus, you need to attend some more skills training sessions as part of your journey. Knowing how the various tools work and in what way data can be queried are important for coding as well. When you get tired of coding and feel like taking a break from it, then it is a good idea to stop by the next skills training session on the query tool. Other tools I can explain by way of example when we go through the remaining research questions for the Schwarzenegger project. The query tool, however, needs theoretical instruction first before we can apply and work with it.

Skills training 5: introducing the query tool

The query tool is used for the retrieval of coded data segments, the ATLAS.ti quotations. You have already seen and practiced the simplest form of retrieval where you double click on a code in the Code Manager. The query tool can process more complex queries by combining codes. For that, 14 different operators are at your disposal.

The results of a query formulated in the query tool are always quotations. If you are interested in the location of codes, for example which of the codes overlap, you need to use the co-occurrence explorer. That will be explained later, when examing R25 on p. 174. For now, I would like you to concentrate on the query tool. The schedule for the skills training session is as follows:

1   We will take a look at the query tool window and I will explain the various components of it.
2   You will get to know the three groups of operators and the retrieval language.
3   Thereafter we will run a few example queries.
4   With this knowledge, we will be ready to return to the research questions of the Schwarzenegger project.

Let's begin by looking at the query tool window:

 • Open the query tool by clicking on the binoculars button in the horizontal toolbar or by selecting the menu option **Tools / Query Tool**.

On the left-hand side of the query tool window (Figure 6.10) you will see the operator toolbar. You will find three sets of operators: Boolean, semantic and proximity operators.

• Move your mouse over each of the operator buttons. A comment pops up showing the name of the operator and a sample query (Figure 6.11).

In the upper left-hand corner of the query tool windows you will see the code family field, listing all code families that can be used in a query. Below that you will see all of your codes. The upper right-hand corner will be filled when you

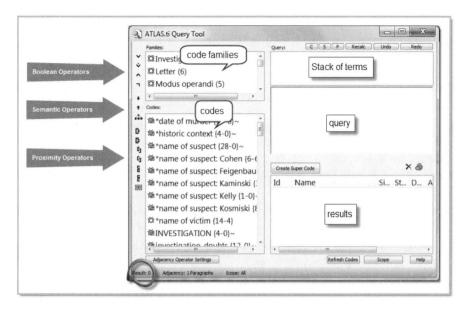

Figure 6.10   The ATLAS.ti query tool: searching for quotations based on code combinations

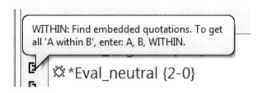

Figure 6.11   Comments explaining query buttons

begin to click a query. It lists all activated terms and is called the 'stack memory'. This is just like other stacks that you know of from everyday life, like a stack of books (Figure 6.12) or a stack of wood. I will return to this comparison later when we start to build queries.

Figure 6.12   The stack of terms is similar to a stack of books

The middle pane on the right of the query tool windows is the place for the evolving query. It is called the feedback pane. Here you can see the arithmetical problem being addressed by the query tool. At the bottom right, you will see the results of a query in the form of a list of quotations. The resulting total number of quotations is shown circled in the bottom left-hand corner in Figure 6.10.

The retrieval language

Queries are formulated following the principle of **reverse Polish notation (RPN)** developed by the Polish mathematician Lukasiewicz. This sounds complicated but is actually quite easy as it does not require you to learn syntax. Every step of the method produces a significant result and it is impossible to formulate a query wrongly. You may have found in statistics programs that you cannot run a query because you forgot the period at the end or a comma somewhere. The reverse Polish way of entering queries demands neither syntactical knowledge like commas, semi-colons, periods, etc., nor the need to enter brackets to control the order of operators.

The basic principle of RPN is that all arguments (codes or code families) are written first, followed by an operator. In RPN, this order is reversed: all arguments are written before the operators. When entering an arithmetical problem into a calculator, we are accustomed to a notation in which the operator stands between two arguments, for example in the term 3 + 4. This form of entering terms is also called **infix notation**.

In the table before you can see some arithmetical problems in two alternative notations, the usual infix notation and reverse Polish:

Infix notation	Reverse Polish notation
3 + 4	3 4 +
3 + (4 * 5)	4 5 * 3 + alternative: 4 5 3 * +
(3 + 4) * 5	3 4 + 5 * alternative: 3 4 5 + *

You will get the hang of it once we enter some example queries.

The three sets of operators

Boolean operators

Boolean operators combine keywords with the use of fixed operations. You probably know and have used at least two of them (OR and AND) when you do a literature search or search the Internet. For the operator OR you usually enter a vertical bar '|':

    OR: A OR B

    XOR: Either only A, or only B

    AND: A and B have to be complied simultaneously

    NOT: Negation of a term

You may remember set theory from your math classes in school. Let's go back a bit in your memory to retrieve some of that knowledge. Below, the four Boolean operators found in ATLAS.ti are explained and for each a Venn diagram is shown. Your task is to mark the area that results from the query for each operator. You will find the solutions at the end of the chapter in Figure 6.51.

OR: The operator OR is the non-exclusive OR. The term 'A OR B' is true if A, B or both are true. Using this operator, the search system will return all quotations that are linked to at least one of the codes in the search term. Therefore, the query tool's mission is to find at least one of the specified arguments. When you want the quotations of a number of codes, then it is easier to create a code family rather than using the query tool. A code family basically consists of codes linked with the **OR** operator: (C1 | C2 | „C3 | „C4" | „C5").

- In the following graphic, mark the area that results from the search A OR B:

XOR: The XOR is the exclusive OR. 'A XOR B' is true if either A or B is true, but it is false if both A and B are true. XOR represents the colloquial 'either–or': 'You can have either chocolate or ice cream.' Thus, XOR means: 'You can have one of the two, but not both.' In contrast, the OR operator allows you to have both.

- Mark the area that results from the search A XOR B:

AND: The operator AND will only find those quotations that meet all conditions of the search term. It is very selective and only finds those segments that you have coded with two codes. Remember 'Skills training 3' on the rules of hierarchical coding and how to avoid the code swamp? I advised you to create different codes for different code levels like theme and dimension. Let's assume you come across a data segment that contains a text about the election results, giving a negative evaluation of it and written in polemic language. Instead of having one code like election results_negative eval_polemic language, it is better to code the text segment with Election results _and_ Eval_negative _and_ Language_ polemic. Coded like that, you can use the AND operator in query tool to find all data segments where the journalists report on the election results in a polemic way; or in a negative way; or both negatively and polemically.

- Mark the area that results from the search A AND B:

NOT: This operator is used to check if a condition is not applicable. Its formal meaning is that all results of the negated term are subtracted from all text segments in question (the 'universe'). You only need to select one code in order to use this operator. Usually it is used to exclude the quotation of one or more codes: all A or B but not C.

- Mark the area that results from the search NOT B:

Example query

In the coded Schwarzenegger sample project, information on Arnold Schwarzenegger's personal and professional biography is coded. The task is to retrieve the quotations of both codes. Remember that we have to enter the query in RPN: first the codes, then the operator.

- In the query tool, double click on Sch_biography_pers, then double click on Sch_biography_prof.

The codes you select appear in the stack of terms (Figure 6.13). In the results pane you will immediately see the results of the query shown in the feedback pane; in this case, the 13 quotations of the code Sch_biography_prof.

- Now click on the OR operator, the top one in the row of operators.

The feedback pane displays the query: ("Schw_biography_pers"|"Schw_biography_prof"). The total number of resulting quotations is 16.

- To review the results in the context of the data, click on each quotation in the results pane. To export the results, click on the printer symbol (see Figure 6.20 below).

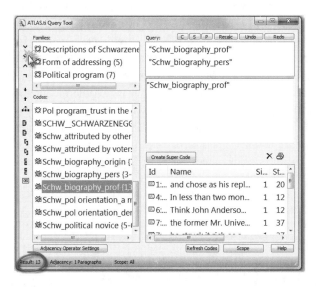

Figure 6.13   Example query with Boolean operators

Congratulations! You have clicked your first query. It was a simple process, and step by step you will get more used to it: first click on the code(s), then select an operator.

Semantic operators

Semantic operators make use of the links between codes. Such links are created with the help of the **network view function**. Codes can be linked via directed or non-directed relations. When you find a causal link – for example, action A is always followed by action B, or B is a consequence of A – then you can use a directed transitive relation to link the two codes. But it is not always possible to define a directed link; at times you just want to indicate that two or more codes relate to each other, or occur at the same time or place, etc. It is neither a cause and effect relation, nor a description of situation and consequence, or anything similar. Therefore ATLAS.ti also offers non-directed relations. In a network view, this looks as shown in Figure 6.14.

Semantic operators make use of directed relations to define a hierarchy between codes. This means you can collect all quotations coded by codes that are hierarchically below, above or on the same level as another. In Figure 6.14, the two codes related to 'reasons for the recall' are below the code 'election results'. You can collect their quotations via the SIB (sibling) operator. If you also want to review the quotations of the data segments coded by 'election results', then you use the SUB operator. If, however, you only want the quotations of one of the 'reasons for the recall' code + the election results quotations, then you need the UP operator.

SUB: all A with subgroups

UP: all A with codes of the next upper level

SIB: all quotations connected with A that are on the same sublevel

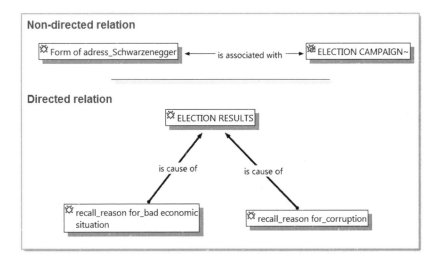

Figure 6.14 Network view showing non-directed and directed relations

Example query

When using any of the three semantic operators, you only need to select one code and then the operator. To collect all quotations linked to the code election results or any of its subcodes:

- Double click on the main category code 'ELECTION RESULTS', which is empty. Then click on the SUB operator.

Following the NCT model of analysis as described here, semantic operators can be used to find and visualize hierarchical relations in your data which do not describe a main category code and its subcodes.

Proximity operators

Proximity operators analyze the spatial relations between coded data segments like overlaps and distances. For a query with proximity operators, you have to select two codes or code families as arguments, as was also the case for Boolean operators. There is one significant difference between these operators and the ones already discussed: proximity operators are non-interchangeable.

This means that you have to pay attention to the order in which you enter the codes (or code families). The query tool can only find quotations, not the lines between them.

The example in Figure 6.15 shows some lines of text where Code A is overlapped by a Code B. The query tool only returns the data segment coded by Code A or the ones coded by Code B. It cannot output lines 2 and 3, the text where the two codes actually overlap. Thus, if you want all data coded by Code A, you need to enter the query:

Code A, Code B, OVERLAPPED BY.

When you want to read the text coded by Code B, you need to enter the query the other way around starting with Code B:

Code B, Code A, OVERLAPS.

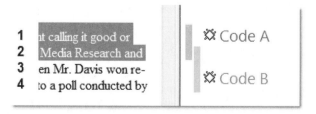

Figure 6.15   Proximity search: A is overlapped by B

For this reason, there are always two versions of a proximity query and respectively two operators.

Finding overlapping quotations

| | OVERLAPPED BY: | A is overlapped by B |
| | OVERLAPS: | B overlaps A |

Finding quotations of embedded codes

With the help of the following two operators, you can find quotations that are embedded in each other:

| | WITHIN: | B within A |
| | ENCLOSES: | A encloses B |

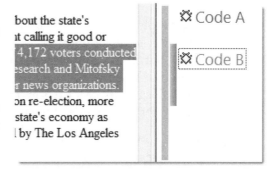

bout the state's
it calling it good or
4,172 voters conducted
esearch and Mitofsky
r news organizations.
on re-election, more
state's economy as
by The Los Angeles

Figure 6.16 Querying data using the WITHIN operator

To find the segment highlighted you need to enter Code B, Code A, WITHIN. This kind of query is useful if, for example, you have coded longer segments by a time period like 'childhood' (Figure 6.17). Within this longer segment, you have coded friendship as 'first year in school', 'relations with mother', etc. If you want to find all data segments related to friendship during childhood, you enter 'friendship', 'childhood', WITHIN. It does not make much sense to enter

childhood

friendship

friendship

Figure 6.17 Example for a useful application of the WITHIN operator

the query the other way around ('childhood', 'friendship', ENCLOSES) as the query tool will then return the long segments on childhood. The general rule is that the first code you select should be the one you are interested in.

Finding quotations within a set distance

The last twin set of operators returns those quotations that do not directly overlap, but occur within a specified distance from each other. The distance can be specified based on the type of document you are working with: paragraphs for text documents, characters for text and PDF files, pixels for image files, milliseconds for audio files and frames for videos.

FOLLOWS: B follows A

PRECEDES: A precedes B

For interview data this option is interesting when looking for coded data segments that occur near each other, for example within two consecutive paragraphs. Thus, the codes do not overlap directly. When coding very small data segments, then the maximum distance can be set to characters instead of paragraphs. This option is also interesting for descriptions of plots or when filming actions and events. Then the sequence of when what is done or happens can be very revealing.

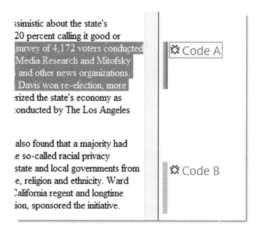

Figure 6.18   Quering data using the PRECEDE operator

When clicking on a query using the precede or follow operators (e.g. Code A, Code B, PRECEDES), a window pops up asking you to enter the maximal distance between the two codes (Figure 6.19).

You can set the default distance for all document types beforehand by clicking on ADJACENCY OPERATOR SETTINGS. Then the window pops in Figure 6.20 up.

Figure 6.19 Determining the maximum distance for two codes

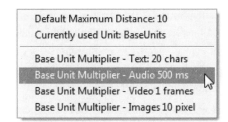

Figure 6.20 Adjacency operator settings

Finding quotations that occur together If it does not matter in which way two codes overlap, you can use the CO-OCCURRENCE operator. This is a combination of AND, ENCLOSES, WITHIN, OVERLAPPED BY and OVERLAPS:

CO-OCCURRENCE: all A together with B

When using the co-occurrence operator it is still important in which way around you enter the codes or code families. Start with the code or code family whose coded segments you want to read.

Miscellaneous useful query tool functions

On the top right hand side of the query tool, you will find some buttons facilitating the process of clicking on queries (Figure 6.21).

> **Clear:** The button C clears the whole stack of terms. After you finish one query and review the results, it is best to click on the C button to clear all entries before you enter the next query.

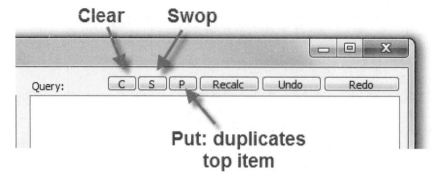

Figure 6.21 Useful buttons when clicking on a query

Swap: When clicking on the button S, the first two elements of the stack switch places. This option is very useful if you have entered the codes or code families in the wrong order.

Put: The **P** button creates a copy of the first element and puts it on top of the stack. This can be used for reproducing a complex expression.

Recalculate: If you have created and coded new quotations while the query tool window is open, you can use the **Recalc** button to recalculate the current query results.

Undo: The **Undo** button removes the element at the top of the stack if you have, for example, selected the wrong code.

Redo: The **Redo** button puts the last removed element back on the stack.

Reviewing results

Even though you can see (at the bottom left of the query tool) how many quotations the query is yielding, the really important result is the content of the quotations. It is essential to read, review or listen to the contents of the quotations to be able to interpret them. The number of results can serve as an initial point of orientation and thus is also meaningful, but only together with the corresponding content. You can either review the results in context by clicking on each quotation in the results pane of the query tool, or export the results as in rich text format.

The various output options can be seen when you click on the printer symbol (Figure 6.22).

The List and the List - Include Comments output only shows a list of the quotation names or the list with comments. This is useful for outputting multimedia (audio, video, image, Google Earth) quotations, when you have used the quotation name as title (see Chapter 4, p. 83).

The Full Content output is useful for text and image documents. The Full Content-No Meta option is quite handy for reducing the number of output pages. The regular output includes a reference for each quotation plus information about other codes, memos and families linked to the segment. This takes up a few lines of space. The no meta option reduces the output to the

Figure 6.22 Query tool output options

minimum necessary, which is often sufficient. You can compare the two output formats in the box below.

Full Content output

P 8: SeatleTimes.rtf - 8:22 [Besides, Arnold is an alpha ma..] (60:60) (Susanne)

Codes: [Form of address_Arnold - Family: Form of addressing] [Schw_attributed by others - Family: Descriptions of Schwarzenegger]

No memos

Besides, Arnold is an alpha male, and alpha males are by nature inclined to strut their power, especially with women.

Full Content - No Meta output of the same segment

Besides, Arnold is an alpha male, and alpha males are by nature inclined to strut their power, especially with women.

<ref>P 8: SeatleTimes.rtf - 8:22 [(60:60)] by Susanne</ref>

If you have written quite a number of quotation comments and want them all to be included in the output, the 'no-meta' option cannot be used. Then you need to use the option **Full Content – Include Comments**.

As usual, you can send the output to an editor or the printer, or save it directly as a text file. The 'File & Run' option is useful when creating Excel tables as output. You will see how this works a little later.

Exploring the data terrain further – the journey continues

Knowing which operators are available to ask questions should give you some ideas about how the data must be coded in order to be able to ask more complex questions. If none of your codes overlaps others, then you can at most use the OR, PRECEDES and FOLLOWS operators. In such a case, your coding system is probably quite simple anyway and you probably won't go any further than simple code retrieval in the Code Manager. The scope button in the query tool may nevertheless be an interesting option for comparing and contrasting groups of documents.

I will now take you on an excursion to explore the Schwarzenegger data terrain in a bit more detail. Our program for the day is to look at the five research questions and subquestions, and how to find an answer to them using the analysis tools that ATLAS.ti provides. These examples prepare you to explore more of the terrain on your own and to transfer this knowledge to investigations of other data landscapes in the form of your own projects.

- Open the coded Schwarzenegger project and inspect the codes in the Code Manager in order to get a feeling for what was coded and what kind of categories and code families are available.

Examining RQ1a (finding co-occurring segments)

To remind you, in research question 1 the aim was to examine the kinds of information transmitted via the headlines. This question was divided into two subquestions. The first one is as follows.

Is direct speech used in headlines?

The codes we need to find an answer to this question are in the code family 'use of direct speech', and we need the code 'layout_1 headline'.

- Open the query tool.
- Remember that you first need to select the arguments in the form of codes or code families and then the appropriate operator. Start with the code or code family you are most interested in, here the headline code.
- As you should be able to click on this query on your own after going through 'Skills training 5', I will leave you to figure it out on your own. The correct solution is provided at the end of this chapter.
- Enter your query below into the research question memo for RQ1a (Figure 6.23). Read through the results and write down your thoughts.
- When you are finished with writing up your answer in research question memo R1a and before you turn to part b of RQ1, close the query tool window.

Examining RQ1b (getting to know the co-occurrence explorer tree view)

Research question 1b is: **Which topics are chosen to attract readers to the article?** In answering this question, you will get to know a new analysis tool, the co-occurrence explorer. The co-occurrence explorer is available in two views, a tree and a table view. To look at the various topics that appear in headlines, the tree view is more suitable. The arguments we need are the code family 'topics' and 'layout_1 headline'.

Figure 6.23   Memo for RQ1a

As the co-occurrence explorer uses all codes when you run it, we need to use filters if we only want to query a particular subset of the data. ATLAS.ti offers a number of predefined filters via the main menus: Documents / Filter **or** Quotations / Filter **or** Codes / Filter **or** Memos / Filter. Creating a user-defined filter that you need for a particular query is best achieved via families.

In our case, the code family 'topics' already exists. Thus, we only need to add the headline code to it:

- Open the code family manager: CODES / EDIT FAMILIES / OPEN FAMILY MANAGER.
- Select the code family 'topics' and add the code 'layout_1 headline' to it. It is not worth creating a new family just for this query. We just have to remember to remove the layout code from this family when we are done.
- Double click on the code family 'topics'. This activates the filter. You can see this in the Code Manager. It now contains only the 34 codes from the family and, in the program, shows a pale yellow background color. This is always the case when you have activated a filter somewhere.
- Minimise the Code Family Manager.
- To run the co-occurrence explorer (Figure 6.24), go to the main menu and select TOOLS / CO-OCCURRENCE TOOLS → TREE EXPLORER.

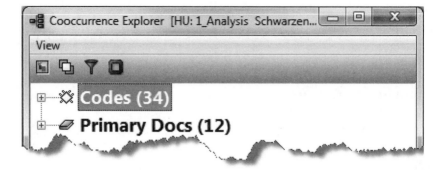

Figure 6.24 Co-occurrence explorer – non-expanded tree view

- Expand the tree by clicking on the line in front of the code symbol or on the plus sign. You need to check what works on your computer. You can also right click on the entry CODES and select the expand option from the context menu.

Then the tree expands and shows all 34 codes with their co-occurring codes. To answer the research question, we are only interested in the 'layout_1 headline' code.

- Take a look at the subtree for the headline code in Figure 6.25.
- The tree can be further expanded to the quotation level by clicking on the plus sign in front of each code.
- What can be seen is that the topics used to attract readers to the article are: the election results; the winner and the loser of the election, Davis and Schwarzenegger; the story line 'from dish washer to millionaire'; and the outsider role of Schwarzenegger as political newcomer.

This short summary of the findings needs to be followed up by further interpretations in your research question memo on RQ1b. This memo should also include the research question and a description of the query (see Figure 6.26). When you find some good quotations that illustrate the points you are making in your memo, attach the memo to these quotations.

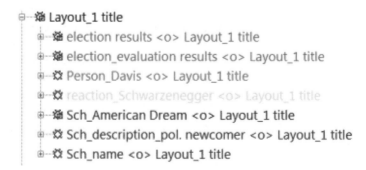

Figure 6.25 Expanded tree view showing all codes that co-occur with the 'layout_1 headline' code

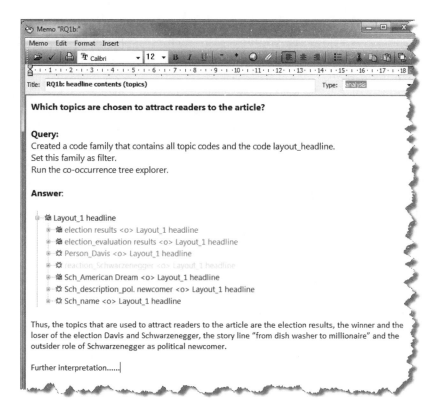

Figure 6.26 Research question memo for RQ1b

- When you are finished examining this research question, remove the code 'Layout_1 headline' from the code family 'topics'.
- Then double click on the code family once again to take out the filter or select the main menu option EXTRAS / RESET ALL FILTERS.

Examining RQ2a (combining code queries with variables + creating superfamilies)

With research question 2a, the aim is to find out: **What is reported about Arnold Schwarzenegger's political program? Are there differences between local and national newspapers?** In answering this research question, you will learn how to use variables together with code searches and how to combine variables to create new ones. So far, we have only created what I call 'base variables' like country, circulation and type of newspaper. But often the combination of certain variables is important as well, such as looking for all headline topics in German (&) national papers as compared to US (&) national papers. There is no need to create such combinations as stand-alone document families. You can combine the base families in whichever way you need them, to form what ATLAS.ti calls 'superfamilies'.

To begin with, I will show you the function **Scope** of the query tool. It allows us to compare and contrast groups of data such as local and national papers, tabloid vs. broadsheet, German vs. American newspapers, male and female, teachers and parents, etc.

Remember that we created groups of documents in Chapter 3 when setting up the project (see Chapter 3, 'Organizing documents into groups'). They helped us to get started when we developed the project and now they will be very useful again when querying the data.

- Open the query tool.
- Double click on the code family 'political program'. All quotations from all subcodes are displayed. Based on the current state of coding at the time of writing, this resulted in 42 quotations.
- Now, we want to filter these codes by local and national papers. Click on **Scope** at the bottom right hand side of the query tool window.
- The scope of query window (Figure 6.27) opens. It is a so-called 'sticky' window. Stick it to the bottom right-hand side of the query tool. When you now move the query tool window, the scope window moves with it.
- Select the P-Doc family 'Cir::national' to narrow your search to quotations from national papers. In my current data set, this results in 23 quotations.

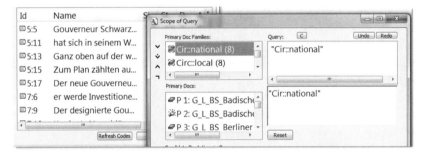

Figure 6.27 Narrowing down the search to quotations from national papers

The resulting quotations are always shown in the query tool window, never in the scope of query window. You can ignore the bottom half of the 'scope of query tool window'. It simply shows you all quotations of the currently selected subgroup.

- Read through these quotations and write down your impressions and interpretations in your research question memo RQ2a.
- Then narrow it down to local papers by double clicking on the P-Doc family 'Circ::local'. Read through the resulting quotations again and write down your thoughts in the memo. You probably can already write about some commonalities and differences.
- Read through the results and write down your thoughts, ideas and interpretations in the research question memo for RQ2a (Figure 6.28):

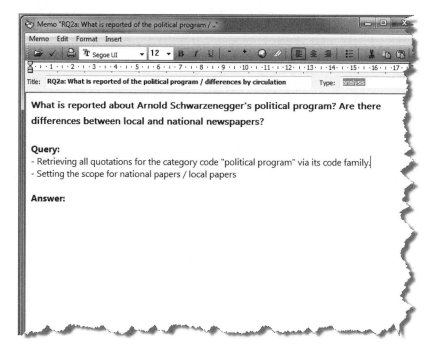

Figure 6.28 Research question memo for RQ2a

As you can see in the scope of query window, you can also use individual documents as a filter instead of P-Doc families, or a combination of documents and P-Doc families. If you are only interested in quotations from particular PDs, select the desired PDs from the PD list and link them with the OR operator.

- To reset the filter, click on the button **C** in the scope of query window.
- Let's assume you want to narrow down the results to national American newspapers. How would you do this?

The solution is shown in Figure 6.28. You select the two families that you want to combine by double clicking on each one. Next, you need the intersection of the two groups. This is achieved by clicking on the AND operator: 'Circ::national & Country::US American.'

Figure 6.29 Combining variables on-the-fly

Creating combined variables (= primary document superfamilies)

If you need a combination of P-doc families more often and you don't want to create it again each time you need it, you can preserve it in the form of a superfamily. Unfortunately, this cannot be done in the scope of query window. You need to open the P-Doc Family Manager first and from there the Superfamily Manager:

- From the main menu select DOCUMENTS / EDIT FAMILIES / OPEN FAMILY MANAGER.
- Within the manager click on the button **superfamily** or select FAMILIES / OPEN SUPER FAMILY TOOL.

After having learned how to click on a query in the query tool, you are equipped to build your own superfamilies. Try creating a few:

- Create the combinations: National (&) US papers; National (&) German papers; Local (&) US papers and Local (&) German papers.
- After you have clicked on a query, click on the button '**Create Super Family**' (Figure 6.30). This saves the query and stores it in a so-called superfamily.

When you add more US newspapers and group them into the base families 'Country: US American' and 'Cir::national' or 'Cir::local', then the superfamily updates itself. Every time you click on it, the query is recalculated and the up-to-date results are shown.

All created superfamilies show up in the scope of query window and can be used as filters to narrow down the results of a query to compare and contrast different groups of data.

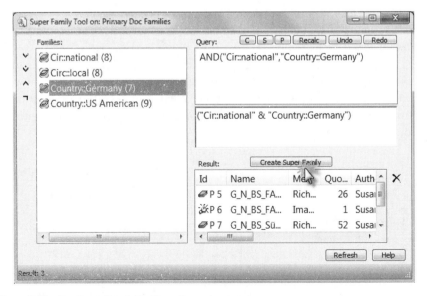

Figure 6.30 The Super Family Tool for primary documents

Following the same logic, you can also create 'supercodes'. This is done in the query tool. The prefix 'super' always indicates that the code is a stored query.

- Close all open family and superfamily managers and the query tool window.

Examining RQ2b (exporting code frequencies per document)

The focus of research question 2b is on the questions: **Which aspects of the political program are reported on? Are there differences among newspapers?** As we have seen so far, the results of a query clicked in the query tool are always quotations. Hence, the answer is qualitative. The various aspects of the political program can, however, best be seen by looking at the subcodes of the main category code PP_POLITICAL PROGRAM and the distribution of them across the newspapers. Such a result can be produced by the **Codes-Primary-Documents-Table**. This table can be created as an Excel file and shows the frequency of all codes by document. ATLAS.ti offers two alternative frequency counts: how often a code was applied or the number of words within the coded segments per code. In addition to the Excel output, you can choose to create the report as a text file within ATLAS.ti. Mostly I use the Excel output option because Excel provides further options to work with the data.

Let's create such an output now in order to see how this works in practice.

- As we only want to output the political program codes, we need to set a filter. I asked you to clear the screen at the end of the last exercise. Hence, the Code Family Manager is no longer open to set the filter. Therefore, we will choose a different route this time: From the main menu select CODES / FILTER / FAMILIES → Political Program.

Next, we also want to set a filter for documents. The political program codes have only been applied to the textual documents and not to the images. Therefore, we do not want to output the frequency count of the image files as it will be zero. ATLAS.ti provides default filters for file formats:

- From the main menu, select DOCUMENTS / FILTER / TEXT.
- To create the table, select CODES / OUTPUT / CODES-PRIMARY-DOCUMENTS-TABLE → QUOTATION COUNT (EXCEL).
- Then select the output option FILE & RUN. This means you first have to save the file and then ATLAS.ti opens Excel (or OpenOffice Calc) for you.
- When the 'Save as:' window comes up, a file name is suggested to you. You can use this file name or enter a different one. If you use a different name, remember to add the **xls** extension to the file name. This is not automatically entered. if you do not enter it, Excel does not recognize the file.

> **Tip:** The software chooses your project folder for storing output files. Create a subfolder within your project folder to store these files so that they are not mixed in with your primary data sources and HU file(s).

Aspects of Schwarzenegger's political program	economic growth	education	environmental issues	grass roots politics	human rights	non-specific pledges	political culture	TOTALS:
Local German papers								
P 1: G_L_BS_Badische Zeitung online.doc	0	0	0	1	0	0	0	1
P 3: G_L_BS_Berliner Zeitung.doc	0	0	0	0	1	0	0	1
	0	0	0	1	1	0	0	2
National German papers								
P 5: G_N_BS_FAZ.doc	5	0	0	0	0	0	0	5
P 7: G_N_BS_Süddeutsche Zeitung.rtf	2	0	0	0	1	0	1	1	5
	7	0	0	1	0	1	1	10
Local US papers								
P 8: US_L_BS_Capital Times_Wisconsin.rtf	0	0	0	0	1	0	2	3
P 9: US_L_BS_Los Angeles Times.rtf	1	1	1	0	0	3	4	10
P10: US_L_BS_SeatleTimes.rtf	1	0	0	0	0	1	0	2
P11: US_L_BS_The Dallas Morning News.rtf	1	0	0	1	1	1	0	4
	3	1	1	1	2	5	6	19
National US papers								
P12: US_N_BS_New York Times.rtf	0	0	0	1	0	2	1	4
P15: US_N_BS_Washington Post.rtf	2	1	3	0	1	4	2	13
P16: US_N_BS_Washington Post.jpg	0	0	0	0	0	0	0	0
	2	1	3	1	1	6	3	17

Figure 6.31   Edited Codes-Primary-Documents Table showing the frequency per code

The results are shown in Figure 6.31. The output which ATLAS.ti creates does of course not automatically include the subheaders, sums for each subgroup and colors. I have done some editing work, but this is easy enough to do in Excel. Pretending this is a fully coded data set, the table could be interpreted as follows.

Schwarzenegger's political program does not seem to matter much to local German newspapers. The national papers pick up on it but, to them, his plans regarding economic growth appear to be of most importance. This is especially true for the FAZ. This result can be explained by the target group of this newspaper: well-situated businessmen over the age of 35.

In comparison, in the US press, Schwarzenegger's political program is reported in both local and national papers. They focus on the issue of improving political culture as well as on the many non-specific pledges that Schwarzenegger has made.

You can visually support your interpretations by creating charts in Excel. Thus, also a quantitative charting of the data terrain is possible. But as can easily be seen from the charts, numbers need to be interpreted with care. The charts shown in Figure 6.32 are based on only a few articles. Visually they transport a lot of information quickly, whether it is true or false.

The memo for RQ2b might look as shown in Figure 6.33.

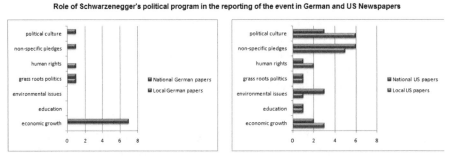

Role of Schwarzenegger's political program in the reporting of the event in German and US Newspapers

Figure 6.32   Excel charts based on the numbers provided by the Codes-Primary-Documents-Table

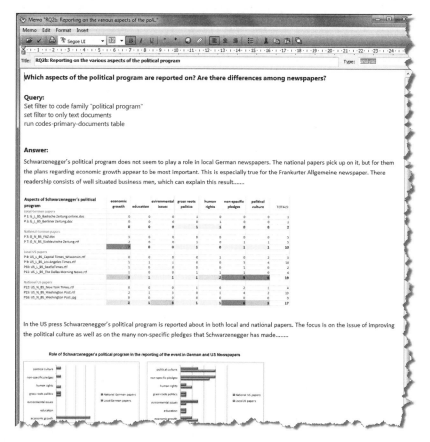

Figure 6.33   Research question memo for RQ2b

Examining RQ3 (exporting code frequencies per document)

Which topics are reported in US vs. German newspapers, local as compared to national papers? Are there differences? Finding an answer to this question is very similar to answering RQ2b. Try it yourself. You will find the answer at the end of this chapter.

- Write down the query and your answer in the research question memo for RQ3 (see Figure 6.34).

Examining RQ4 (finding co-occurring segments in combination with variables)

In research question 4, we want to know: **How is Schwarzenegger presented visually in the articles?** In order to answer this, we need the query tool again. The following codes and code families are of interest in this query.

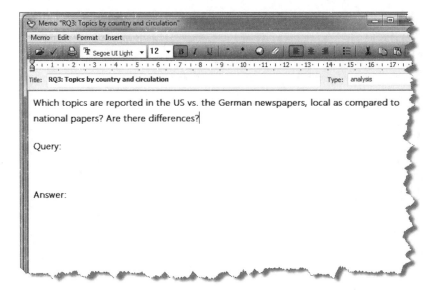

Figure 6.34 Research question memo for RQ3

Within the pictures, gestures and facial expressions have been coded. These codes are summarized in the code family 'non-verbals'. In addition, the various elements in the pictures have been evaluated in terms of whether the portrayal of Schwarzenegger is positive or negative. As evaluation codes are on a different level than topic codes, their label starts with an asterisk (*) and thus you find them on top of the code list. As a first step, we want to find out whether Schwarzenegger is portrayed more often in a positive or negative way, and how. In a second step, a comparison by country might yield interesting results as well. For that comparison, we need to use the scope button again.

- Open the query tool.
- The focus of interest is on the different elements of the picture and how the coder has evaluated them. Thus, we first select the code family 'non-verbals' and then one of the evaluation codes before we select the operator (Figure 6.35).
- Double click on the code family **non verbal**. Double click on the code *Eval_negative. Then select the co-occur operator.
- After selecting the operator, check the feedback pane. The query looks like this:
- ("non-verbal stuff" COOCCUR "*Eval_negative")
  Given the current state of coding, this results in seven quotations.
- Click through the quotes to get an idea as to why these picture elements were coded as negative.
- Repeat the query for positive evaluations. You can click on the undo button twice and then add the code Eval_positive to the stack. Then once again select the co-occur operator.

The result also shows seven quotations. Thus, there seems to be quite a balanced selection of pictures. Look at the positively evaluated elements. Even though the numbers are small and it is easy to recognize which of the

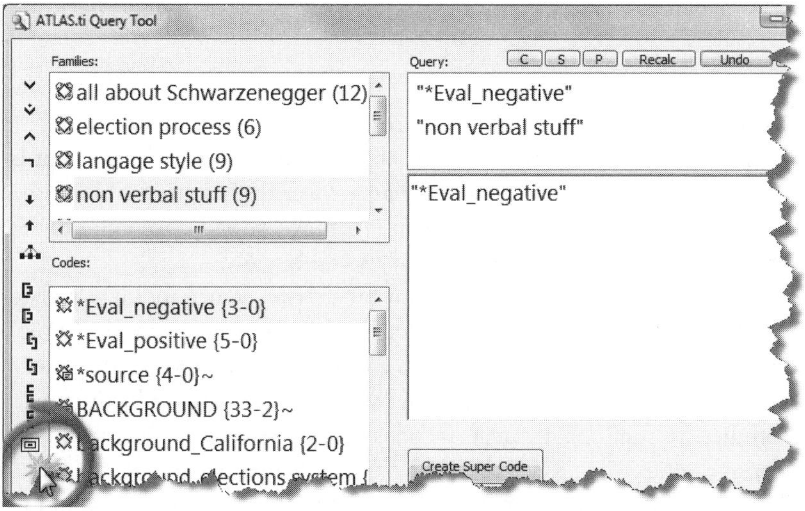

Figure 6.35 Looking for negatively evaluated picture elements

quotations come from German and which from US newspapers, let's still go through the motions and filter the results by country.

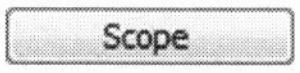

- Click on **Scope** and select **Country::Germany** with a double click. Then set the family **Country::US American** as the scope. There are four positive elements from two German newspapers and three elements from two US newspapers. No differences are apparent.
- Redo the query on negatively evaluated elements and then compare the results by country. Again, we cannot see a big difference, although there seem to be slightly more negative elements in the NYT.
- Write down your observations in research question memo RQ4 (Figure 6.36).
- Close the query tool.

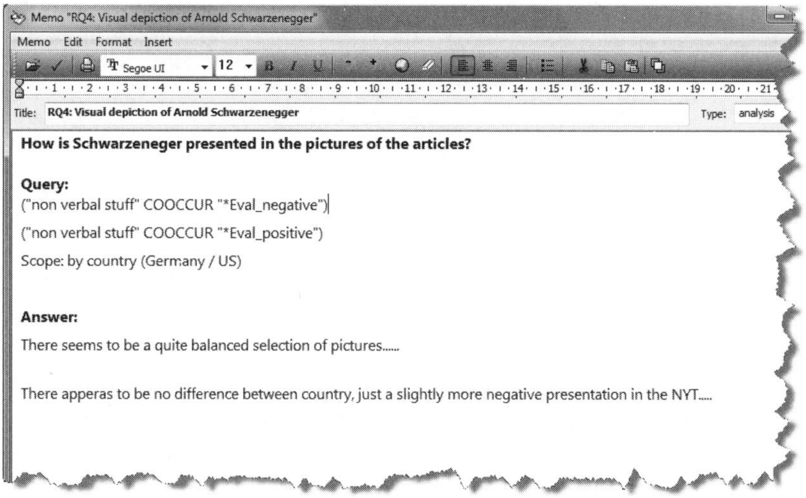

Figure 6.36 Research question memo for RQ4

Examining RQ5 (getting to know the co-occurrence explorer table view + creating superfamilies)

The last question that I would like to explore with you on this day excursion is: **For what kind of topics did the journalists quote direct speech? What is the effect of it on the reader?** In looking for an answer to this question, we need to work with the co-occurrence tool again. We have already used the co-occurrence tree view for RQ1b; now we need the table view.

As was the case in RQ1b, when we run the co-occurrence tool it correlates *all* codes with each other unless we set a filter. What we need here are the 'topic' and the 'direct speech' codes. Thus we need to create a filter suitable for this query and this is best achieved – as you have learned by now – via a family. I habitually create code families from all main category codes as they always come in handy when formulating queries. Thus, as we already have a family for 'topics' and one for 'direct speech', the easiest way is to combine these two in the form of a superfamily.

- Open the Code Family Manager via the main menu: CODES / EDIT FAMILIES / OPEN FAMILY MANAGER.
- From there, open the **Super Family Tool** for codes.
- Then click on the two families in question and the OR operator as we need all codes from both families. Double click on the code family **topics**. Double click on the code family **Use of direct speech**. Double click on the OR operator.
- Then click on the button CREATE SUPER FAMILY. Accept the suggested name or enter a new one and click on **OK**. The default name starts with an asterisk (*) and therefore it will appear at the top of the list of families (Figure 6.37).
- Close the **Super Family Tool**.

Figure 6.37 Creating a superfamily in preparation for the query

You will see the superfamily with a red/yellow symbol (in the program) at the top of the list if you accepted the default name.

*topics + use of direct speech

- Set the newly created superfamily as a filter by double clicking on it in the Code Family Manager. It then appears in bold letters and the list fields and managers affected by this filter show a pale yellow background color (in the program).
- Now, run the co-occurrence table tool: TOOLS / COOCCURRENCE TOOL / TABLE EXPLORER.

A window pops up showing something that looks like a correlation matrix. By default, each code is correlated with another. Therefore the table is divided by a diagonal line. The table shows identical results above and below this line. To optimize the view, you can select those codes that should be shown in the rows and those that should be shown in the columns. The codes are listed on the left-hand side of the window in two panes. Multiple codes can be selected using common Windows procedures like holding down the Ctrl key.

- Select the direct speech codes in the top pane. They will then be used for the columns.
- Select the topic codes in the bottom pane as rows.
- Then activate the field **Use selected codes** on top of the two panes (see Figure 6.38).

In order to produce the table shown in Figure 6.38, I selected only those codes that co-occurred with another at least once. The cells can be displayed on-screen in green, blue or red. Green is the default setting. The lighter the color of a cell, the higher is the frequency of co-occurrence. To change the color scheme, click on the colored circle in the toolbar.

A coefficient indicating the strength of the relation between two codes is automatically displayed. You can deactivate it by clicking on the c-coefficient button on the toolbar. The c-coefficient is generally a number between 0 and 1, similar to a correlation coefficient in statistics, but it needs to be interpreted in light of the different data material you are analysing in ATLAS.ti. If it is purely qualitative data and you use an inductive approach for coding, then it is best to disregard the coefficient value. If you import open-ended questions from 500 respondents in an online survey, say then it makes much more sense to look at this value.

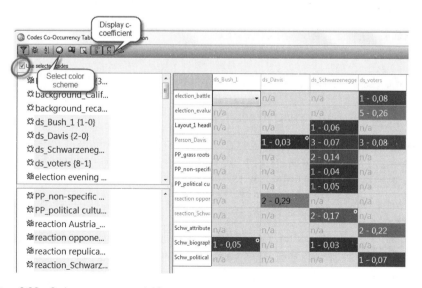

Figure 6.38 Codes co-occurrence table

2 - 0,09

Normally, the value of the coefficient is somewhere between 0 and 1. But as we are not dealing with standardized quantitative data, it might be that the value is higher than 1. If this is the case, you will see on-screen a red circle next to the coefficient. When the c-coefficient is low but the data segments overlap quite considerably, then the field is marked by a yellow circle. The message is: even if the coefficient is small, it might be worthwhile to look at the data behind the cell.[1]

For anyone interested in the mathematics behind the c-coefficient

The coefficient is based on the "Normalized Co-Occurrence" measure as used for quantitative content analysis. Garcia (2005) defines the normalized co-occurrence as the "Co-Occurrence Index" or C-index. In the case of pair wise co-occurrence, that is co-citation frequency between two and only two terms k1 and k2, the C-index is given by:

Eq 1: C12 – index: $n_{12} / (n_1 + n_2) - n_{12}$

where:

* $c_{12} = 0$ when $n_{12} = 0$, i.e., k1 and k2 do not co-occur (terms are mutually exclusive).

* $c_{12} > 0$ when $n_{12} > 0$, i.e., k1 and k2 co-occur (terms are non-mutually exclusive).

* $c_{12} = 1$ when $n_{12} = n_1 = n_2$, i.e., k1 and k2 co-occur whenever either term occurs.

- To look at the data behind the numbers, double click on any of the fields that show a result. A drop-down list with the list of quotations will opens (Figure 6.39).

The drop-down list contains more quotations than are indicated by the frequency. Remember from 'Skills training 5' that ATLAS.ti can only find something that is a quotation and not the stuff in between? Thus, when looking for co-occurring codes, ATLAS.ti always finds two versions unless the segment is double coded by two codes, (i.e., an AND co-occurrence). If not, then the alternatives are:

- A is overlapped by B and B overlaps A.
- A within B and B enclosed A.

All of these quotations are shown in the drop-down list.

Exporting results

If you want to continue to work with the resulting numbers, you can export the table as an Excel file. A direct Excel output containing the data is not yet available.

Clustering

If you have coded multiple segments within a larger segment with the same code, for example all parts of an interview

---

1 See also: www.atlasti.com/395.html.

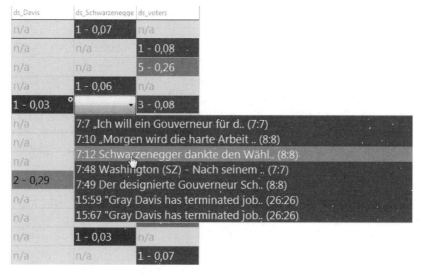

ds_Davis	ds_Schwarzenegge	ds_voters
n/a	1 - 0,07	n/a
n/a	n/a	1 - 0,08
n/a	n/a	5 - 0,26
n/a	1 - 0,06	n/a
1 - 0,03		3 - 0,08
n/a	7:7 „Ich will ein Gouverneur für d.. (7:7)	
n/a	7:10 „Morgen wird die harte Arbeit .. (8:8)	
n/a	7:12 Schwarzenegger dankte den Wähl.. (8:8)	
	7:48 Washington (SZ) - Nach seinem .. (7:7)	
2 - 0,29	7:49 Der designierte Gouverneur Sch.. (8:8)	
n/a	15:59 "Gray Davis has terminated job.. (26:26)	
n/a	15:67 "Gray Davis has terminated job.. (26:26)	
n/a	1 - 0,03	n/a
n/a	n/a	1 - 0,07

Figure 6.39 Data behind the co-occurrence table explorer

where the interviewee talks about friendship during childhood (the larger segment), then you may not want to count these as five co-occurrences but as one. This can be achieved by clicking on the clustering button.

- Try out the various options so that you become familiar with the tool.
- Explore the results and write down your observations in the research question memo for RQ5 (Figure 6.40).

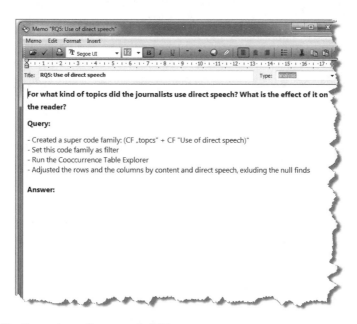

Figure 6.40 Research question memo for RQ5

Saving a query for later reference (or working with supercodes)

We have already come across superfamilies, which are a combination of already existing families. They are created with the help of Boolean operators. In fact, a superfamily is a saved query, for example 'Country::Germany AND Circ:: local'. Every time you click on this family, ATLAS.ti retrieves all articles from German and all local papers. If you add more German articles over time and sort them into the respective families, the superfamily returns the most current result. In other words, it is dynamic and every time you click on it, the query behind the superfamily is recalculated.

There is a similar option for code queries. If you want to rerun a query in the future, you can save it as a supercode. When you add, modify or delete quotations during the progress of your work, this will be detected by the supercode. Every time you click on a supercode, the query will be newly calculated and the results will reflect the current state of your coding.

Depending on the chosen analytic approach, supercodes could be regarded as 'frozen' hypotheses and thus be used to test hypotheses based on newly collected data.

Properties of supercodes

- Supercodes have a red symbol (Figure 6.41) instead of a yellow one (in the program).
- You can select supercodes just like other codes in the Code Manager or network view and display their virtual connections to the quotations.
- Supercodes can be part of a code family or a network view. They can also be an argument in other queries. With the aid of supercodes, you can therefore create highly complex queries in a few steps. Supercodes can contain supercodes, which contain supercodes, etc.

What supercodes cannot be used for

- Coding: supercodes cannot be directly linked to quotations. Thus, drag and drop from the Code Manager is not possible and supercodes are not shown when selecting the option 'code-by-list'.
- Supercodes do not remember filters. A filter set in the scope of query window is ignored during the creation process of a supercode. The list of results always displays the quotations from the entire project. Thus, when rerunning a supercode, you need to apply filters again if you want to break down the results to a subgroup of data.

Creating supercodes

The first step in creating a supercode is the formulation of a query. For that matter, it is irrelevant whether the query returns any results or not. Supercodes

Figure 6.41   Supercodes can be recognized by their red color

are 'intentional', meaning you can also create them based on a query without results. This saves the trouble of having to reformulate the same query later in the analytic process.

- Open the query tool and click a query.
- Then click on the button **CREATE SUPER CODE**.
- Accept the default name suggested by ATLAS.ti or enter your own name and click on **OK**.

> Create Super Code

The suggested default name contains the query details and starts with an asterisk (*). This means supercodes are displayed at the top of the Code Manager when sorted alphabetically (Figure 6.42). If you change the name or if it is too long, remember to add the query as a definition to the code to indicate what the supercode is based on.

If you want to use a different name, I suggest that you leave the default name at first, then go to the Code Manager, copy the default name (= query) into the comment field and enter a new name as the code label.

The quotation frequency is not displayed immediately since the supercode is dynamic; you will only see an asterisk (see Figure 6.43). Only when you

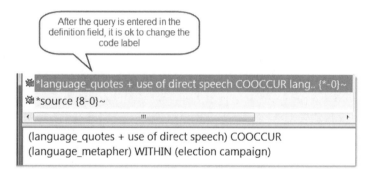

Figure 6.42 Naming convention for supercodes

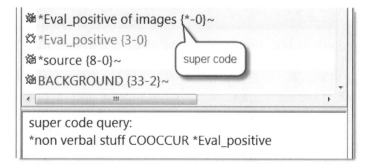

Figure 6.43 Supercodes display a wild card for the code frequency until you activate them

activate the supercode will the valid number of quotations be displayed for the duration of the current work session. If you close and reopen the project, you will see the wild card until you activate the supercode.

Editing supercode queries

If you get into the habit of clicking on queries and develop a taste for complicated queries that you want to store as supercodes, you have the option to edit the query directly. Some ATLAS.ti users will definitely want to use this option, so this is how it is done:

- Right click on the supercode and select **MISCELLANEOUS / EDIT QUERY**.

Figure 6.44 shows what the syntax for a supercode query looks like and provides some instructions on how to edit it. You can see the instructions when you click on the help button in the editor window.

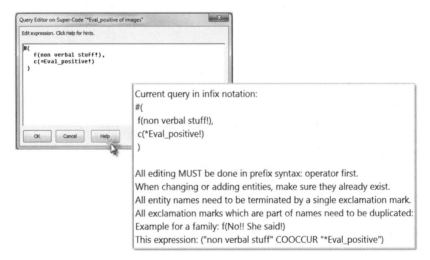

Figure 6.44 Editing a supercode query

Climbing the hills and clicking more complex queries

So far we have only combined two codes or one code and a code family. Queries can, however, be more complex and much longer. It all depends on what you need to retrieve in order to answer your research questions.

Using the Schwarzenegger data as an example again, we could look for segments where *metaphoric language* is used in the form of *quotes* or *direct speech* in relation to reports on the *election campaign*. The metaphoric language code has been used to code the data segments with references to Arnold

Schwarzenegger's Hollywood films. The codes and code families we need for this query are:

- Language_metaphor
- Language_quotes
- CF: direct speech
- CF: Election campaign

The first step is to create a set of all quotations where quotes or direct speech are used. Then we need to see where these segments co-occur with metaphors used in the text (2), and then where these occur in the context of the election campaign. (3).

1 Double click on the code family 'use of direct speech' (Figure 6.45). Double click on the code 'language_quotes'. Select the OR operator.
2 Double click on the code 'language_metaphor'. Select the COOCCUR operator.
3 Double click on the code family 'election campaign'. Select the COOCCUR operator.

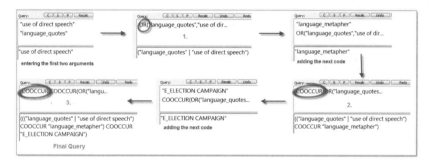

Figure 6.45   Entering a more complex query

Did I promise too much? Qualitative researchers can and do ask sophisticated questions and it is not all chit-chat and subjective interpretation. At this point in my coding, the query gives me two quotations. As I am not yet finished with coding, I will save this query as a supercode so that I can reuse it later.

Let's try one more query, as I still have to explain to you why the stack metaphor is useful.

You may have noticed by now that all newly added codes or code families are entered on top of the stack and the previously entered one moves one line down. This is similar to building up a stack of books or a pile of wood. We put the next item on top. When we need one of the books from the stack or want to fetch some wood for the fireplace, we start at the top; we do not drag one piece out from lower down. If we did that, all the books or our wood pile would tumble down. The ATLAS.ti query tool behaves in the same way. It first makes use of the argument on top of the stack.

What we want to find out now is where use of *direct speech* is used in reports on the *election campaign*, but we *do not want* to retrieve any of the *direct speech segments from Schwarzenegger*. Thus, the codes we need are:

- CF: direct speech
- Ds_Schwarzenegger
- CF: Election campaign

Excluding quotations from a query is at first sight not so easy, but once you have seen how to click it, you can remember the operator combination for future queries. First we need to exclude the direct speech quotations of Arnold Schwarzenegger from all direct speech quotations.

- Double click on the code family 'use of direct speech'. In Figure 6.46, this is everything within the large circle.
- Next, double click on the code 'ds_Schwarzenegger'. The result is the inner gray circle.

However, we do not want the Schwarzenegger quotes. Therefore we need to negate them with the NOT operator. The NOT operator needs only one argument. This means that the direct speech Schwarzenegger code now needs to be on top of the stack, otherwise we would not be able to negate it.

- Click on the NOT operator.

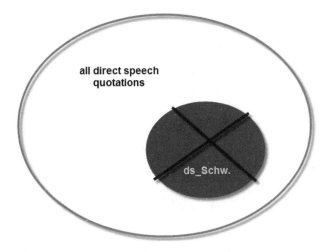

Figure 6.46   Excluding quotations from a query

The result is the entire universe of quotations except the direct speech quotations of Schwarzenegger. The visual equivalent is the squared area in Figure 6.47 minus the grey circle.

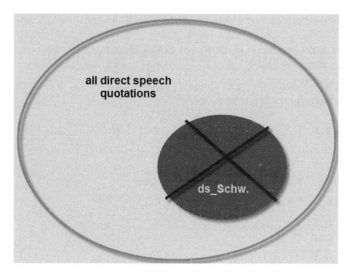

Figure 6.47 The entire universe of quotations minus the Schwarzenegger direct speech quotes

The next step is to combine the two arguments now listed in the stack of terms: the 'use of direct speech' quotations and the universe of everything else that isn't direct speech by Schwarzenegger. Thus, we need the light gray area within the large circle. This is the intersection of the two terms currently in our stack and therefore we need to click on the AND operator.

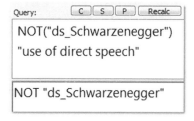

When looking at the resulting query in the feedback pane, it is easy to see what we did. You can read it as 'Use of direct speech' *but not* 'direct speech of Schwarzenegger'. The visual equivalent of the results is the light gray circle outer circle with a 'white hole' in the middle (Figure 6.48).

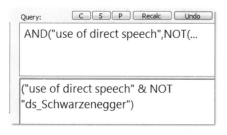

Figure 6.48 Exclusion query – read as A but not B

Remember, to exclude quotations from a code or code family you must:

1 Select the code or code family where something should be excluded.
2 Select the code/code family whose quotation should be excluded.
3 Negate it with NOT.
4 Combine the two resulting terms with AND.

We are not finished yet! Our aim was to search for all of these direct speech quotations within the context of the election campaign. So now:

• Double click on the code family 'election campaign'.
• Select the co-occur operator. The final query looks like this:

(("use of direct speech" & NOT "ds_Schwarzenegger") COOCUR

You are probably somewhat exhausted by now. This is normal when you're going uphill, but the view from the top is your reward (Figure 6.49). I hope that at least sometimes you felt, 'Yeah, I am getting there. This is great. I can see things in my data landscape that I did not dream of when I started to explore.'

While you take a rest, open your backpack, take out something to eat and drink, maybe a notepad to write down some notes as well, and let me point out a few last issues.

Figure 6.49   Rewarding view from the top

Intermezzo

On the use of code families

In Chapter 5, I briefly mentioned that it is best not to use code families to aggregate codes. I didn't show you how *not* to do it, I just showed you how to go about developing subcategories and how to aggregate codes from a lower level to a conceptual level without using code families. You have also seen how useful code families are in formulating queries. For this reason, I generally create code families from all main category codes once the code scheme is developed. But I advise against using code families solely for the purpose of creating categories. This results in an unstructured list of codes that is difficult for you to handle and for others to comprehend.

What also happens when code families are used to aggregate codes is that early descriptive codes are bundled using code families without developing them further into 'proper' codes. As I mentioned in Chapter 5, neither ATLAS.ti nor any CAQDAS package can recognize the different levels of codes. It is up to the software user to make this distinction. If a code remains at the descriptive level and is not conceptualized, there is no warning sound or flashing red light indicating: 'Please take a look at this code; it is not a proper code yet. You need to work on it a bit more!'

To the software, a code is just an object that can be attached to various other objects and whose content can be searched and retrieved. Everything else is up to you.

A second consequence of using code families to aggregate codes is that network views are empty of content. I am jumping ahead of you now, I realize, but let me explain. You have seen what a network view looks like in Chapter 1, when I introduced the main features of ATLAS.ti. I also showed you two network views in Chapter 5 explaining that it isn't a good idea to use the network view function to structure a code list.

Code families can be included in network views, but they can be linked neither to each other nor to other codes using named relations. Figure 6.50 shows a network view based on codes that are linked via a named relation.

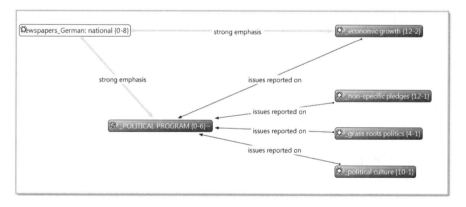

Figure 6.50   Network view based on codes that are linked via named relations

If I had not developed a main category code in the Code Manager and instead used a code family for collecting the codes, the codes probably would have remained unsorted in the Code Manager. Another consequence is that I

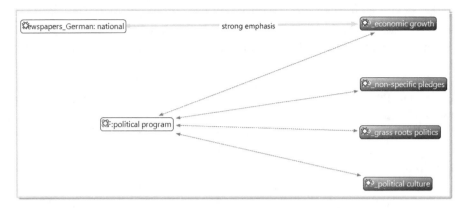

Figure 6.51   Network view including a code family and some of its members

cannot use named relations. I can only visualize that the codes are part of a family, in this case 'Political Program', but I cannot link this family to other codes using named relations (see Figure 6.51).

If I were to link the code family 'Political Program' to the code 'newspapers_ German: national', then it immediately becomes a member of the code family (Figure 6.52).

Thus, there are some technical issues limiting the use of code families.

A second reason for not using code families as categories is methodological rigor. The first step should always be to develop the coding system in a proper manner. This means that codes should not be all over the place on different levels with no indication of which code is which and what kind of meaning it has. If you use the code family function in ATLAS.ti too early, it undermines this process and the families will get in the way of building a systematic, transparent and comprehensible coding system.

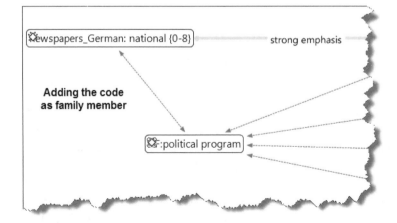

Figure 6.52   Linking a code to a code family in a network view

Summary

After learning how to build up a coding system in Chapter 6, in this new chapter you have learned all you need to know about second-level conceptual analysis. We started by looking at the memo function and, apart from the technical know-how, you learned about different types of memos and what kind of information to store in them. I emphasized the role of memos as containers for ideas and explained in detail how to set up research question memos so that they can be used as building blocks for the research report. Then it was time for some further skills training to get to know the ATLAS.ti analysis tools. You learned how to click on queries in the query tool, how to combine code queries with variables, how to ask ATLAS.ti to tell you which codes co-occur, and how to set filters and export a frequency count of codes across documents. While exploring the Schwarzenegger terrain in greater detail by working through some research questions, you learned how to apply the analysis tools in conjunction with writing research question memos. You can test your knowledge now by taking the next open book assessment.

'Open book' assessment of analysis tools

Can you answer the following questions on ATLAS.ti analysis tools? If so, you have already gained a good understanding of the second phase of analysis. Congratulations! If you are not sure about some of the answers, fortunately this is a book and not a fleeting lecture. You can go through the chapter again at your own pace and review what you're not yet sure about. Use the provided sample data and click on the instructions to see what is happening on the screen. Or wait until you have coded your own data and can then apply the analysis tools with your own questions in mind. I have often seen the 'Aha!' effect when users apply the analysis tools to their own data and suddenly see the light.

Here are the questions for you to work through:

1 What kinds of analysis tools are available?
2 Explain the query tool window.
3 Which operators are available to create queries? Explain them.
4 How do you click on a query in the query tool?
5 How can code searches be combined with variables?
6 How would you go about developing a coding system?
7 How do you store a query for later reuse?
8 How do you create reports from query results?
9 What is the purpose of the co-occurrence tool?
10 When would you use the tree explorer, and when the table explorer?
11 What does the c-coefficient indicate? When is it useful to use it?
12 How do you create and apply filters to restrict a query to a particular part of the data set?
13 Which function do you need to create a frequency table showing code frequencies by documents?

Further reading

On memos and writing

Birks, Melanie (2008). Memoing in qualitative research: probing data and processes, *Journal of Research in Nursing*, January, 13, 68–75.

Charmaz, Kathy (2006). *Constructing Grounded Theory: A Practical Guide Through Qualitative Analysis*. London: Sage. Chapter 4.

Corbin, Juliet and Strauss, Anselm (2008). *Basics of Qualitative Research: Techniques and Procedures for Developing Grounded Theory* (3rd ed.). London: Sage. Chapters 6–12.

Lewins, Ann and Silver, Christine (2007). *Using Software in Qualitative Research: A Step-by-step Guide*. London: Sage. Chapter 9.

Richardson, Laural (2003). Writing: a method of inquiry, in S. N. Hesse-Biber and P. Leavy (eds.), *Approaches to Qualitative Research: A Reader on Theory and Practice*. Oxford: Oxford University Press. Chapter 22.

Wolcott, Harry E. (1994). *Transforming Qualitative Data: Description, Analysis and Interpretation*. London: Sage.

Wolcott, Harry E. (2009). *Writing up Qualitative Research* (3rd ed.). London: Sage.

On querying data

Ayres, L., Kavanaugh, K. and Knafl, K. (2003). Within-case and across-case approaches to qualitative data analysis, *Qualitative Health Research*, 13(6), 871–83.

Bazeley, Pat (2002). Issues in mixing qualitative and quantitative approaches to research. Presented at 1st International Conference on Qualitative Research in Marketing and Management, University of Economics and Business Administration, Vienna. www.researchsupport.com.au/MMIssues.pdf.

Kelle, Udo (ed.) (1995). *Computer-aided Qualitative Data Analysis*. London: Sage. Part III.

Kelle, Udo (2004). Computer-assisted qualitative data analysis, in C. Seale et al. (eds.), *Qualitative Research Practice*. London: Sage. pp. 473–89.

Lewins, Ann and Silver, Christine (2007). *Using Software in Qualitative Research: A Step-by-step Guide*. London: Sage. Chapter 8.

Miles, Matthew B. and Huberman, Michael (1994). *Qualitative Data Analysis* (2nd ed.). Thousand Oaks, CA: Sage. Chapters 5–10.

GLOSSARY OF TERMS

Co-occurrence tools: The co-occurrence tools can be used for a cross-tabulation of codes. Before you run the tool, it is often advisable to set code or supercode families as filters. The quantitative results of the co-occurrence table explorer can be exported in the form of an Excel table.

The **Codes-Primary-Documents-Table** shows the frequency of codes across documents. It can be exported as an Excel table. Before creating such a table, it is often useful to set a primary document and a code family as the filter.

Memos in ATLAS.ti: Regard memos in ATLAS.ti as containers for ideas. Do not create a memo for every single idea. If the idea cannot be developed or expanded over time, then consider whether your thoughts might better be entered as a comment for a quotation.

Operators: ATLAS.ti offers a total of 14 operators that you can use to formulate a code query:

Boolean: OR, XOR, AND, NOT

Semantic: DOWN, UP, SIBLING

Proximity: WITHIN, ENCLOSES, OVERLAPPED BY, OVERLAPS, FOLLOWS, PROCEEDS, COOCCUR

Within a given project, you will probably never use all operators.

Query tool: The query tool can be used to build queries based on codes or code families and a number of different operators. ATLAS.ti provides three set of operators: Boolean, semantic and proximity operators. The result of a query formulated in the query tool is a list of quotations. Furthermore, code queries can be combined with variables via the scope button within the query tool. Variables are created via the so-called primary document families (see Chapter 3).

Research question memos: Research question memos form the building blocks for the results section of the research report. They begin with a well-formulated research question, a description of how the answer to this question was found (e.g. in the form of the query that was run) and how it was developed by the analyst over time, and some linked quotations that provide good examples. These linked quotations might later be used as citations in the research report. Research question memos can be added to the project at any time. Some research questions might be known already from the beginning; others may be added or existing questions may be modified throughout the analytic process.

Reverse Polish notation: A code query in the query tool is entered using reverse Polish notation (RPN). This means that you first select the codes or code families and then select one of the operators. Thus, you enter **Code A, Code B, OR** instead of **Code A OR Code B**. The logic of reverse Polish notation bypasses the need to set brackets in longer queries.

Role of families in the analytic process: Primary documents and code families are very handy when it comes to querying the data. You need them as filters to ask focused questions. In addition to the filter options from the main menu and the Family Manager, primary document families can also be set as filters via the scope button in the query tool.

Supercodes: Supercodes are a saved query. They can be created within the query tool after having clicked a query. They appear by default in red in the Code Manager and only show frequencies once selected. Each time you activate a supercode, the query that it consists of will be run. Thus, a supercode is always up to date and changes when the code content that it is based on changes.

Superfamilies: When you need a combinations of two or more families (e.g. to prepare a special filter for a code query in the query tool or a Codes-Primary-Documents-Table, or before you run the co-occurrence tool), you can create superfamilies. This option is available within the Family Managers.

Solutions

A reminder of set theory for understanding Boolean operators

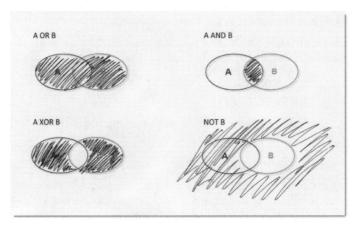

Figure 6.53   Solutions to Boolean queries

Query for RQ1a: is direct speech used in headlines?

1 Double click on the code 'layout_1 headline'.
2 Double click on the code family 'use of direct speech'.
3 Select the COOCCUR operator.

Query for RQ3: which topics are reported in US vs. German newspapers, local as compared to national papers? Are there differences?

1 Select the code family 'topics' as filter: **CODES / FILTER / FAMILIES.**
2 Create an Excel table by selecting **CODES / OUTPUT/ CODES-PRIMARY-DOCUMENTS-TABLE** → **QUOTATION COUNT (EXCEL).**
3 Create the subtotals for US and German newspapers and for local and national papers in Excel. This is easier than exporting separate tables from ATLAS.ti to Excel for each group.

SEVEN

Working with network views

The ATLAS.ti network view function is a tool that allows you to explore your data visually. It can be used throughout the analysis and toward the end as a tool to integrate all your findings. We started the journey by looking at an unknown landscape (see Introduction, 'Computer-assisted analysis is like exploring a data landscape'). Then we began to explore it by noticing interesting things. After a while we were able to label what we noticed and we gained a better understanding of the data landscape during the process of first- and second-cycle coding (see Chapter 5, 'The journey begins'). At first this was a descriptive understanding. With a prolonged stay and further exploration we were able to describe the various aspects of our data landscape and their specifications in the form of a well-developed code system (see Chapter 5, 'Skills training 2'). This enabled us to dig a bit deeper and to ask more specific questions utilizing a number of different tools provided by the ATLAS.ti toolkit (see Chapter 6). Our notebook became even more of an indispensable companion. In order to be able to explain later how we discovered something, we noted down every step of the analytic process and described each examination in detail, writing down what we found. We collected some sample materials and added these to our notes so that later we would be able to illustrate our findings to others. All this was achieved by writing research question memos. By writing these memos, step by step we gained an understanding of what the data landscape is like and how the various aspects are related and linked to each other.

Visualizing these links in the form of the ATLAS.ti network views is the natural next step. Graphic illustrations enable a different kind of exploration. Images, as compared to words, activate different parts of the brain and lead to different ways of processing (e.g. Khateb et al., 2002). The ATLAS.ti network views illustrate findings in the form of concept maps. Concept maps are known to aid creativity and to help in detailing the entire structure of an idea or a line of argument. They enhance metacognition in the form of elucidating and thinking about knowledge. On the receiver end, they support the creation of a shared understanding and help to communicate complex ideas and arguments (Novak and Cañas, 2006; Novak and Gowin, 2002).

In Figure 7.1, you can see the end result of the exploration of our data landscape. Previous explorers found out which people belong together, who is living where and related to whom, and furthermore the secret attraction of this valley: the cairn of wisdom. Not everybody has access to the cairn of wisdom;

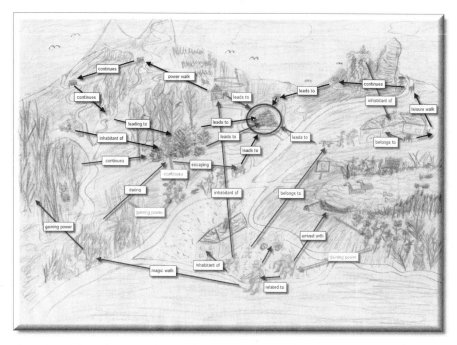

Figure 7.1 Concept map of the data landscape

some can only observe from the outside while others undergo various rituals in order to gain entry – however, this requires such mental strength and will power that not all inhabitants of the valley or its visitors will succeed. If you enjoy storytelling, look at the concept map laid over the data landscape and try to continue the story. You can embellish it with further detail, mystery and possibly a happy ending.

In this chapter you will learn the technical steps of creating network views in ATLAS.ti. Once again this will require some skills training. You will need to learn some new terminology, how the network view function is integrated within the HU, and of course how to create links and relations.

Skills training 6

Learning terminology

The ATLAS.ti concept maps are called **network views** because each of the views you create offers some insight into the whole network, which is your HU. Basically, everything you do in ATLAS.ti – each link you create, be it a code–quotation link, a code–memo link, a memo–quotation link, a code family linked to its code members, and so on – can be visualized. The entire HU consists of links and thus represents the total network. The process of coding has already generated a great number of links between individual codes and the data segments they encode.

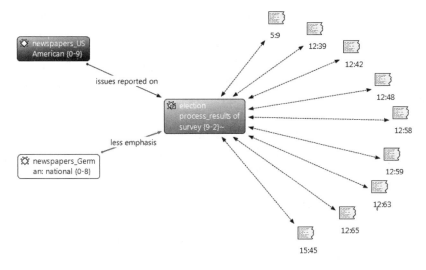

Figure 7.2 Coding visualized

Figure 7.2 shows the code 'election process_results of survey', which codes nine data segments and is linked to two other codes. By the way, each object that becomes part of a network view is called a **node**.

As you can see from the network view here, there are different types of relations – just a line linking two objects or a line plus a name for the link. The named links are referred to as **first-class relations** and the unnamed links as **second-class relations**. First-class relations can only be created between two codes or between two quotations. All other links are second class. In Figure 7.3 you will see an overview of possible links.

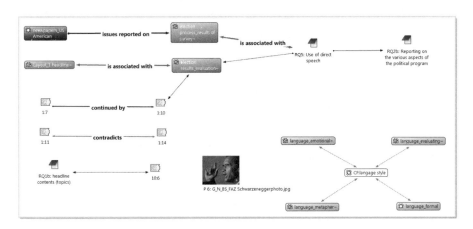

Figure 7.3 Examples of the various possible links and visualization options

First-class relations can be **directed**, that is pointing from A to B (A → B), or **undirected** (A <--> B). In the figure you can see an example of each. The property of directed relations is **transitive** and those of undirected relations **symmetric**. We need to know these terms when creating new relations, as I will show on p. 203ff.

One of the code–memo relations shown in Figure 7.3 looks like a first-class relation, but it is deceptive. The 'is associated with' link is created automatically when linking a code to a memo. When you link a memo to a code, the link is shown as a line without a label. Other second-class relations you see are between memos and quotations, codes and quotations, memos and other memos, and between families and their members. When visualizing families, the members are linked to the family name via a second-class undirected red arrow (on-screen). There is no need to draw these arrows. As soon as you open a network view for a family, the lines are shown automatically.

In addition to the various object types, an image PD has been imported into the network view in Figure 7.3. You cannot link the image PD to anything, unless it is part of a PD family, but it can be included as a thumbnail image (see p. 207ff).

You can choose from a number of display options. I will not describe all of them in this chapter as most are self-explanatory, but here is a list of things you can do. Figure 7.3 only shows quotation IDs, but you can extend the display up to the full text for each quotation. Video and audio quotations are played when you click on them in a network view. Code nodes can be shown with and without their groundedness and density counts. If you don't like the node bitmaps, you can deactivate them. Double clicking on a memo in a network view will display the memo text.

Creating network views

Over the next few pages, you will learn about various ways of linking and how to create new relations or modify existing ones. I will show you how to save network views and how to export them to other applications like a word processor or presentation program. In the section 'Removing nodes' I will warn you of a hazardous option in order to stop you deleting something you did not intend to.

Learning how to link

- Open the Code Manager and choose a code word. Then click on the network symbol in the toolbar of the manager.
- A network view editor will open. As a title, the name of the selected code is chosen. The window so far contains only the code you have selected. Let's add some more codes.
- Move the network view window next to the Code Manager and drag and drop three more codes into the network view.

Linking nodes using the main menu option

- Select one of the code nodes with a left mouse click.
- From the main menu of the network view select **Links / Link Nodes**. The movement of the cursor will be traced by a rubber band (in red on-screen).
- Move the cursor to the target node and left click. A list of relations will open.
- Select the '**is associated with**' relation.

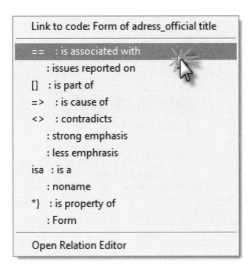

Figure 7.4 List of code–code relations

The 'is associated with' relation is a symmetric relation showing a double-ended arrow. It indicates that the two codes are related somehow but no direction can be specified.

The list of relations on your computer screen is probably shorter than the one shown in Figure 7.4. The image is taken from my computer; in addition to the default relations that ATLAS.ti provides, I have created new ones. Basically, you can create any relation you want and need, and in any language you want.

Let's try out another way of linking. This time, let's select a transitive relation.

Linking nodes using the toolbar option

- Select another code. This time, click on the link button in the toolbar and move the line (red on-screen) to another code. Left click and select the 'is part of' relation (Figure 7.5).

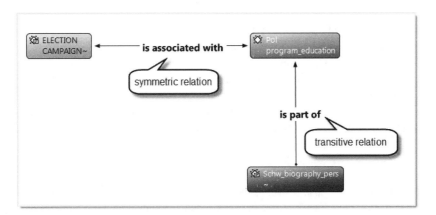

Figure 7.5 Examples of a symmetric and a transitive relation

Figure 7.6 Context menu for links

Linking nodes using the mouse and the Shift key

- Select one of the code nodes in your network view. Now press the Shift key on your keyboard, left click on the mouse and drag the cursor to the target node. You will see the (red) line again.
- When you reach the target node, release the Shift key. Let go of the left mouse button. The window with the relations opens again. Select one of the relations offered in the window.

Exploring the links

- The link labels are interactive. Right click on a link label and explore the options like flipping a link, changing the relation or cutting a link (Figure 7.6).
- Each link can be commented individually. Try it out. All commented links are marked with a tilde (~) as you already know from other commented objects in ATLAS.ti.
- End this exercise by unlinking all codes from each other.

Next, I want to show you how you can link multiple objects to each other at the same time. For this we need free unlinked nodes.

Linking multiple nodes simultaneously

- Select three of your nodes by holding down the **Ctrl**-key, or by drawing a frame around the three nodes with the mouse cursor.

- Now you need to select either the main menu option **LINKS / LINK NODES** or the toolbar button. The number of the (red) rubber bands that show up corresponds to the number of selected nodes.
- Move the cursor to the target node, left click and select a relation. The chosen relation is used for all links. If the relation does not apply to all links, you can change the relation later via the link context menu as explained above.

> The various ways of linking explained here apply to all objects that can be linked to each other in network views. When linking codes to codes and quotations to quotations you are offered a list of link labels to choose from. You won't be able to link any others.

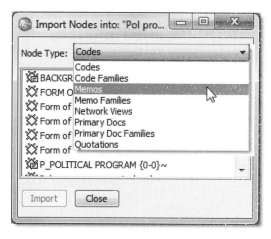

Figure 7.7 Importing nodes into a network view

Importing nodes

- You can import objects into a network view editor via drag and drop from all managers or the margin area. Another option is via the menu **NODES / IMPORT NODES**. Select this menu option (Figure 7.7).
- Click on the down arrow to select a different node type. Then select the objects to be imported and click on the button **IMPORT**.
- The imported nodes are placed in the upper left-hand corner. To distribute them evenly in the network view, select **LAYOUT / SEMANTIC LAYOUT** from the network editor menu.

Removing nodes

If you want to remove an item from a network view, you must be careful to select the correct option. When right clicking on a node in a network view, you have two options: **Remove from View** and **Delete Node** (see Figure 7.8).

As all objects inside a network view are called nodes, users often think that the node is not the 'real' object. But it is. When you delete a node in a network view, the object is deleted from the HU itself (i.e. from your entire project). When selecting **Delete Node**, you are asked whether you really want to do this. Regardless of this warning, many users have learned the hard way by clicking on this option. So, if you no longer want an object to be visible in the network view, select the **Remove from View** option or press DEL. The delete key on your keyboard is the equivalent of the 'remove from view' option.

You may wonder why the 'delete node' option exists at all when it is so dangerous. It can be useful, for example when creating new code nodes or memo nodes as placeholders or modifiers of relations (see p. 209: Dealing with

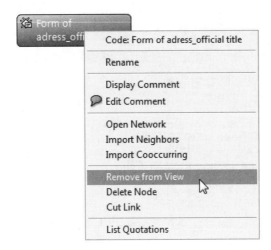

Figure 7.8 Removing vs. deleting a node

case-based network views). However, if it turns out that they do not work in your network view as you hoped and you want to get rid of them, it is quite handy just to right-click and delete them instead of having to go to the Code Manager.

Moving nodes

If you want to move the whole or parts of the network view within the editor, first some nodes need to be selected:

- To select all nodes, use the key combination **CTRL+A**. To select only a few nodes, hold down the **Ctrl** key.
- Then point to a node with the cursor, press the **Ctrl** key and move the selected nodes by dragging the cursor to a different location.

Layout options

Take a look at the semantic or topological layout of your network: LAYOUT / SEMANTIC LAYOUT or LAYOUT / TOPOLOGICAL LAYOUT.

- The **semantic layout** can be used to evenly distribute all nodes in a network view. This is especially useful when importing a number of objects at once.
- The **topological layout** arranges your codes from the upper left-hand corner to the lower right-hand corner, based on the relation types. This is useful when you want to visualize a sequence of events or activities.

If you don't like the result of an automatically created layout, you can use the undo function by selecting the option NODES / UNDO POSITIONING or use the hotkey Ctrl+Z.

The REFRESH option (F5)

Sometimes when you edit or modify a network view, you may notice that the contents of a node are no longer displayed correctly or that a link is not drawn properly. If that is the case, press **F5** on your keyboard to refresh the page. The F5 key is also useful if you change some preference settings under the specials menu and want to see the effects of the changes immediately.

Displaying code families in network views

As you have already seen, code families can also be displayed in network views. This is useful when creating a code book or explaining your category system to a third person or an audience. As standard procedure, I create a code family from every category I develop in the Code Manager. As seen in Chapter 6, these come in handy when formulating queries. Also, they can be used to improve the layout of otherwise dull-looking code books (see Figure 7.13). This is how you do it:

- Open the Code Family Manager and select a family.
- Click on the network view button to open the network view for this family.
- Arrange the nodes manually by dragging them to the desired position with the mouse.

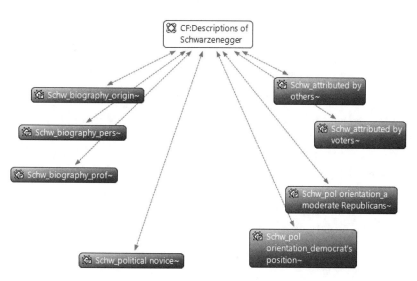

Figure 7.9 Example of a code family displayed in a network view (Display option: 'Rounded Nodes with Gradient Fill' – see 'Display menu' below).

Exporting network views

You can save the network view as a graphic file or use the copy and paste option to export it to word processing or presentation software.

- To save a network view as a graphic file, you need to open it in the network view editor.

There are two options for exporting network views. The first is to export them as graphic files; the second is to copy and paste them:

1 To save a network view as a graphic file, select the option **NETWORKS / SAVE AS GRAPHIC FILE**. You can save it as Bitmap (.bmp) or as Enhanced Windows Meta File (.emf).
2 To copy and paste a network view, select **NETWORKS / COPY TO CLIPBOARD**. Here you have the option to copy all nodes or only selected ones. Let's output the entire network by selecting **COPY ALL NODES**. The network view is placed on the clipboard. Open your word processor. Pasting the network view (e.g. via **CTRL+V**), will insert it as text only. To insert it as an image, select the **paste special** option. In older Office versions of Word, this option can be found under the Edit menu. In Office 2007 and 2010 it is the first option under the Start tab. In the Paste Special window, select one of the graphic formats (e.g. image (enhanced windows metafile) and click on OK.

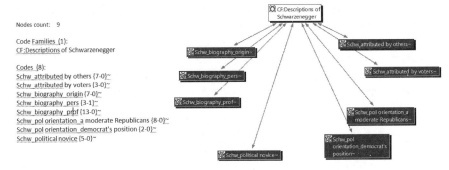

Figure 7.10   Exported network view as text and image

Figure 7.10 shows the network view pasted as text and image. As mentioned above, the gradient-fill and rounded colour layout gets lost when exporting a network view. In Version 7, you can export and print network views as you see them on-screen.

Saving network views

- To save a network view, click on the menu option **NETWORK / SAVE AS** and enter a name for the network view.

All saved network views (Figure 7.11) are listed in the **Network View Manager** that you can access from the main menu NETWORKS / NETWORK VIEW MANAGER.

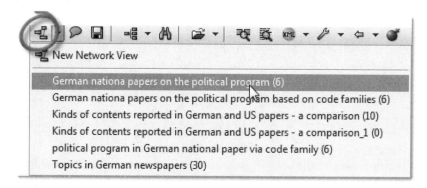

Figure 7.11   How to open existing network views

Or click on the network view button in the main toolbar. It is the first button on the left-hand side under the main menu FILE.

When you link objects in a network view and you do not want to save the image itself, there is no need to save each network view. The relations that you create between two objects are saved in the HU. The network views listed in the Network View Manager or as shown above under the main toolbar are only saved images of a particular constellation.

Display menu

Click your way through the different options and try out the display options. Here are a few exercises and explanations:

- Display the nodes with and without the bitmaps for the respective object type. Option: **DISPLAY NODE BITMAPS.**
- Switch between the normal view of the nodes and a three-dimensional (3D view. Option: **DISPLAY NODES 3D**. Which one do you like better?
- Hide or show the 'groundedness' and 'density' for your code nodes. Option: **EXTENDED CODE LABEL.**
- Display additional code definitions. Option: **CODES WITH COMMENTS.**
- A new display button was added to the network view editor in version 6.2. You can now display nodes with rounded edges and a gradient fill. Click on the display button in the toolbar as shown in Figure 7.12.

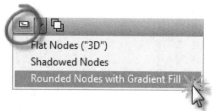

Figure 7.12   New display options in v6.2

With this knowledge about the network view function, you can now create code books as shown in Figure 7.13.

Code Book – Project Newspaper Analysis Schwarzenegger

Description of Schwarzenegger:

This category collects the various ways Arnold Schwarzenegger is described and characterized.

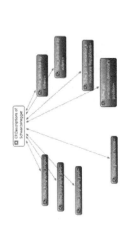

Schw_attributed by others: Positive and negative characteristics attributed to Schwarzenegger by the author of the article

Schw_attributed by voters: Positive and negative characteristics attributed to Schwarzenegger by voters

Schw_biography_origin: References to his Austrian roots

Schw_biography_pers: References to personal elements of his biography like age or family, persons that are close to him

Schw_biography_prof: References to his previous professions and professional life

Schw_pol orientation_a moderate Republicans: References to Schwarzenegger that name him directly to be a Republican of some sort. This code is not about the political position, just about names.

Election Process:

All events leading up to the election and closely following the election

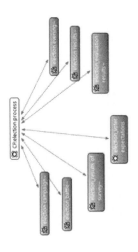

Election campaign: All reports on the election campaign

election evening: Reports from the election evening, reactions, atmosphere

election results: Facts on the election results, numbers, percentages

election_battle: Reports on the sexual allegations

election_evaluation: All reports where the results are evaluated and anaylsed

election_results of survey: Results of the exit polls

Election_voter expectations: Voter opinions on the candidates

Figure 7.13 Excerpt of a code book

ATLAS.ti offers three alternatives for displaying the label of a link. These are called label 1, label 2 and menu text. You could, for example, use label 1 as an empty label in case you don't want the name to show, label 2 for labels in English and the menu text for labels in another language. You can set the alternative displays under: DISPLAY / LINK DISPLAY.

- Try out the three options to see what happens when you select LABEL 1, LABEL 2 and the MENU TEXT.

The default relations that come with the software show a symbol for label 1, a letter for label 2 and a text for the third label (menu text). But you can define the labels in any way you want. This is done in the Relations Editor, which I will explain next.

Relations Editor

The Relations Editor gives you an overview of the existing relations and their attributes. Additionally, you can define new relations. In the following, you will learn how to customize relations so that you can illustrate the kinds of relations that are relevant for your data material.

Above, I introduced you to the concept of first- and second-class relations. We have seen that codes can be linked to other codes and quotations to other quotations via first-class relations. For this process, ATLAS.ti offers a distinct set of link labels for each of the two object types, as the nature of the relations between codes is different from that of the relations needed for quotations. The link labels offered for quotations include 'discusses', 'justifies' or 'explains' as compared to 'is a', 'is associated with' or 'is part of' for codes. Accordingly, there are also two **Relations Editors**: one for code–code relations and one for quotation–quotation relations. The latter types of relations are called **hyperlinks**. In terms of handling, there is no difference between the code–code relations editor and the hyperlink relations editor. When you know how to create new code–code relations, you also will know how to create new hyperlinks.

Explaining the Code-Code-Relations Editor

- In the main menu of the network editor, select the option **Links / Edit Relations / Code-Code-Relations**.

The Relations Editor can also be accessed from the main menu of the HU. From the main menu, select **Networks / Relations Editor / Code-Code-Relations**. The window in Figure 7.14 will open. If you do not see the main menu, increase the size of the window by dragging it with the mouse.

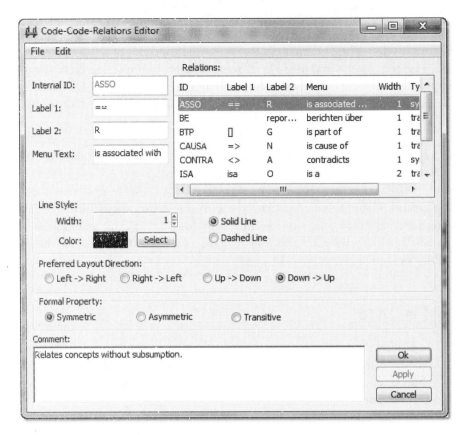

Figure 7.14 Code-Code-Relations Editor

Description of the data fields

Internal ID: Each relation has an internal ID by which it is recognized. By default it uses capital letters, but this is not a requirement. When creating a new relation, you just need to make sure that this ID has not already been used. My suggestion is to continue to use capital letters and to use the first three or four letters of the new relation as ID.

Link labels: Next you can define the three link labels. You can leave label 1 and label 2 empty, but it is necessary to create an entry in the menu text field.

Line style: You can define the width, color and representation (dashed or solid) of the line. Try out different colors and widths. The width allows you to add some more graphic elements to your network view (I think this is an unintentional option, see Figure 7.15). For instance, when you use a width of 40 characters, the line can be shown as a triangle.

When using a symmetric relation, you can make it look like a star. You achieve this by using a width of eight points and by leaving one of the link labels blank. Then move the two linked codes or quotations close to each other and choose to display the link that has no label.

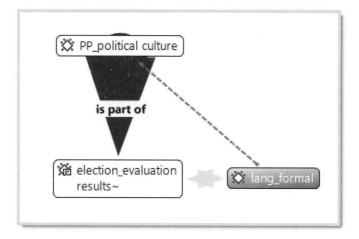

Figure 7.15 Customizing link displays

Preferred layout direction: You can influence the automatic layout algorithm by defining the layout direction of the different relation types. Most of the time, however, one drags the nodes manually to the desired position in the network view.

Formal properties: The definition of the formal properties is more important. It not only has a cosmetic effect, but also affects the representation of the codes in the **code forest** and the use of the semantic search operators in the **query tool** (see Chapter 6).

All codes can be displayed in a sideways tree called the **Code Forest** in ATLAS.ti.

- Select **CODES** / **MISCELLANEOUS** / **CODE FOREST** from the main menu, or select the option from the main toolbar as shown in Figure 7.16.

Figure 7.16 How to open the code forest from the main tool bar

The display is not strictly hierarchical. All codes appear at the first level. If you link two codes via a transitive (directed) relation, you begin to arrange them in a hierarchical order. However, if you link two codes using a symmetric (undirected) relation, then the codes point reciprocally to each other. This is shown in Figure 7.17.

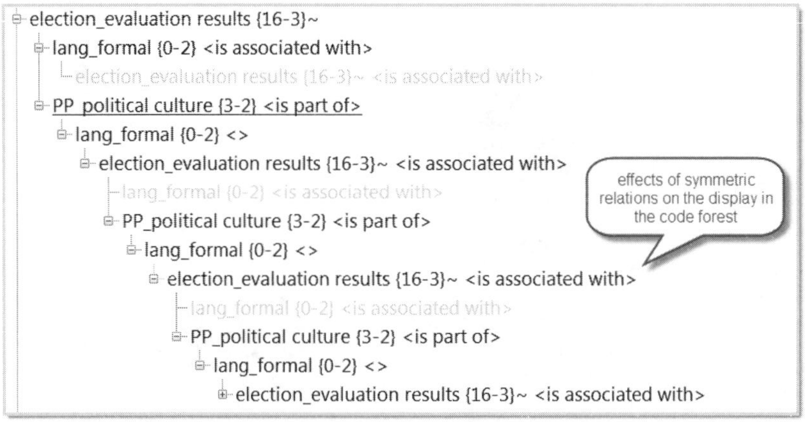

```
election_evaluation results {16-3}~
  lang_formal {0-2} <is associated with>
     election_evaluation results {16-3}~ <is associated with>
  PP_political culture {3-2} <is part of>
     lang_formal {0-2} <>
        election_evaluation results {16-3}~ <is associated with>
           lang_formal {0-2} <is associated with>
           PP_political culture {3-2} <is part of>
              lang_formal {0-2} <>
                 election_evaluation results {16-3}~ <is associated with>
                    lang_formal {0-2} <is associated with>
                    PP_political culture {3-2} <is part of>
                       lang_formal {0-2} <>
                          election_evaluation results {16-3}~ <is associated with>
```

effects of symmetric relations on the display in the code forest

Figure 7.17   The ATLAS.ti code forest

Thus, the code forest is not equivalent to the code tree in other CAQDAS packages and I advise against using it in such a way unless you do not want to go beyond descriptive-level analysis. I explain this at greater length below on p. 211ff.).

Comment: The comment field allows you to describe each relation and how you intend to use it.

Modifying an existing relation

- Activate one of the entries in the Relations Editor and customize the relation according to your preferences.
- For example, edit the relation '*is associated with*'. Think of a more meaningful name for label 2, change the width of the line and select a different color.
- Click on **APPLY** to save the changes.
- Then go to network view and link two codes using the 'is associated with' relation and see how it looks now.

Creating a new relation

Let's create the relation '**is reason for**':

- In the Relations Editor, select the menu option **EDIT / NEW RELATION**. All input fields are empty and can now be filled with new information.
- Enter an internal ID (e.g. **REA**).
- Enter label 1, label 2 and the menu text (see Figure 7.18).
- Then, select the width and color for the line.
- Set the formal property to **Transitive**.
- Click on **APPLY** to accept the new entries.

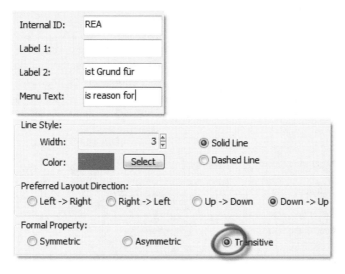

Figure 7.18 Creating a new relation

In order to make this relation available to all HUs in the future, you need to save it:

- Select **File / Save Relations**. Accept the default setting and save the relation to the standard relation file DEFAULT.REL by clicking on **Save**.
- You are asked whether it is OK to overwrite the existing file. Click on **Yes**.

Note: If you want to add new relations to the set of existing relations and you use Vista or Windows 7, you need to start the software in administrative mode. This means right-clicking on the program icon instead of launching the program via a double click. From the context menu that opens select 'Run as administrator'.

Use of colors and images in network views

There are various ways to utilize colors in network view displays. For instance, in the window **Network Preferences**, you have the option to set fonts and colors for nodes and the background (Figure 7.19). The modifications you make here apply to all network views and not just to individual ones.

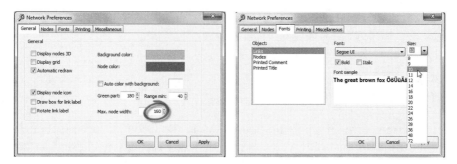

Figure 7.19 Setting network view preferences

Select the menu option SPECIALS / PREFERENCES.

- Click on the tab GENERAL and set a new background and node color.
- Click on the tab FONTS and select a different font and size (e.g. for the links).
- If you want to include thumbnail images based on image PDs, then click on the tab NODES and activate the option 'Full image for PDs' and select the width (Figure 7.20).
- Then import an image PD into a network view and see what it looks like (Figure 7.21).

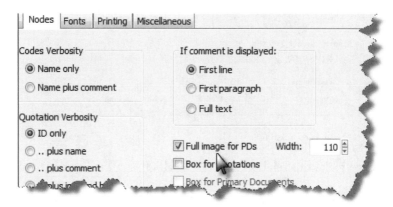

Figure 7.20   Setting network view preferences – Full image for PDs

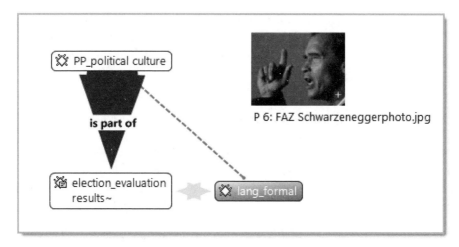

Figure 7.21   Network view including thumbnail image

Code colors in network views

You probably have set colors for your codes in the Code Manager. If they do not show up automatically, you can find the color settings by clicking on the colored circle in the network view editor (Figure 7.22).

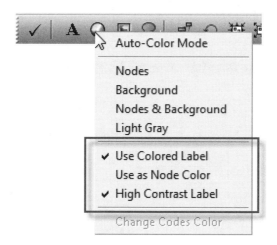

Figure 7.22   Use of code colors in a network view

If you activate the option 'Use Colored Labels', then only the label is colored. If activating the 'Use as Node Color' option, the label is shown in black and the node is filled with the code color. It is advisable to activate the high-contrast option as well. This changes the node label to white when a dark color is used for the node itself (Figure 7.23).

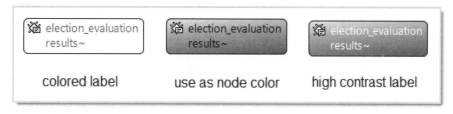

Figure 7.23   Variations of displaying code colors

Utilizing code colors to show patterns in the data

For the following example I am indebted to Eddie Hartmann for allowing me to use his data material (Hartmann, 2011). He conducted 20 interviews and developed a case structure for each person. For each case he developed a network view based on four main criteria: **affirmation, negation, rejective negation** and **positive substitution**. As you can see in Figure 7.24, each type shows a different pattern visualized (on-screen) by the colors used for the different criteria. Quotations were added to each network view to show the sequence of arguments that comprise the story of each interviewee.

Dealing with case-based network views

When you link two codes to each other in one network view, the link is not just a private link for this one view. It is used for these two codes in the entire HU.

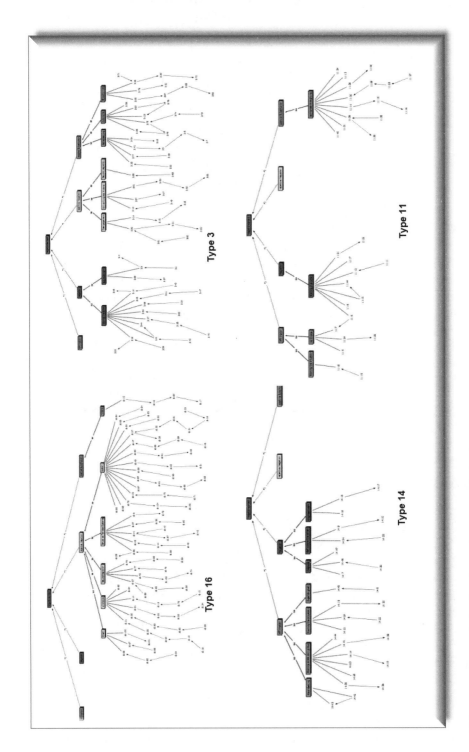

Figure 7.24 Using the network view function to show patterns in the data

Thus, if you pull the two codes into another network, the link between these codes immediately becomes visible.

But what if you want to link Code A with Code B using the relation 'is a consequence of' in a network view in the case of Paul, but need to use the label 'is a prerequisite of' for the network view in the case of Mary? The solution is to add more information to the network. If A is a consequence of B for Paul, there is probably a reason for this that you know from reading the data. If A is a prerequisite for B in the case of Mary, there are likely to be circumstances that explain this relation too. This information is what you need to add to the net-work view. Thus, it becomes even more meaningful as you add more to it.

If the reason that applies to Paul and the circumstances relevant to Mary are not yet covered by existing codes, you need to create them. These codes then will not contain data; you use them as modifiers to show the kind of relations that exist in your data. The term for such codes in ATLAS.ti is **abstract codes**. The frequency is zero and the density is at least one or higher. Creating abstract codes occurs quite regularly when creating network views. You often need to add codes at this stage to let the network view visualize the story you want to tell. Codes as compared to memos have the advantage that you can link them via first-class (i.e. named) relations.

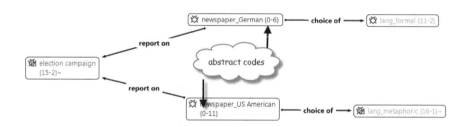

Figure 7.25   Using abstract codes to modify relations

In Figure 7.25, the two codes "*newspaper_German*" and "*newspaper_US American*" have not been used for coding. The frequency is zero but the density is high. Thus they are linked to a number of other codes not shown in this network view. Both codes are needed, however, to show that the US American press uses mostly metaphoric language to report on the election campaign whereas in the German press formal language is used.

On the use of network views for structural purposes

After 'Skills training 3' on p. 121ff., I told you about the advantages of a sorted and structured code list and presented my own dissertation research as an exam-ple of how not to do it. Instead of utilizing the Code Manager, I used the network view function to put some order into my thoughts. The danger of this is that the code system remains messy. The brain work is done, but one forfeits transparency. The code list is difficult to handle, remains incomprehensible to an outsider, and the different levels of analysis get mixed up. If you use the Code Manager to represent the various levels of your codes instead, the network view function is still at your disposal for higher order conceptual-level analysis.

Most packages I know of offer a tree structure for the code list. Thus, you can immediately sort codes into higher and lower order categories in the tree. Even though you don't have to do so – one could still start out with a flat code list – just by having the tree available it is tempting to sort codes into subtrees right from the start. Whether the codes on the main and sublevels are already proper conceptual codes also needs to be worked out when using these programs. Whether this is easier or more difficult because of the visual display the tree offers, I cannot say. User studies are very rare and so far have not dealt with such issues (Schmieder, 2009).

Whether a hierarchical tree display of codes is available or a flat code list as in ATLAS.ti, at some point during the analysis most users get to the point where they ask, 'What shall I do next? The data are coded, so what is the next step?' Some programs offering a hierarchical tree display allow you to print out the trees, which are basically the main category codes with their subcodes. This form of visualizing the coding system gives a false impression that there are already associative links and interesting relations in the data. You can also do it with the aid of the network view function in ATLAS.ti as shown in Figure 7.26.

If you link codes in this way, you can open a tree view for your codes in ATLAS.ti similar to those you may have seen in other packages. In ATLAS.ti this is called the **Code Forest**. To open it, select CODES / MISCELLANEOUS / CODE FOREST from the main menu, or select the equivalent option from the main toolbar (see also p. 205).

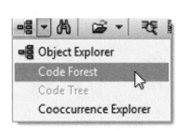

This works as long as you only use hierarchical links. The codes shown in Figure 7.27 are all linked via an 'is a' relation. You could also use 'is part of' or another label that you feel suits your data as long as it is a directed relation. As soon as you choose a symmetric relation like '*code_A is associated with code_B*', then the code forest is no longer hierarchial (see Figure 7.17 for an example).

That's not to say that the tree view is of no use at all. It always depends on the type of project and what you want to achieve. The tree view, for example, has been used quite successfully in team projects where the coding work needed to be allocated to the various team members. When dividing the work into categories, each team member goes through the data applying the codes of one or two main categories, in which case using the code forest works quite well.

If you use the network view function to link higher and lower order categories, you visualize first-level descriptive analysis. Moving forward, looking

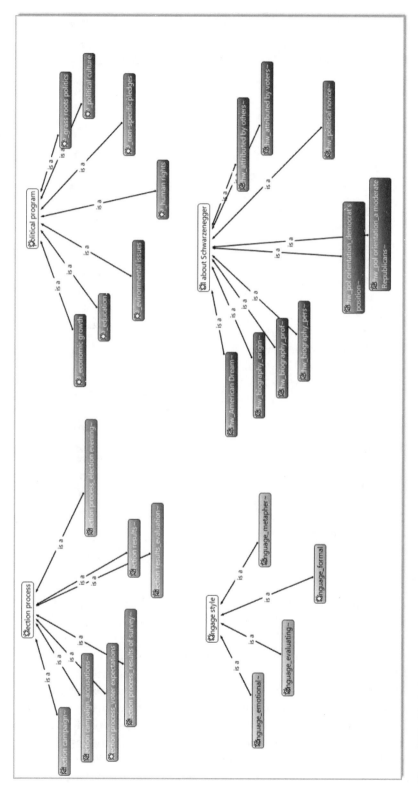

Figure 7.26 Displaying categories in the form of hierarchical trees

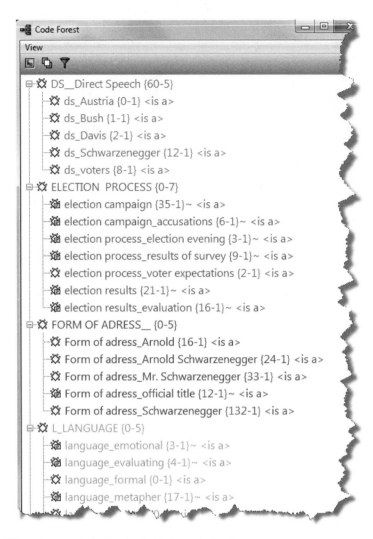

Figure 7.27 Hierarchical display of codes in the code forest

beyond the top-downward view of the categories and approaching the data with research questions in mind – querying the data and writing research question memos as explained in Chapter 6 – the 'is a' links between higher and lower order categories get in the way. Second-level conceptual analysis is about linking data across categories (Figure 7.28).

The aim of using network views for conceptual-level analysis is to illustrate the answers to research questions instead of just displaying the categories. Such network views are likely to contain subcodes of a variety of categories, but only those that are relevant in the context of the research question. For a cleaner methodological approach, I suggest that you define and visualize higher and lower order codes in the Code Manager and reserve the network

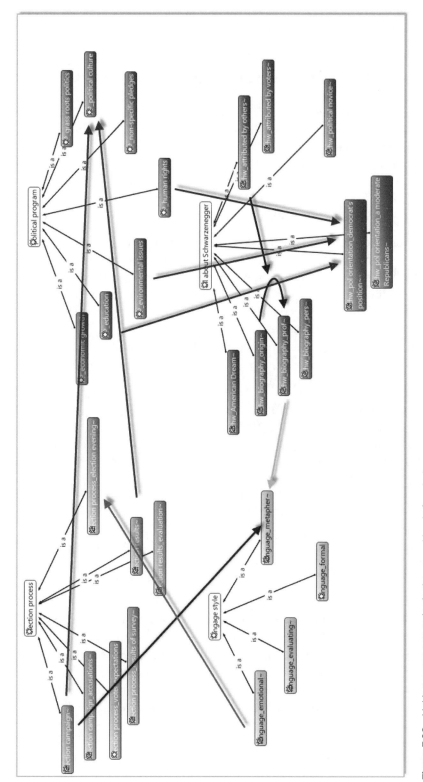

Figure 7.28 Linking across categories in the second level of analysis

view function for advanced conceptual-level work, when you begin to find relations between codes and across categories.

Using network views to present conceptual-level analysis

Before you get to this point of being able to integrate the major findings in network views, you will probably have created a number of smaller network views to explore your research questions in a variety of ways. It might be possible to integrate all findings in just one network view, but sometimes several are needed. Below, I will show a few examples.

Illustrating results from the Schwarzenegger project

The network view shown in Figure 7.29 illustrates a result from analyzing the Schwarzenegger data, that is the differences in topics covered by the German local and the German national press. As can be seen from the network view, the local press did not provide background information on the recall process; instead it focused on the election results, the reactions to the results and the person of Arnold Schwarzenegger.

In comparison, the national press provided background information as well as reporting on the person and the election results, with a strong focus on Schwarzenegger's political program.

- You have the data at your disposal. Go ahead and analyze them so that you can create the companion network view for the US American press.
- To explore the data further, you could add a network view on the type of language primarily used, either within the different newspapers or by types of newspapers or topic.
- Another issue you may want to illustrate is the presence or absence of various topics on cover pages, editorials, etc., and within different parts of an article like the headline or body of the article.
- Based on these network views covering one specific aspect each, create an integrative network view that elucidates all your major findings.

Illustrating results from a media analysis on the financial crisis

Figure 7.30 shows the results of a study comparing media reports from 2008 and 2009 on the financial crisis.[1] The codes in the upper portion of the figure (green on-screen) represent the contributing factors and the three groups of codes linked to the research question memos refer to immediate, long-term and individual consequences. The codes at the bottom (violet on-screen) indicate the source: expert opinion, political opinion, statistical figures, news agencies and personal experiences.

---

1 The study was developed as a sample study based on a small data set. Therefore the results are fictitious.

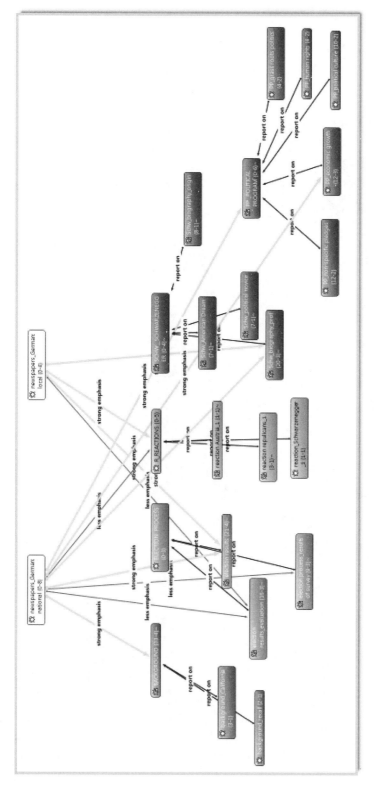

Figure 7.29 Network view on the issues covered by the German local and national press

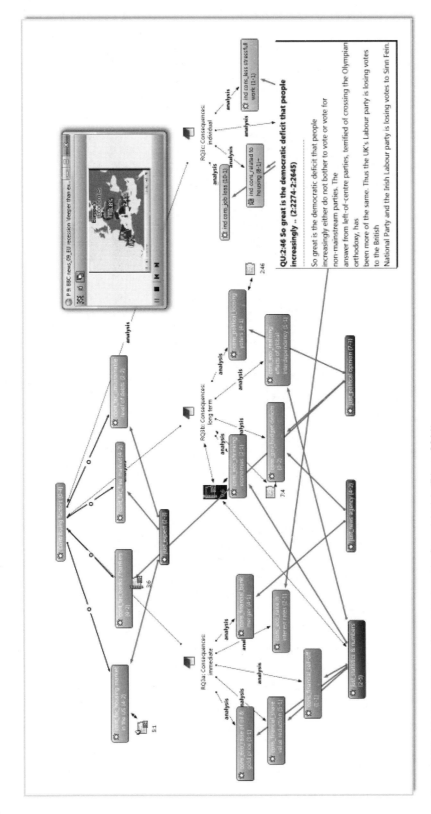

Figure 7.30 Integrating findings from a study on the financial crisis (Friese, 2011)

Also shown are an activated video and a text quotation. If the quotations are not included in the network view, you can always right click on a code node and select the option LIST QUOTATIONS (Figure 7.31).

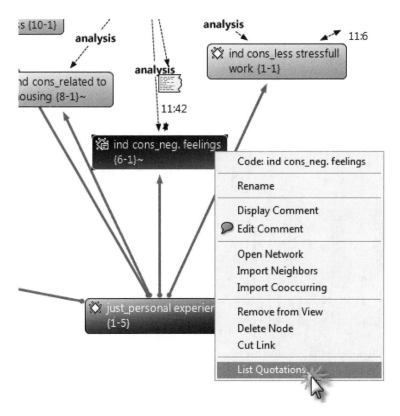

Figure 7.31 Bring your data to life by showing quotations linked to nodes in a network view

Illustrating results from the study on shopping addiction

Figure 7.32 shows one result of my dissertation research illustrating the phases of an addictive buying experience. The original network view I created did not contain colored codes, as this option was not available at the time in ATLAS.ti version 4. I have also modified the original code label.

When presenting your findings at meetings, at a conference or in a seminar, try using ATLAS.ti. You will be able to:

- present your project setup and sampling showing the Primary Document Manager and the families;
- explain your major categories by showing the coding scheme;

(Continued)

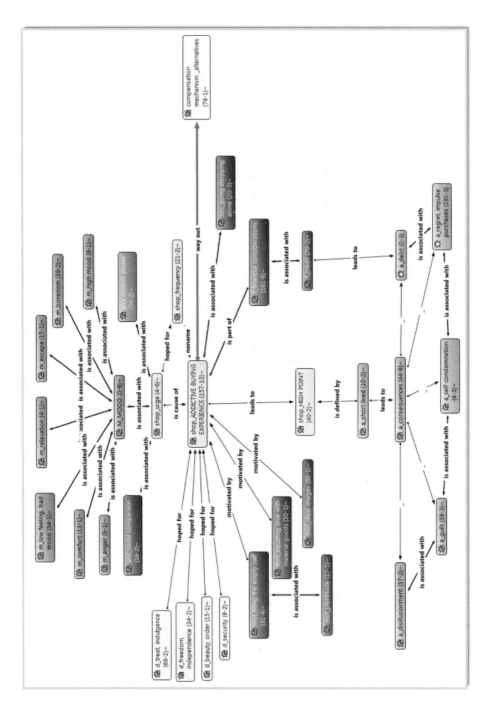

Figure 7.32 Illustrating the addictive buying experience (adopted from Frise, 2000)

- show the major findings in the form of network views;
- bring the data to life by showing or playing quotations that illustrate the results;
- show a few of your research question memos if anyone questions how you derived your conclusions.

You find an example of a presentation based on ATLAS.ti screen shots on the companion website.

Hyperlinks in ATLAS.ti

As explained above, hyperlinks are relations between quotations. You can create hyperlinks in network views by applying the various techniques as shown for code–code relations. The practice of using hyperlinks, however, is different. Therefore I have added a further section to this chapter specifically on hyperlinks. I will provide some examples on how to use hyperlinks and show an alternative way of creating them which stays closer to the data than using network views.

Examples for using hyperlinks

Linking repeated occurrences of the same idea

Sometimes an idea or subject is repeated again and again without adding further information. If you code each instance, then the frequency of the code goes up, distorting the code frequency count. The solution is to code only the first segment and connect the repetitive segments via hyperlinks.

Linking different aspects within a document

Take, for instance, an interview situation. The interviewee tells you something and halfway through the interview he or she tells you the exact opposite. Depending on the type of interview you are conducting, you can either query the contradiction on the spot or leave it till later. In order to easily access the contradictory information, you can link the statements via hyperlinks.

Another common issue in interviews is that people don't always stick to chronological order. Hyperlinks can be used to add a chronological structure to an anecdote or statement. Perhaps, while involved in telling a story, your interviewee does not start at the beginning of events but fills in important details later. If this makes it difficult to understand the logic of the argument, one option is to code the section that marks the beginning of the train of thought and link the rest of it via hyperlinks.

As shown in Figure 7.24, hyperlinks can also be used to link various statements that build on each other and that are typical of a particular speaker or illustrate an important line of reasoning.

Linking across documents

Linking across documents is likely to occur when you have several documents on one case, or when using different media types as your primary document. Pictures, for example, can be used as ice breakers to start an interview. Another data collection procedure may require people to provide visual material themselves and the interview is set up to talk about this material. Drawing diagrams or concept maps can be used as a way to summarize the main aspects of an interview in agreement with the interviewee. This results in data that contain images as well as the discussion of these images. Hyperlinks can be used to link the verbal and the pictorial aspects of the data.

Furthermore, the possibility of working with geo data using the Google Earth function in ATLAS.ti provides further reasons to create links across data, for example between a quotation in a Google Earth document and the verbal description of the location.

Skills training 7: working with hyperlinks

When linking quotations, you begin by setting one quotation as the source link. Then you select a second quotation as the target. As you continue to link more quotations, you can create a **star** or a **chain**. Creating a star means using the same quotation as the source and linking more target quotations to it. Creating a chain means beginning with one quotation as the source, and selecting a quotation as the target; this quotation then becomes the source and you select a new quotation as the target. This is illustrated in Figure 7.33.

You already know how to link quotations within a network view as shown above. Below, I would like to show you how to create hyperlinks while staying close to the data level. Let's try this out using text data. Later you can apply your skills to different types of media.

Linking two quotations

- Select a text segment that already is a quotation (e.g. by clicking on a code in the margin area). Right click on the highlighted segment.
- Select the option CREATE **Link Source** from the context menu that pops up. ATLAS.ti marks this quotation as the start anchor. This can be seen in the status bar at the bottom of the screen: it displays the text START ANCHOR DEFINED.
- Select a second quotation as the target. Right click and select the option CREATE LINK TARGET.
- A selection of relations will open in a new window. Select one of the relations with a left click.

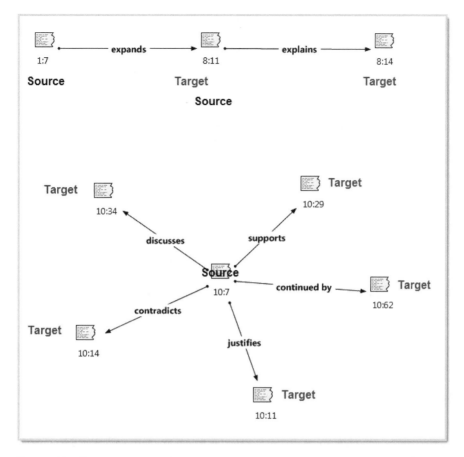

Figure 7.33   Star and chain hyperlink structures

Linking multiple quotations – creating a chain or a star

When you want to link a number of quotations one after the other, you need to use the buttons in the vertical toolbar.

- Select a text segment that already is a quotation. Click on the button **Create Link Source** in the vertical toolbar.
- Select a second quotation as the target. Click on the button **Create Link Target**.
- The window with the selection of relations will open. Select one of them.
- Another window will open where you can choose to create either a chain or a star, or whether to end the link.

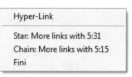

The newly created hyperlink (1) becomes visible in the margin area and (2) is shown in the form of a symbol at the beginning of a hyperlinked quotation in the Quotation Manager. The symbol '<' in front of a quotation means that it is a source link; the symbol '>' means that

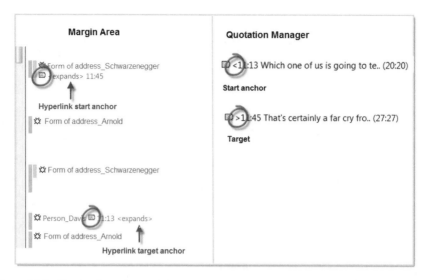

Figure 7.34   Display of hyperlinks in the margin area and in the Quotation Manager

it is a target link. In the margin area, the bitmap image for quotations indicates that a hyperlink exists (see Figure 7.34).

Browsing hyperlinks

- You can display the contents of a hyperlinked quotation by double clicking on the hyperlink icon in the margin area. If the quotation is linked to a text quotation, the contents of this quotation are shown in a comment field; if linked to a video or audio quotation, the linked quotation is played (see Figure 7.35).
- You can go directly to the hyperlinked quotation by holding down the **Ctrl**-key and then double clicking on the hyperlink in the margin area.

Visualizing hyperlinks in network views

- Right click on a hyperlink and select the option **Open Network**.

The network view displays those quotations that are immediately linked. If you have created a chain, then it is possible to expand the network view to show it all:

- Right click on a hyperlink node in the network view, hold down the **Ctrl** key and select the option **IMPORT NEIGHBORS**.

The option **Import Neighbors** is available for all types of nodes. If you want to import only nodes of the same type, you have to hold down the **Ctrl** key while clicking the option. In case you unintentionally import all neighboring objects and not just those of the same type, there is an undo option: **NODES / UNDO IMPORT NEIGHBORS**.

Linked text quotations

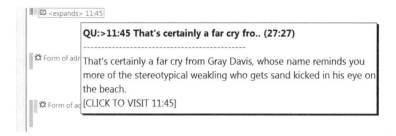

QU:>11:45 That's certainly a far cry fro.. (27:27)

That's certainly a far cry from Gray Davis, whose name reminds you more of the stereotypical weakling who gets sand kicked in his eye on the beach.

[CLICK TO VISIT 11:45]

Linked text and video quotation

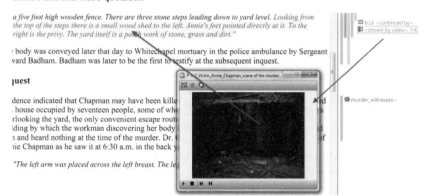

a five foot high wooden fence. There are three stone steps leading down to yard level. Looking from the top of the steps there is a small wood shed to the left, Annie's feet pointed directly at it. To the right is the privy. The yard itself is a patch work of stone, grass and dirt."

: body was conveyed later that day to Whitechapel mortuary in the police ambulance by Sergeant vard Badham. Badham was later to be the first to testify at the subsequent inquest.

quest

dence indicated that Chapman may have been kille house occupied by seventeen people, some of wh rlooking the yard, the only convenient escape rout lding by which the workman discovering her body n and heard nothing at the time of the murder. Dr. ie Chapman as he saw it at 6:30 a.m. in the back y

"The left arm was placed across the left breast. The le

Linked GE and video quotation

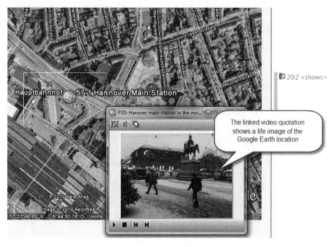

The linked video quotation shows a life image of the Google Earth location

Figure 7.35 Examples of hyperlinked quotations

Summary

In working through this chapter, you have learned two new technical skills: linking objects within network views and creating hyperlinks at the data level.

Regarding the process of data analysis, the creation of conceptual network views is most likely to occur toward the end of the analytic process, after a deeper exploration of the data material has been made. Hyperlinks and exploratory network views may be created throughout the analysis.

'Open book' assessment on the network view function

1　What are network views?
2　What can you do with network views?
3　Which objects can be contained in network views?
4　What is meant by first- and second-class relations?
5　Which objects can be linked via first- and second-class relations?
6　How can you modify existing relations or create new relations?
7　Think of a suitable way to make use of the three alternative link labels.
8　How can you save a network view and when do you need to do so?
9　How can you export network views?
10　Why should network views not be used for organizing your codes into higher and lower order codes?
11　Explain the code forest and why it cannot be used in the same way as a hierarchical tree display of codes.
12　What are hyperlinks?
13　How could you use hyperlinks in your own project to enhance data analysis?
14　What are the steps involved in creating hyperlinks?
15　How can you recognize hyperlinks in the margin area and the Quotation Manager?
16　How can you browse hyperlinks?
17　How do you use the network view function in creating a code book?

GLOSSARY OF TERMS

Hyperlinks: These are links between quotations. Quotations can be linked via named relations and thus are first-class relations.

Link: A link is the line that you draw between two objects in a network view.

Network views: These visualize the various ATLAS.ti objects and the links between them. Objects that can be included are: primary document codes, quotations, memos, all object families and the network views as icons themselves. Image PDs can be visualized as thumbnail images.

You can link codes to codes, codes to quotations, codes to memos, memos to memos and quotations to memos. Families can be visualized as well by showing the links between the family name and each member. The family name cannot be linked to other objects. Links between two codes and between two quotations are considered to be first-class relations as the links can be named. All other links are unnamed and therefore 'second class'.

In NCT analysis, network views play a major role in the conceptual level of analysis, when the analyst begins to see relations in the data during the process of writing research question memos.

Nodes: All objects inserted into a network view become nodes. They are visualized as code nodes, memo nodes, quotation nodes, etc., but the generic term applies to all of them. Therefore you need to be extremely careful when deleting a node: you will not just remove the object from the network view, but also delete it from the entire HU.

Relations: These are the names that you can give to a link. This is possible for code–code links and for quotation–quotation links.

Relations Editor: This is the window where you can define new relations or modify existing ones. It can be accessed from within a network view via the menu **Links** or via the main **networks** menu.

Further reading

Attride-Stirling, J. (2001). Thematic networks: an analytic tool for qualitative research, *Qualitative Research*, 1(3), 385–405.

Lewins, Ann and Silver, Christine (2007). *Using Software in Qualitative Research: A step-by-step Guide*. London: Sage. Chapter 10.

Miles, Matthew B. and Huberman, Michael (1994). *Qualitative Data Analysis* (2nd edn). Thousand Oaks, CA: Sage. Chapters 8–13.

Novak, Josef D. and Cañas, Alberto J. (2006). The theory underlying concept maps and how to construct and use them. Institute for Human and Machine Cognition. http://en.wikipedia.org/wiki/Concept_map (accessed 11 December 2010)

Slone, Debra J. (2009). Visualizing qualitative information. *The Qualitative Report*, 14(3), 488–97. Retrieved from www.nova.edu/ssss/QR/QR14-3/slone.pdf.

EIGHT

The method of computer-assisted NCT analysis

While working through this book, you have probably noticed that I'm not completely reinventing the wheel. At times I draw on basic methodological principles that have been described for manual methods of data analysis. The implementation of these principles, however, is different when using software.

The basic steps of the NCT method of analysis can be understood very easily. It enables novices to work in a systematic manner instead of declaring the software to be the method in itself. With more experience, the cyclical nature of the basic steps becomes more apparent and one learns to apply the method in a more sophisticated manner. In this book, I explain the application of the method within the context of ATLAS.ti. However, it can also be applied when analyzing data using other software tools.

The cyclical nature of analysis: Notice–Collect–Think

As you have seen already, noticing, collecting and thinking play a recurrent role in the analytic process. Researchers begin with noticing things in the data and as soon as they have an idea for a label, they begin to collect what they notice in the form of codes. After coding a few documents, and if no new ideas for further codes arise, the coding system is reviewed. On the one hand, your aim is to identify any codes that are still too descriptive and need to be collected under a more abstract conceptual label; on the other, you need to take a closer look at codes which collect a lot of quotations – perhaps too many. Within those you are likely to find a number of interesting new aspects that need to be explored further. While doing this, noticing and collecting takes place again. The task then is to identify those data segments that are most similar, collecting them under a subcategory label, and those that are most dissimilar, collecting them under a different subcategory label. Once the coding system has developed satisfactorily, the next step is to apply it to the rest of the data; and once the data are coded, questions can be posed. Later in this stage, the memos

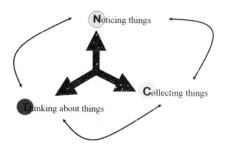

become containers for collecting ideas. Reviewing the results of a query requires you once again to notice things of interest and to summarize them (collect them) in your own words while thinking about them. This process continues until you begin to see how the elements of your data landscape relate to each other and you can collect these elements and draw maps and visual representations of your findings.

Below, I will briefly remind you of the various steps of the analytic process described in detail in Chapters 5, 6 and 7. For the sake of clarity I will treat each step as a separate entity. In everyday analytic practice this is not always so clear cut, but some processes build on others and so some steps need to be taken in order.

Descriptive level analysis

The computer-assisted NCT method of analysis consists of a descriptive level and a conceptual level. The tasks of the descriptive-level analysis phase are to explore the data, to read or to look through them and to notice interesting things that you begin to collect during first-stage coding. Based on these first ideas, the code list is developed further with the aim of describing everything that is in the data, naming it and trying to make sense of it in terms of similarities and differences. This results in a structured code list which can then be applied and possibly adapted to the rest of the data during second-stage coding. This concludes the first-level descriptive analysis phase.

First stage-coding

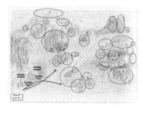

You begin by reading through transcripts, field notes, documents or newspaper articles, viewing video material or images, or listening to audio files. As soon as you start to notice things, you write notes, mark segments and attach first preliminary codes. At this point, the level of a code does not matter. It may be descriptive or already conceptual. The point is to mark things that are interesting in the data and name them. On reading further, you are likely to come across data segments

that are similar to others that you have noticed before. The segments may even fit under an already existing code label. This is when the process of collecting data segments under a common code name begins. If a similar issue doesn't quite fit under the same heading, you can rename the code or subsume two codes. Even if the term is not yet the perfect code label, it does not matter. When continuing to collect other similar data segments and later reviewing them, it becomes easier to think of better, more fitting code labels that cover the substance of the material that has been collected.

The first phase of coding ends when you no longer notice anything new, when no codes are added and you can only apply already existing ones. Then a first saturation point has been reached. As a rule of thumb, in an interview study, this point is generally reached after three to five interviews, depending on the length and diversity of the data. With shorter texts like newspaper articles, around 20 to 30 articles need to be coded before you get to this point. These are only approximate numbers depending on the type and length of data, the diversity within them and across the sample. The researcher needs to develop a feeling for this first saturation point and will do so as a result of experience over time. A good indicator is when no new codes are added and you only apply already existing codes via drag and drop from the Code Manager.

Depending on the focus of the coding, their style of analysis and individual ways of thinking, some researchers may end up with 70–100 or even a few hundred codes after this first phase of coding. At this stage I do not want to restrict anyone. Coding should be done in whatever way works best for the coder in relation to the data and the research goal. For most codes, the label at this point is not yet the final label. What needs to be done at this stage is to add more structure to the code list. This means developing more abstract conceptual-level codes and developing codes into categories and subcategories.

Adding structure to the code list

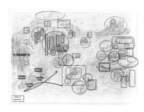 Codes in computer-assisted analysis are a technical device provided by the software. The software cannot distinguish between different levels of codes. It is during the process of analysis that a code is turned into a methodological device by the researcher. The danger of not properly understanding the meaning of a code in a computer-assisted context has been pointed out by Seidel and Kelle (1995). They were primarily concerned about losing the phenomenon and the context by reifying the codes, thus pointing out the risk of just playing with the codes and forgetting the raw data behind them. For a code to reach methodological status the researcher needs to arrive at a point where he or she can clearly define a code and determine its level. In ATLAS.ti, this is achieved via naming codes in a specific way and by adding a code definition.

As a general rule, it is very useful to look at frequencies when deciding what might be a candidate for a category code (see also Charmaz, 2006: 57). As the substance is non-standardized qualitative data, the outlined procedures need to be regarded as rules of thumb and code frequencies as pointers. There might be codes that are only applied a few times but are nonetheless very important, and the researcher may feel that it is not appropriate to subsume them under another code. Such codes may indicate that more data material needs to be collected. Or perhaps, due to the nature of the content that is coded, there are not many data segments that can be collected, for instance when coding epiphanies in narrative interviews, therefore, evaluating numbers always needs to occur within the context of reading and reviewing the data. The decision about which code might be developed into a higher or lower order code (i.e., category or subcategory) is still made by the researcher and not by numbers produced by the software.

Code labels that have been applied quite a few times show that it is possible to collect a number of similar items under one heading. Often these are candidates for developing subcategories based on the content coded within them. Here the process of noticing and collecting is repeated within the smaller cosmos of the code. The researcher reviews the coded segments at this point and the process of noticing sets in once again. This time the focus is on similar data segments within the code, which can then be collected under a new code label as subcategory code. This process continues until all data segments of codes with high-frequency counts have been reviewed. Whatever cannot be determined at this point remains coded as main category code.

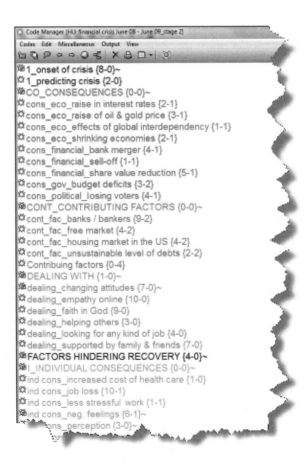

Next, one looks for code labels that have been used only a few times. These codes are likely to be descriptive, thus referring to specific data segments but without the ability to unite a lot of them. Such codes are candidates for a closer examination, either to merge them with similar codes under a higher order conceptual label or to evaluate whether they can be collected under a common category label. Noticing and collecting thus also play a role when developing codes on an aggregate level.

The aim of the above-outlined process of developing categories and subcategories is to add structure to a previously shapeless list, forcing the researcher to rethink the initial codes and to develop them conceptually. This prevents drowning in what I call the code swamp: that is, creating too many codes that look like codes in the software but have not yet achieved methodological status.

To the software, a code is just an object; to the analyst it is a tool for opening containers full of data. Creating too many containers that only hold a few items, or too few that hold a whole flood of information, creates analytic problems in the long run. Hitting the right level and knowing when a code is a proper code – when it has achieved methodological status – is a matter of experience. You become better at it with each project you analyze. This is independent of your software. Software has neither a positive nor a negative influence on learning how to develop codes methodologically. It is the analyst who needs to come up with the right ideas and labels. Software only facilitates the process of handling data, creating and applying codes, renaming and modifying them; it does not teach you about good and bad labels and when or when not to apply a code (see also Lewins and Silver, 2007).

Second-stage coding

After the structured code list has been developed, the researcher continues coding the remaining or newly collected data. This second phase of coding serves as a way to validate the code list. If the code list has been developed usefully, then not many new codes are added at this stage. If the coder has problems applying the codes to additional data, the noticing and collecting process needs to be continued. A code list probably never reaches 100 percent perfection; small modifications like refining a code label or adding more subcategories to already existing category codes are quite normal. The purpose of the code list for an NCT analysis is to be able to access the data in a systematic manner. A well-developed NCT code list describes what is in the data, but it does not represent a theoretical framework. If theory development is the aim then this occurs when writing memos, using the codes to query and access the data content.

Conceptual-level analysis

At some point, all data will have been coded; then the analyst enters the next phase. Until now, he or she was immersed in the data, working from the inside out. The aim now is to look at the data from the perspective of the research questions by approaching them from a different angle. This means asking questions using the various analytic tools like the query or the co-occurrence tools and the various table outputs that the software provides. Based on this exploration, you will once again begin to notice things in the data but this time, specifically, the relations between them. You move the analysis a step further, dig deeper, look at details and begin to understand how it all fits together. Accompanying the process of querying are what I have labeled *research question memos*.

Writing research question memos

In writing research question memos, I borrow from standard procedures on how to write up quantitative research findings. My suggestion is to begin the memo by clearly stating the research question to be examined. This may have been formulated right at the start of the project or developed during the process of analysis. The next step is to think about how an answer to your question can be found using the coded data. In order to make this thought process transparent, the query needs to be added to the memo as well. This query can be a simple retrieval based on one code, a retrieval based on code combinations, a cross-tabulation of codes, code queries combined with vari-

ables, and so on. The purpose of this is to tell fellow researchers and other interested parties what you did, so they can evaluate the quality of the results and the research project as a whole. Qualitative data analysis procedures too often remain opaque, and writing a short entry in a memo about which codes were queried does not take much time. It adds a lot to the transparency of the research process.

Next, the analyst runs the analysis, reads or looks through the data and writes down his or her thoughts and interpretation. While reviewing the data and writing about them, the analyst is likely to come across data segments that very nicely illustrate the interpretation written up in the memo. The memo can then be linked to these data segments and later retrieved as quotes for the research report. The content of a research question memo may begin at a descriptive level, but over time and with progressive analysis it is likely to become more conceptual and theoretical. Once you actually begin to write research question memos, you will be surprised how much analytic progress you are making. Coding the data is only one aspect; working with the codes and the coded segment adds a different dimension to the analysis. As this is about qualitative data, there is no p-value to look for, nor can you calculate an effect ratio, or see whether the result is significant. The only real guidance is to say: 'Just do it!' Query the coded data and write!

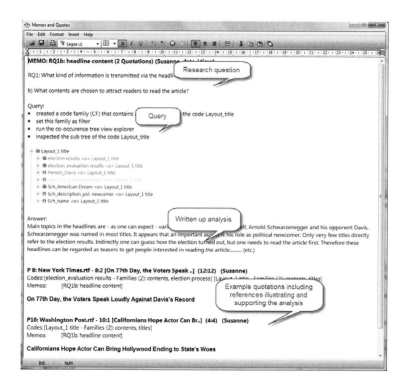

MEMO: RQ1b: headline content (2 Quotations) (Susanne...

RQ1: What kind of information is transmitted via the headli... *(Research question)*

b) What contents are chosen to attract readers to read the article?

Query:
- created a code family (CF) that contains ... *(Query)* the code Layout_title
- set this family as filter
- run the co-occurence tree view explorer
- inspected the sub tree of the code Layout_title

⊟ 🔲 Layout_1 title
 ⊞ 🔲 election results <0> Layout_1 title
 ⊞ 🔲 election_evaluation results <0> Layout_1 title
 ⊞ 🔲 Person_Davis <0> Layout_1 title
 ⊞ 🔲 ...
 ⊞ 🔲 Sch_American Dream <0> Layout_1 title
 ⊞ 🔲 Sch_description_pol. newcomer <0> Layout_1 title
 ⊞ 🔲 Sch_name <0> Layout_1 title

Answer: *(Written up analysis)*
Main topics in the headlines are - as one can expect - vari... f, Arnold Schwarzenegger and his opponent Davis. Schwarzenegger was named in most titles. It appears that an important asp...s his role as political newcomer. Only very few titles directly refer to the election results. Indirectly one can guess how the election turned out, but one needs to read the article first. Therefore these headlines can be regarded as teasers to get people interested in reading the article........ (etc.)

P 8: New York Times.rtf - 8:2 [On 77th Day, the Voters Speak ..] (12:12) (Susanne)
Codes: [election_evaluation results - Families (2): contents, election process] [La... *(Example quotations including references illustrating and supporting the analysis)*
Memos: [RQ1b: headline content]

On 77th Day, the Voters Speak Loudly Against Davis's Record

P10: Washington Post.rtf - 10:1 [Californians Hope Actor Can Br..] (4:4) (Susanne)
Codes: [Layout_1 title - Families (2): contents, titles]
Memos: [RQ1b: headline content]

Californians Hope Actor Can Bring Hollywood Ending to State's Woes

Then you will find out for yourself how much more you start to see in your data. If you need some input about writing, see, for example, Wolcott (2009) or Charmaz (2006).

The aim of writing research question memos might be simply to find answers to questions, or more elaborately, to identify patterns and relations in the data to see how various aspects of the findings can be integrated.

Visualizing

When beginning to see how it all fits together, visualization tools like the network view function in ATLAS.ti, or modelers and maps in other programs, can be used. Working with network views stimulates a different kind of thinking and allows further explorations in different ways. It can also be used as a means of talking with others about a particular finding or about an idea to be developed. Before you reach the final step of the analysis, a number of network views will probably have been drawn, redrawn, deleted and newly created. The ultimate aim is to integrate all of the findings and to gain a coherent understanding of the phenomenon studied; or, if theory building was your aim, to visualize and to present a theoretical model.

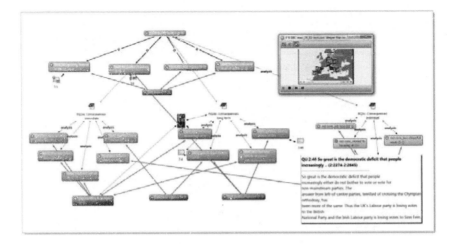

The role of memos in NCT analysis

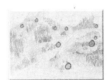 Writing memos is useful throughout the entire process of analysis, and different types of memos can be attributed to different phases of the analytic process. However, as I said before, I often come across projects where the memo function provided by the software is used very little or not at all. Often the memo function is misused as a comment function and users drown in a large number of 'memos' that are not really memos at all (see, e.g., Corbin and Strauss, 2008; Dey, 1993; Gibbs, 2005; Morse, 1994; Okeley, 1994). This does not mean that software users never write memos, but many do so using a word processor. This is a pity, because then they are a step away from the data and unable to link memos directly to them. This is also emphasized by Lewins and Silver (2007).

Within the context of software, I suggest making a clear distinction between comments/annotations and memos. The danger of writing in the context of software is that you write bits and pieces all over the place. You notice something and you write it down wherever the software provides an editor for it. What is often forgotten is the process of collecting. Frequently, users often do not even add a proper memo title as the software adds an automated title like a date and timestamp. Therefore, I suggest you create a number of memos right at the beginning of the analysis by thinking about issues you want to write about, such as the research process, a to-do list, ideas for further analysis, issues related to the coding scheme, or the research questions you want to find answers for. And throughout the analytic process, collect everything that fits under a certain theme within the appropriate memo. Further memos are likely to be added during the analytic process if other issues are noticed and you want to collect them under a common theme in the form of writing.

Software functions throughout the NCT process of analysis

There are certain ATLAS.ti tools that are more relevant than others for each step of the process. Before you even open ATLAS.ti, you should think about data management and how you want to set up your project (see the worksheets on project management on the companion website, www.quarc.de/qualitative-analysis-with-atlasti.html). Good project management begins with thinking about which file formats to use, how to name files and where to store them. When these decisions are made you can set up a project in ATLAS.ti, primarily using the functions of the main menu Documents. Grouping documents into primary document families adds further structure to your project and facilitates moving toward the actual first stage of the analytic process, namely coding. For the first and second stage of coding you basically need the functions provided by the main menu Codes and the Code Manager. Memos and comments are used throughout the analytic process, although a shift of emphasis occurs over time. Comments are likely to be written more frequently at the beginning; memo writing becomes more extensive over time. A space for writing comments can be found in each Object and Family Manager. Other objects like relations in network views offer a comment field via a right mouse click. All memo-related options can be found under the main menu Memo.

The logic of the analysis tools in ATLAS.ti is based on the existence of codes. Therefore you will use these tools primarily after the data are coded for conceptual-level analysis. At this stage, the following functions under the main menu Tools may be used: simple and complex retrieval options provided by the query tool; retrievals of coded segments in combination with variables, also offered by the query tool in combination with the scope function; the co-occurrence tools, tree and table explorer, to explore relations among codes; the Codes-Primary-Documents-Table to review the frequencies of codes across documents;. In Version 7, you will find all of these analysis options gathered under a main menu **Analysis**. Visualizing the findings in network views is a natural next step. All options that you need at this stage can be found under the main menu Networks.

When it is time to write up the research report, the research diary provides input for the method section, the research question memos provide the building blocks for writing up the results, and the network views can be used to illustrate the findings.

To sum up, the method of computer-assisted NCT analysis is illustrated in Figure 8.1.

Teaching computer-assisted NCT analysis

In the Introduction I suggested that this book can also serve as a textbook for various levels of qualitative data analysis. The dashed line in Figure 8.1 indicates that the focus of the analysis shifts when you move from coding to asking

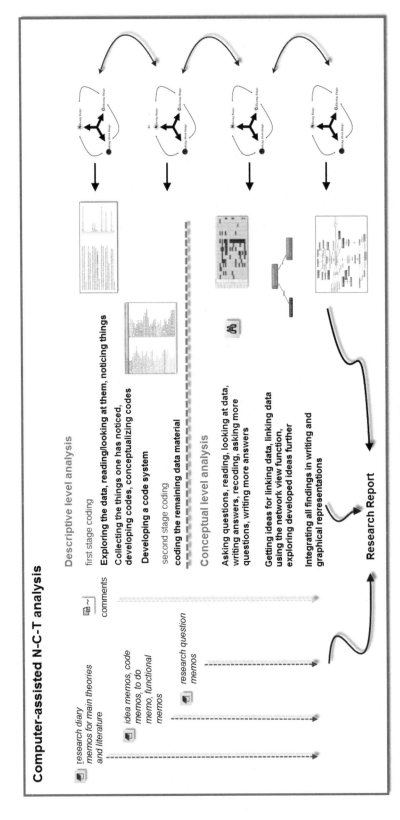

Figure 8.1 The steps of the NCT analytic process and the tools most relevant for each step

questions. Smaller student and classroom projects with a focus on description may stop here. At this stage, students have learned how to set up and manage projects (Chapters 2 and 3), how to code data (Chapter 4) and how to build up a coding system (Chapter 5). They probably have already learned a lot about their data and gained some insights. They have mapped out their data landscape (see Figure 5.14). At this level, you can also teach them how to write various types of memos, including research question memos (in the first half of Chapter 6). They have not yet learned the various, more complex retrieval options, but queries can also be based on simple retrievals (i.e. querying single codes). From my experience, students by this time are motivated enough to take a look at the network view function on their own and begin to visualize their findings.

For advanced, Master's and PhD courses, you can take the students one step further and teach them how to analyze data on the conceptual level. This means teaching them about the various analysis tools described in Chapter 6, talking more extensively about writing memos, inserting a lecture or two on issues of reliability and validity in qualitative research, and showing the students, how this can be achieved with the support of software. All this can be rounded off by providing more details about the network view function, including the possibilities of working inter-textually using hyperlinks (see Chapter 7).

Addenda

The addenda provide further technical information related to project management in ATLAS.ti. Here you will find information on editing primary documents, on merging projects when working in teams, on backup options and a section on troubleshooting. The aim is to cover areas which, in my experience, frequently throw up problems or user questions. Often, however, problems cease to be problems if users keep an up-to-date backup copy of their entire project. If they make a mistake, whether by accident or ignorance, they won't lose much data as long as a backup file or folder is available. Therefore backup options are explained in detail as well. The troubleshooting section will hopefully help to prevent panic if something does not work as expected, such as a data file not loading. I want to help users to help themselves, or at least to understand why something isn't working. The ATLAS.ti help desk will always provide further support if necessary.

Editing primary documents

Editing documents may become necessary in order to correct typing errors, insert pictures and tables, transcribe directly within ATLAS.ti or create internal documents. Users often do not consider the consequences of editing a coded document and in most cases are unaware of what happens technically behind the scenes. Below, you will find some reasons why it may be necessary to modify an already coded document and what you need to pay attention to if you decide you must do so.

Why you may want to edit a document

Correcting typing errors

Transcripts often contain typing errors. This may not be an obstacle for some kinds of data analysis; however, it can become rather tiresome to have to correct these mistakes every time you want to export data. Also, due to typing errors, the text search function may not be able to find the requested text passages. If you are using a linguistic approach for analysis, it is important that the words are written in the same way they are used. Misspellings should be corrected, otherwise the entered search terms will not yield adequate results.

Inserting pictures, tables and other objects

ATLAS.ti supports the insertion of objects like pictures, Excel tables, PowerPoint slides, illustrations, etc. into a document. The function is similar to that which a word processor offers. Pictures can be used to illustrate interview situations, show an environment and the like. Excel tables and graphics can supply additional figures and overviews. If inserted at relevant points, they can be of great value to the analysis and reduce the need to keep switching between different programs and documents. Integrated objects can be coded as one unit. If you want to code segments of inserted objects like images or tables, consider using PDF files that already include these objects, or assign them as independent primary documents.

'Visual coding'

The ATLAS.ti menu **Edit** offers similar options to the WordPad menu. You can underline text passages, display them as **bold**, *italic* or in another color, highlight whole passages and use different font sizes. These options can be used to highlight important passages in your documents and thus 'code' them with a certain color or font size.

Preparing transcripts, writing field notes, creating internal documents

When using the on-board transcription function, or if you want to type your field notes directly into ATLAS.ti or work with internal documents, you need the edit option. For typing a transcript or field notes, you can either assign an empty rich text document or create an internal document (see 'Scenario 2' on p. 55ff.). Rules No. 1 and 2 of editing (see below) only apply to external documents. When you use internal documents, you do not have to worry about them.

What you should know about editing

Required data file format

The edit option is only available for text-only or rich text documents. As doc or docx files are converted on-the-fly when loaded, they cannot be edited. PDF documents are write protected by definition. In ATLAS.ti versions later than 6.2, doc and docx files will be converted to rich text files and stored as packaged files in rich text format. Then editing will also be possible.

What is changed?

If you modify a document that is linked to the HU, then you modify the original document on the hard disk. Thus, the changes are not just visible inside ATLAS.ti – if you open the document in Word or elsewhere outside ATLAS.ti, the changes are also visible.

Mind the following rules!

There are two rules you need to bear in mind when editing a primary document if you do not want to get in trouble.

Rule no. 1: always edit within ATLAS.ti

Editing a document outside ATLAS.ti (e.g. in Word) endangers the congruency of the coding. Everything you do within the HU can be understood as a layer on top of your document. This applies to your codings as well. Each coded segment has a reference pointing to the part of the document that it codes. If you modify a document outside ATLAS.ti, the references may point to the wrong section in your text and if so you will end up with a misaligned coding system (see Figures A.1 and A.2).

If you correct a document in a word processor outside of ATLAS.ti, the HU does not know where changes have been made or where adjustments need to be made to the coded segments. If the HU were to load such a document, the codes would no longer show up where they were supposed to, as illustrated by Figure A.1. In order to avoid such a situation, the HU controls the size and modification date of a document before it is loaded. If a mismatch is found, the document is not loaded and you see only a blank HU editor.

As it would be very restrictive if ATLAS.ti did not allow you to rescue such a document, there is an option to reset the last access information and this forces ATLAS.ti to load the document (see 'Troubleshooting' section on p. 258). However, this does not mean that your codes will magically appear where they are supposed to. If you have modified a document outside of ATLAS.ti, it is up to you to check all codings and adjust them manually if necessary. But this might be better than starting from scratch and recoding the entire document.

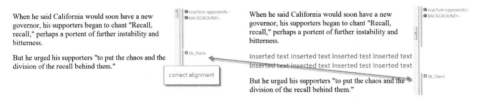

Figure A.1 Editing outside of ATLAS.ti.leads to misaligned codes

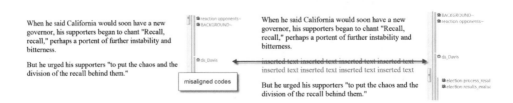

Figure A.2 Correct alignment when editing inside of ATLAS.ti

When setting up projects using the new data handling methods in version 7, you can no longer accidentally edit an assigned file outside of ATLAS.ti, in which case rule no. 1 becomes obsolete.

Rule no. 2: never delete or modify the auxiliary log file

To understand the second rule, you need to understand what happens when a primary document is properly edited within ATLAS.ti. As soon as you save your changes, an auxiliary file is created. This auxiliary file has the same name as the original source file that was edited, plus the file extension '.log'. It is stored within the same folder as the original.

Naming convention including file extensions

Original source file: Washington Post.rtf
Auxiliary log file: Washington Post.rtf.log

The default setting of your file manager is set to 'hide commonly known file extensions'. This is an unfortunate setting because the ability to see the file extensions can be useful in many contexts. You can easily change this setting under the view options in your file manager. In the event that the file extensions are not shown, you will see the following file names.

Naming convention without file extensions

Original source file: Washington Post
Auxiliary log file: Washington Post.rtf

You can only see in the column 'type' of your file manager that the first one is indeed the rich text document and the second one a text file. The characters '.rtf' are part of the file name and do not mark the file extension.

As they are just plain text, log files are very small, usually just a few kilobytes in size. Log files contain information for the HU about how to adjust the codings according to the modifications that have been made. There is an example of a log entry:

```
<LOGSESSIONS>
<LOGS SECS_1901="3243616859" ISODATE="2003-10-14T20:40:59">
<TransformMod oldSel="1@10,1050@10" newSel="1@10" afterOldSel="1051@10"
beforeOldSel="1052@9"/>
```

(Continued)

(Continued)

```
<TransformMod oldSel="1@10,1@10" newSel="1@10" afterOldSel="2@10" before-
OldSel="1052@9"/>
<TransformMod oldSel="1@10,1@10" newSel="1@10" afterOldSel="1@11" before-
OldSel="1052@9"/>
</LOGS>
```

As a user, there is no need to understand the content of a log file or even to open it. You just need to know that it is there and that it is best not to touch it. If you delete a log file and it cannot be rescued from the recycle bin, you have lost the coding for this document. The only option that remains is to disconnect the document from the HU, then newly assign and recode it. By the way, deleting a log file is the one single activity that will cause permanent data loss (apart from losing your HU file of course). All other problems related to data management can generally be solved.

As for rule no. 1, In version 7 if working with managed files, you no longer have to worry about log files as they are not visible and users cannot touch them. Rule no. 2 then also becomes obsolete.

How to edit

By default, all documents are loaded in write-protected mode. To enter edit mode:

- Load a primary document that can be edited. When loading such a document, a second toolbar appears underneath the main toolbar.

- Either select the main menu item **EDIT / DOCUMENT ACCESS / ENTER EDIT MODE** or click on the edit button in the second toolbar.

All edit options in the second toolbar can now be used. Try out the various options like enlarging or reducing the font size, changing colors, putting text into bold or italics, using the highlighter, etc.

To exit the edit mode:

- Click on the edit button in the second toolbar and select **SAVE AND LEAVE EDIT MODE**. This is the moment when a log file is created.

If you edit a file multiple times, more information is written into the already existing log files. Thus, there will always only be one log file per edited document.

Log and lok files

At times users are confused because they find log and lok files. **Lok** files are temporary files and are created when you open an HU or load a document. They indicate to the software that a file is already loaded or open. This prevents you from opening an HU a second time. If you do so, you can only open it in read-only mode. This has probably already happened to you when using other applications.

When a primary document is loaded it is put into the cache, a kind of intermediate storage space. This enables the software to show the document or its quotations quicker when accessing it several times during a work session. When you close ATLAS.ti, the lok files are usually deleted. If your system or ATLAS.ti crashes, it could be that there is no time to delete them and you still see them in your project folder. If you find **lok files** when ATLAS.ti is not open, it is safe – and advisable – to delete them.

If you are working on your own and have not set up a server-based team project, you can deactivate the creation of lok files: EXTRAS / GENERAL / GENERAL PREFERENCES → tab: GENERAL, option: DATA SOURCE LOCK PROTECTION.

Editing primary documents in team situations

If you want to allow your team to edit primary documents, you need to add an additional layer of complexity to your project. It is possible, but it should be managed with care. When your team accesses the project folder containing the data and the HUs on a server (see Chapter 3, 'The server-based setup'), then ATLAS.ti controls the process. Thus, you do not need to do anything more than instruct each team member to leave the log files where they are, and that they should not modify, delete or move them. If your team members are working at different locations, then editing needs to be tightly controlled.

Editing in teams using a server-based project setup

Using such a setup means that every team member is working within his or her own HU, but all are accessing the same data (Figure 3.12). Let's assume Peter discovers a typing error in P7. He enters the edit mode to correct the error. Michelle discovers the typo at about the same time and also wants to enter the edit mode. The software will tell her that she currently cannot enter it as Peter's computer is currently editing the document. Half an hour later she tries again to edit P7. This time she sees a note ordering her to synchronize her HU. She needs to accept this message in order to load P7. Then her HU file is synchronized. This means that the quotation references in her HU are adapted to the changes made by Peter. All other users must synch their HU files as well. This is done at the latest by the software while the project administrator is merging the various sub-HUs into the Master HU. For all these processes, the log files of all edited documents are needed.

Editing in teams when working at different locations

If editing is allowed, you need to decide whether documents should only be edited at one central location by the project administrator, or whether each team member has the right to edit a specific set of documents.

If the project administrator only is allowed to edit With this option, it is best to edit documents after merging the various sub-HUs. For the next round of coding or work on the data, it is not sufficient to send the new Master HU to each team member – you need to send or upload the entire project folder containing the edited documents and the log files. It is best for each team member to replace the entire project folder with the new master version.

If each team member is allowed to edit specific subsets of documents This option requires a strict agreement about who is allowed to edit which subgroup of documents. If the same document is edited at two locations, you will lose one version of it. Take a look at Figure 3.15. Peter, Michelle, Marie and Claus are working together on a project and accessing the files at various locations. Marie is the project administrator. Let's assume that the project contains 40 rich text files. The team has agreed on the following:

- Peter is allowed to edit PD 1 to PD 10.
- Michelle is allowed to edit PD 11 to PD 20.
- Marie is allowed to edit PD 21 to PD 30 (she is also the project administrator).
- Claus is allowed to edit PD 31 to PD 40.

When it is time to merge the various sub-HUs, Peter sends Marie his HU file '*Newspaper analysis_Peter.hpr6*' and the rtf and log files for PD 1 to PD 10, Michelle sends Marie her HU file '*Newspaper analysis_Michelle. hpr6*' and the rtf and log files for PD 11 to PD 20, and Claus sends Marie his HU file '*Newspaper analysis_Claus.hpr6*' and the rtf and log files for PD 31 to PD 40.

   Marie copies all four sub-HUs into one folder, along with all 40 rtf files and all 40 log files. Then she opens each sub-HU and synchronizes it. ATLAS.ti will recognize any modification when merging HUs and goes through the synchronization process, but I recommend that you update each HU and check it yourself before beginning the merge process.

Best practice rules for editing primary documents

- Documents must be saved and assigned as text (*.txt) or as rich text (*.rtf) files.
- Never open or modify a file that is assigned to an ATLAS.ti project in Word or any other application outside ATLAS.ti.
- Never change or delete log files.
- For teams: Discuss the necessity of editing primary documents. If editing is allowed, discuss the two rules of editing with each team member and decide who is allowed to edit what.
- Regularly create **Copy Bundle** files as project backup. A copy bundle file contains the HU, all documents assigned as PD (unless you exclude them from the bundle) and all log files. See the section on project backups below for further information.

Merging projects

Merging projects is a complex procedure for the software, but easy to do for a user. You can merge two projects at a time. In larger team projects, you have to go through multiple merges to create a Master HU, but it won't take you longer than just a few minutes.

Prerequisites for merging

1   If the sub-HUs reference the same documents, the documents need to be in the same order in each HU. PD 1 needs to be associated with the same source file in HU1, HU2 and HU3; PD 2 needs to be the same in each HU, and so on. If the order is not the same, the software will let you know and you can still change the position of the PDs via drag and drop. This no longer applies in version 7, because GUI Ids are used for each object. This means that each document gets a world-wide unique Id and this is independent of the location of the document in the HU.
2   The project setup should be the same for each sub-HU to be merged. As I'm sure you followed my advice and used the one-folder setup (i.e. the HUPATH for each document in your HU), this should not be an issue.
3   The documents assigned to the sub-HUs should be available and stored in the same folder as all HUs to be merged. You can also merge the HUs without the associated documents, but the software will let you know that you have no access to the documents.

How to merge

- Open the first HU. This will become the target HU.
- Save it under a new name like Master + date. Now, if you accidentally select a wrong merge option, you can safely delete the master copy and start again.

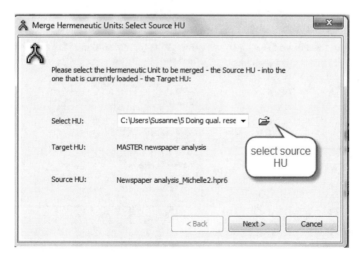

Figure A.3   Select source HU to be merged

- Open the merge tool: TOOLS / MERGE WITH HU.
- Select the second HU (the source) to be merged into the target HU (Figure A.3).
- Click on the button NEXT.

Now you need to define a merge strategy. This consists of two steps. First you need to define a main or stock strategy on the left-hand side of the window and then you can fine tune this strategy on the right-hand side.

Let's assume you want to merge two projects that contain the same documents. The Peter and Michelle team started out with an agreed set of codes, but each of them is allowed to add additional ones. The stock strategy that needs to be selected is: **Same PDs and Codes** (Figure A.4) This means that all the same codes and PDs are unified and all objects that are different are added.

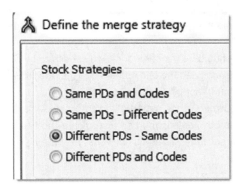

Figure A.4   Selecting a stock strategy on the left-hand side

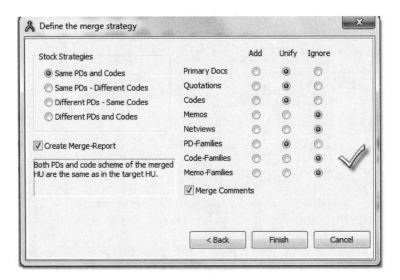

Figure A.5   Fine tune your strategy on the right-hand side

Users are often afraid of losing newly added codes when selecting this strategy, but this won't be the case.

- Check whether all options on the right-hand side will yield the result you want (Figure A.5). You may want to add memos or network views, for example – or you may choose to select whether you want to receive a merge report and whether comments should be merged or not.
- Click on the button **Finish** to start the merge process.

Here is a summary of a merge report:

Object sizes and selected strategy per object type before merge:

Object Type	Source-HU	Target-HU	Strategy
Primary Docs	15	15	Unify
Quotations	115	135	Unify
Codes	11	14	Unify
Codings	123	145	-
Memos	7	7	Ignore
Network views	6	6	Ignore
Primary Doc Families	4	4	Unify
Code Families	12	12	Ignore
Memo Families	0	0	Ignore
Code-Links	3	7	Target
Hyper-Links	0	0	Target

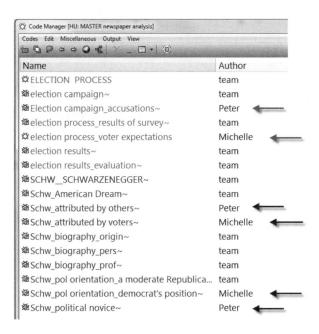

Figure A.6 Code Manager after merging Michelle's and Peter's work

Thus, the target HU contains a few more codes, codings and code links than the source. If we take a look at the Code Manager, we see that Michelle and Peter have each added three codes (Figure A.6). All other codes were previously created and agreed upon by the team. This is visible because objects created by the team are marked with the author 'team', objects created by Peter and Michelle with the author names 'Peter' and ' Michelle' respectively. This has been achieved by creating user accounts and by logging in (see chapter 3).

- If everything turns out as you intended, save the Master HU.

Let's take a look at a different example: Susanne and Berta are cooperating on a project where each of them codes parts of the data using a common coding scheme. Susanne codes the German data, Berta codes the US data.

The main merge strategy for such a project is: Different PD – Same Codes. This time the fine tuning looks as shown in Figure A.7.

After merging, the Primary Document Manager looks as shown in Figure A.8.

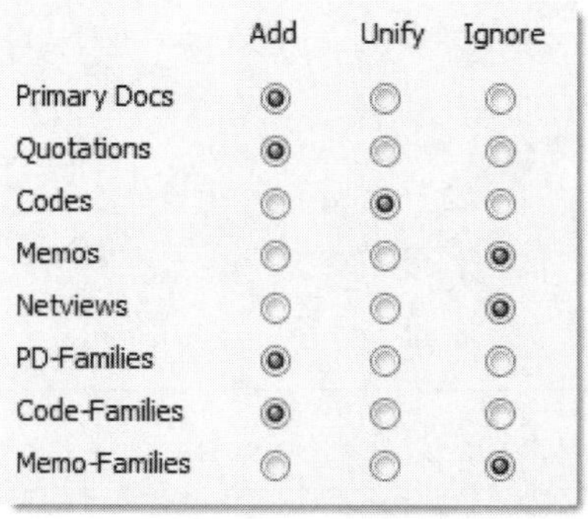

Figure A.7 Fine tuning options for merging HUs containing different PDs and the same codes

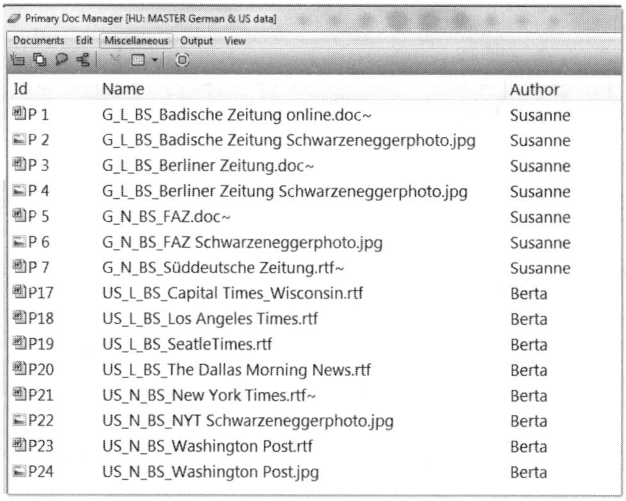

Primary Doc Manager [HU: MASTER German & US data]

Id	Name	Author
P 1	G_L_BS_Badische Zeitung online.doc~	Susanne
P 2	G_L_BS_Badische Zeitung Schwarzeneggerphoto.jpg	Susanne
P 3	G_L_BS_Berliner Zeitung.doc~	Susanne
P 4	G_L_BS_Berliner Zeitung Schwarzeneggerphoto.jpg	Susanne
P 5	G_N_BS_FAZ.doc~	Susanne
P 6	G_N_BS_FAZ Schwarzeneggerphoto.jpg	Susanne
P 7	G_N_BS_Süddeutsche Zeitung.rtf~	Susanne
P17	US_L_BS_Capital Times_Wisconsin.rtf	Berta
P18	US_L_BS_Los Angeles Times.rtf	Berta
P19	US_L_BS_SeatleTimes.rtf	Berta
P20	US_L_BS_The Dallas Morning News.rtf	Berta
P21	US_N_BS_New York Times.rtf~	Berta
P22	US_N_BS_NYT Schwarzeneggerphoto.jpg	Berta
P23	US_N_BS_Washington Post.rtf	Berta
P24	US_N_BS_Washington Post.jpg	Berta

Figure A.8 P-Docs Manager after merging the work of two coders

After the merging process

After merging projects, it is generally a good idea to check for redundant codings. Redundant coding occurs when part of a segment is coded with the same code twice (Figure A.9).

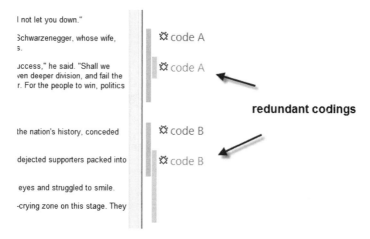

Figure A.9   Redundant codings

ATLAS.ti offers a tool to let you find such false coding in your data.

- Select **Tools/ Coding Analyzer.**
- Click on an entry.
- Then click on the two alternative codings that are offered (Figure A.10), view them in context and decide whether you want to merge the two, remove one of them completely, or unlink one of them in case the data segment is also coded by another code.

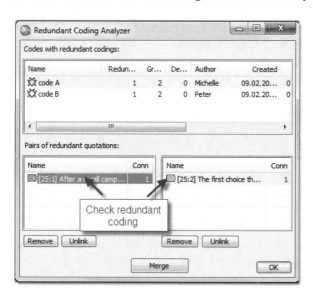

Figure A.10   Redundant coding analyzer

Running the coding analyzer is also useful when working alone. Even if it does not make sense to code parts of the same segment with the same code, it does happen and the coding analyzer helps you to catch it.

Creating backups

Backup options for the HU

ATLAS.ti offers the following standard backup options:

- creation of an auto recovery file; and
- creation of a file with the name '**Backup of YourFileName.hpr6**'.

Auto recovery file

The auto recovery file is created at regular time intervals and restores an HU in case of a crash. If you close ATLAS.ti normally, the auto recovery file is deleted. In case of a crash, however, this file is not deleted and it is available as an alternative next time you start the program. You are probably familiar with this procedure from other applications. If you are sure that you saved your HU shortly before the crash, your own HU file is probably newer than the auto recovery file, which you can then ignore. If you had not saved for a while, you will probably be glad of the auto recovery file.

The name of the recovery file consists of the letters **HPR** and a computer-generated alphanumeric combination with the file identification *.tmp (e.g. HPR7C4.tmp). The file is saved in the so-called User System Folder. You can easily access this folder from within ATLAS.ti via the menu option Extras / Explorer / User System Folder. The time interval and the storage location of the auto recovery file can be set in the preference window (see below).

'Backup of ...' file

The 'Backup of ... hpr6' file is created when actively saving an HU via File/ Save or with a click on the floppy disk symbol. The previously saved HU will then be saved as a 'backup of ...' file and stored in the same folder as your HU. As there is no 'Undo' function in ATLAS.ti (or only a very limited one), saving frequently is a good idea. If you make a careless mistake like deleting a frequently used code (yes, it does happen), then you will be glad that your last saved version is only 10 minutes and not six hours old. You can simply close the HU without saving it and open the last or the 'backup of' version having lost only 10 minutes of your work.

When opening an HU file, be careful not to open the 'backup of ...' file. Because of the naming convention, the 'backup of ...' file might well be stored above the actual HU file, as its name begins with the letter B. This happens to me once in a while when opening an HU directly from the file manager, and I see it happening all the time to others: if you open the *'backup of project name.hpr6'* file, work on it and save it, the program creates a file named *'backup of backup of project name.hpr6'* – and I have even seen *'backup of backup of backup of project name.hpr6'* files. This is undesirable because (apart from the silly name) you're working on an older version of your project and wondering why something is missing. As a safeguard, double check the project name in the title bar after opening it, or always open ATLAS.ti first. The default setting is for ATLAS.ti to open the most recently used project, so you can be sure of working on your actual project instead of a 'backup of' version.

Customizing HU backup options

- Select the main menu option under EXTRAS / PREFERENCES / GENERAL PREFERENCES.
- Select the STORAGE tab (Figure A. 11).

If you are a very anxious or cautious person, you may want to reduce the auto recovery interval to 10 minutes. Keep in mind that saving the HU in the background uses up computer resources. If you experience problems with the auto recovery backup, check the backup path and make sure you have sufficient space to store files at this location.

Backup or transfer of the completed project via copy bundle

The two backup options described above apply only to the HU. If you want to back up your entire project, ATLAS.ti provides a copy bundle function. When using the proposed HUPATH setup for your project, a copy bundle file is more

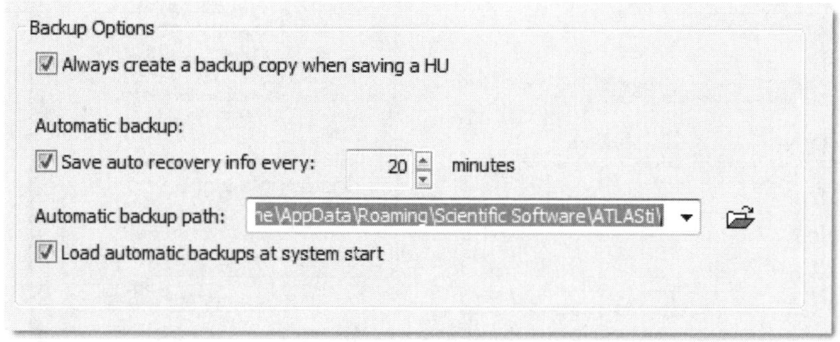

Figure A.11 Default settings for HU backups

or less the same as a zip file of your project folder. It is a single file that stores all project files in a compressed format. It can also be used to transfer your project to a different location. As it is just one file, you can for instance attach it to an email.

When to create a copy bundle file

I recommend that you create a copy bundle file after each work session as a backup. Store this file at a safe location. You can overwrite the file each time with a new version or keep two or three rolling copies.

A copy bundle file can also be used to 'freeze' a certain state of your analysis (e.g. your first stage of coding). When writing the methodology section for your thesis or research report, you can review the frozen stages to remind you how your analysis progressed over time.

Copy bundle files are also useful for transferring projects between computers or for sending them to others via email. Then you need to unbundle or (as ATLAS.ti calls it) 'install' the file (see below). When you use the HUPATH setup, you can also use WinZip or WinRAR to create a compressed file of your project. Use whatever you are comfortable with.

Consider file size when creating copy bundle files

A copy bundle file should not become too large, otherwise it might not be possible to unbundle it. Too large means a few gigabytes in size. Thus, do not include large audio and video files in the bundle. You will have the option to exclude certain items before creating the bundle file.

How to create a copy bundle file

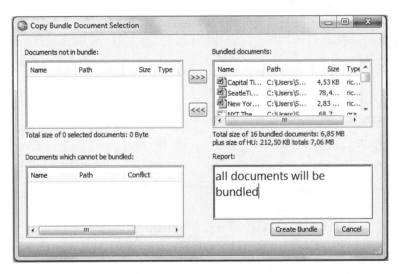

Figure A.12   Creating a copy bundle file

- Save your HU.
- From the main menu, select **Tools / Copy Bundle / Create Bundle**. The window in Figure A.12 will open.
- If the window appears as shown in Figure A.12 then you can simple click on **Create Bundle** to save the bundle file.
- Next, you need to choose a location for your copy bundle file. The default file name is the name of the HU. The extension is .acb, for atlas copy bundle. You can give the copy bundle file a different name, for example adding the date or a version number to the project name.
- After a short time a message pops up letting you know that the copy bundle file is ready (**Copy Bundle finished and saved**).

> Do *not* save the acb file in your project folder. Save it to an external drive, a network drive, in the cloud – anywhere it will be safe. If you store both your project folder and the acb file on the same hard disk and it fails, you will lose all your work.

To remove documents from the bundle   In the **upper right section of the window** you will see the list of all primary documents that can be bundled. To remove documents from the bundle:

- Double click on a document to move it to the left-hand side; or select all documents to be removed and click on the button with the errors pointing to the left.

Potential problems when creating a bundle file   If one or more documents cannot be bundled, you will see a message (in red) in the report pane. On the left-hand side will be listed the reasons why a document cannot be included, like a wrong file path, a missing source file, a wrong version of a source file, or a missing log file. If you want these files to be included, close the copy bundle window and fix the problem(s). See 'troubleshooting' on p. 258.

Installing an acb (atlas copy bundle) file

The 'unbundling' of a copy bundle file is named **installation** in ATLAS.ti. Such an installation can only be done with ATLAS.ti. You can double click on an acb file in your file manager but first you need to tell your computer which application is associated with such a file. If you don't know how to do that, then open ATLAS.ti first and select:

- **Tools / Copy Bundle / Install bundle.** The 'install copy bundle window' will open.

Next, you need to select a location where you want the HU file to be stored. If you work with the recommend HUPATH setup, then this will also be the location where all documents can be found after installing the bundle. If you

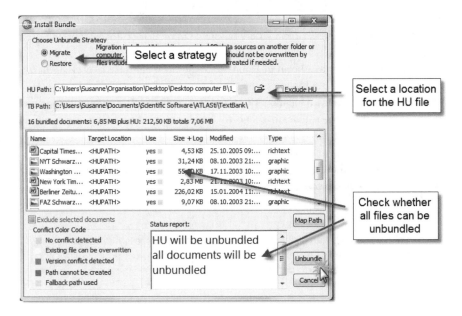

Figure A.13 Install bundle window

use subfolders for your documents, all necessary subfolders will be created and the documents are unbundled there.

If you store the HU file and the documents at different locations and thus your project setup is based on absolute path references, you can only freely select the location for the HU file. The documents will be unbundled to the locations indicated by the path references stored in the HU. Thus, if you transfer a project from computer A to computer B, ATLAS.ti duplicates the necessary folder structure so that the unbundled HU can load the documents.

As already explained in Chapter 3 on project management, working with absolute path references is not a desirable project setup. Imagine a situation where you have set up your project in that way and at some point you want another person to take a look at it. You therefore send him or her a copy bundle file. When this person installs it, ATLAS.ti creates a bunch of new folders and subfolders on the target computer just so your project can be loaded. The person at the receiving end probably does not like this very much, because it messes up his or her computer. If I receive projects like that, I usually move all files – including the HU file – into one folder, change the project setup to the HUPATH and delete the new folder structure that was created during the unbundling process.

There are two installation strategies to choose from: MIGRATE and RESTORE (Figure A.13). Choose MIGRATE if you want to transfer a project to another computer. Older files are then replaced with newer files. Choose RESTORE to restore a previous state: for example, if you have made a mistake, if a document is corrupt, if you have lost your HU, etc. By selecting the restore option, all files are overwritten.

- Select one of the two installation strategies.
- Choose a location for the HU in the field HU Path.

Check the color of the boxes in the column 'Use' to see if there are conflicts and correct them if needed. Green and yellow are OK: if you are transferring a project for the first time or into an empty folder, you will see **green** boxes on the screen. When migrating a project between computers multiple times, the boxes will be **yellow**. This means the files already exist on the target computer and will be overwritten with newer versions.

- If no conflicts are reported and nothing needs correcting, click on **UNBUNDLE**.

The acb file is then unpacked, and all the documents will be copied into the corresponding directories. The unpacked HU opens in a new HU editor window.

Possible conflicts

Version conflict detected: If you see a pink box on the screen, ATLAS.ti has noticed that there are several HUs accessing the same file, but they have different information for this document in terms of file size or date of last saving. Unbundling this document would mean that the other HUs could no longer access it. It is possible to install such documents in RESTORE mode.

Path cannot be created: If a necessary path does not exist on the target computer, it is usually created by ATLAS.ti. But there are situations when this cannot be done. This happens, for instance, when the reference of a document points to a network drive like an H or L or Z drive that does not exist on the target computer, or if a user does not have access to a specific drive. In these cases, the path can be mapped. Click on MAP PATH. Then another window will open. On the left-hand side enter the path that produces a conflict; on the right-hand side enter a path that exists on the target computer to use as location for installing the file.

Fallback path used: A light green box on the screen indicates that the HU can access the document, but not via its original path reference. This happens when an absolute path reference was used in the first place. At some point all documents were moved into the same folder as the HU file, but the original path references were not changed to reflect the new setup (see the rection 'Modifying the project setup' on p. 263).

If you do not optimize paths after changing the project setup to the HUPATH, then ATLAS.ti first follows the original path reference. When it does not find the files there, it checks the folder where the HU file is located as an alternative or 'fallback' location for the files.

When light green boxes are displayed, you can still unbundle the file. But it is advisable to optimize the path references immediately after unbundling:

- To optimize the path references, select **DOCUMENTS / DATA SOURCE MANAGEMENT / OPTIMIZE PATHS.**

Best practice rules

When should you create a **copy bundle** file?

- After each work session as a backup file of your project. Store this file in a safe location like a server or an external drive. You can overwrite this file after the next work session, or you can keep two or three rolling copies.
- To preserve or 'freeze' a certain stage of your project, for example the first stage of coding before sorting and structuring.
- When transferring a project between computers. When using the HUPATH setup, you may as well use WinZip or WinRAR to create a compressed file of your project folder.

Troubleshooting: what to do if primary documents become unusable

If a primary document cannot be loaded, the USABLE column of the **P-Docs Manager** displays No and nothing is displayed in the HU editor. Depending on the kind of problem, the entries in the P-Docs Manager are displayed in a different color.

- Gray indicates that the data source is missing.
- Bright red denotes a problem with editing.
- Dark red means the document can only be loaded via the fallback path (see 'Possible conflicts' above).

Pay attention to the status bar

If there is a problem, ATLAS.ti displays a message at the bottom left of the screen, in the status bar. However, users often do not pay attention to this status bar.

Not found: C:\Users\Susanne\5 Doing qual. research with ATLAS.ti\Example material\Analysis Schwarzenegger project\Los Angeles Times.rtf

Figure A.14   Message in the status bar when a document cannot be loaded

Document cannot be found

The message in Figure A.14 indicates that the HU is expecting the file 'Los Angeles Times.rtf' to be stored in the folder 'Analysis Schwarzenegger project' within the folder hierarchy of the user Susanne.

Solution
If you see such a message, you should search for the file in your file manager (or anywhere else it may be) and move it to the location expected by the HU.

Document cannot be synchronized

A 'not syncable' message indicates that there is a problem with editing (Figure A.15). You have either modified a file outside ATLAS.ti (e.g. in Word) or edited the file in ATLAS.ti as you should, but have misplaced, deleted or modified the log file (see 'What you should know about editing' on p. 241ff.).

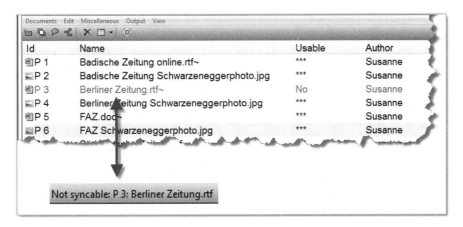

Figure A.15 A synchronization error indicates a problem with editing

Solution
Before you hastily try out all the options you can find that might remedy a synchronization problem, create an accessibility report first and read what ATLAS.ti identifies as the problem.

Creating accessibility reports

To create an accessibility report for all files:

- Select DOCUMENTS / DATA SOURCE MANAGEMENT / ACCESSIBILITY REPORT from the main menu.
- Select one of the output options, for example EDITOR.
- To create an accessibility report for just one primary document:

- Open the Primary Document Manager and select the relevant document.
- Right click on the document and select: **DATA SOURCE MANAGEMENT / ACCESSIBILITY REPORT**.
- Select an output option.

Understanding the accessibility report

Expected log file not found

Document Accessibility Report for: PD-Selection

HU: Analysis Schwarzenegger election 2003
File: [C:\Users\Susanne\5 Doing qual. research with ATLA...\Analysis Schwarzenegger election 2003.hpr6]
Edited by: Susanne
Date/Time: 02.04.2011 22:02:16

Current Special Paths:

<HUPATH> = "C:\Users\Susanne\5 Doing qual. research with ATLAS.ti\Example material"
<TBPATH> = "C:\Users\Susanne\Documents\Scientific Software\ATLASti\ TextBank"

Primary Documents (1):

P 7: G_N_BS_Süddeutsche Zeitung.rtf {52}~
Source: Doc_7
Source reference: "<HUPATH>\Süddeutsche Zeitung.rtf"
Source location: ditto
Last accessed: "<HUPATH>\Süddeutsche Zeitung.rtf" (31.10.2010 22:26:29)
Revision: 18.01.2010 13:37:14
State: loading rejected
Problem report:
Synchronization failure: expected log file not found

This report tells me that the expected log file was not found. Further, I can see that I last revised the document on 18 January 2010 at 13:37:14. The name of the original source file is 'Süddeutsche Zeitung.rtf '.

This means I need to search for a log file with the name 'Süddeutsche Zeitung.rtf.log', last saved on 18 January 2010 at 13:37:14. If I find it, I know from rule no. 2 that I need to move it to the same folder where the original source file is stored (see 'What you should know about editing' on p. 241ff.). The report tells me that this is the HUPATH (see Source reference), thus the same folder where my HU file is stored. In case I don't know the location of the HU file, it is shown at the top of the report:

<HUPATH> = "C:\Users\Susanne\Doing qual. research with ATLAS.ti\Example material\Analysis Schwarzenegger project"

> **If you deleted the log file** and you cannot recover it from the bin or an acb file, there is no solution but to disconnect the primary document from the HU and to recode it!

Source-log mismatch

> **P 3: G_L_BS_Berliner Zeitung.rtf {55}~**
> Source: Doc_1
> Source reference: "<HUPATH>\Berliner Zeitung.rtf"
> Source location: ditto
> Last accessed: ditto (17.02.2011 20:41:35)
> Revision: 17.02.2011 20:41:33
> State: loading rejected
> **Problem report:**
> Source-log mismatch (check document sources table at: Doc_1)

This part of the report indicates that the file was last accessed and revised on 17 February 2011 at 20:41:35. As it was revised, a log file is expected. ATLAS. ti can find a log file, but it is not the correct one. There is a mismatch. In order to get more information about the file, you need to take a look at the document sources table in the second half of the report:

> P 3: G_L_BS_Berliner Zeitung.rtf
> Location: "C:\Users\Susanne\Doing qual. research with ATLAS.ti\Example material\Analysis corrupt\Berliner Zeitung.rtf"
> Modified: 17.02.2011 20:41:33 (expected from log: 15.01.2004 11:17:39!!!)
> Size: 232312 (expected from log: 231219!!!)
> Availability: OK
> Loaded: yes
> Source-Log-Mismatch: yes (copied/moved file without log file?)
> Log sessions: 1
> Last log entry: 15.01.2004 11:17:39

The currently available log file is from 15 January 2004 and it expects the original .rtf file (here the file 'G_L_BS_Berliner Zeitung.rtf') to be 231.319k large (approx. 231k). As the file was last revised on 17 February 2011, the correct log file should be from 17 February 2011. After the revision, the expected file size is 232.312k (approx. 232k).

To solve such a mismatch, you need to search for the expected log file. Then, replace the currently available log file with the correct one. If you cannot find the correct log file, check your acb backup files and hopefully you can retrieve it from there. As above, if the correct log file cannot be found, you will need to disconnect the document and recode it.

Data source changes detected

> **P 8: US_L_BS_Capital Times_Wisconsin.rtf {38}**
> Source: Doc_8
> Source reference: "<HUPATH>\Capital Times_Wisconsin.rtf"
> Source location: ditto
> Last accessed: "<HUPATH>\Capital Times_Wisconsin.rtf" but <HUPATH> was:
> "C:\Users\Susanne\Organisation\Desktop\Project book_sample data eng. AS"
> (31.10.2010 22:26:42)
> Revision: n/a
> State: loading rejected
> **Problem report:**
> Data source changes detected - size changed since last access from: 4638 to:
> 41414

If data source changes have been detected, then you have modified the document outside ATLAS.ti. This should never be done, but let's assume this happened by accident. This problem can be remedied, but you should be aware of its potential consequences.

When you modify a document outside ATLAS.ti, your coding references stored in the HU are not modified and therefore a mismatch between text and attached codes can occur (see Figure A.1). When loading a document, ATLAS.ti checks the file size and date of saving. Based on this information, the software recognizes whether a document was modified outside its boundaries. If so, the document will not be loaded.

You can nonetheless force the program to load the document:

- Open the P-Docs Manager and right click on the document.
- Select the option **DATA SOURCE MANAGEMENT / RESET LAST ACCESS INFORMATION**.
- Read and accept the warning messages.
- Go through all coded segments for this document and modify misaligned segments. At any rate, this is better than disconnecting the document and starting over from scratch.

Source not available

> **P12: US_N_BS_New York Times.rtf {94}~**
> Source: Doc_12
> Source reference: "<HUPATH>\New York Times.rtf"
> Source location: ditto
> Last accessed: "<HUPATH>\New York Times.rtf"
> State: loading rejected
> Problem report:
> **Source not available (check document sources table at: Doc_12)**

If the problem report indicates that the source is not available, then you have to search for the file and move it to the location that is expected by the HU. The name of the document and its expected location are shown in the line 'Source reference'. In the example provided above, the primary document name that is used inside of ATLAS.ti has been changed. Therefore the name of the primary document P12 is not the same name as the file name on the computer disk. The file name is 'New York Times.rtf' whereas the PD name is 'US_N_BS_New York Times.rtf'.

Modifying the project setup

In case you had already set up your project before reading Chapter 3, below you will find instructions about how to change a project setup based on absolute path references to a setup based on the optimal HUPATH:

- If ATLAS.ti is open, close it.
- Create a new folder; let's call it the project folder.
- Move the HU file and all documents that you have assigned to this HU into the new folder. In case you have edited some or all of your primary documents, remember to move the log files as well. *Do not move lok files, delete them!*
- Open the HU and check whether you can load all documents.
- If all documents can be loaded, select the main menu option **DOCUMENTS / DATA SOURCE MANAGEMENT / OPTIMIZE PATHS**.

This creates the HUPATH for each document. You can see this in the P-Docs Manager in the column 'Origin'. If you update to version 7, then the advice is to turn your project into a managed project. This means ATLAS.ti takes over data and project management and you no longer have to worry about it.

Exchanging doc or docx files with rtf files (changing paths)

Let's say that after reading the section on editing primary documents, you realize that you have assigned doc or docx files rather than rtf files. This means you can no longer modify them. Editing within ATLAS.ti version 5 or 6 is not possible and editing outside ATLAS.ti gets you into trouble. There is a solution to this:

- If ATLAS.ti is open, close it.
- Open your doc or docx files in Word and save them in Word as rtf files. Store them in the same folder as the doc or docx files.
- Open ATLAS.ti and then the P-Docs Manager. Right click on a file and select **DATA SOURCE MANAGEMENT / CHANGE PATH**.

ATLAS.ti asks you whether you really want to do this as there are currently no problems related to the path reference. Accept the warning.

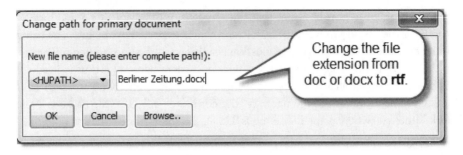

Figure A.16   Change the path reference for a document

Assuming you use the HUPATH setup, you will see the display shown in Figure A.16.

- Change the doc or docx extension to rtf and click on **OK**.
- Load the document. If it does not load immediately, you may need to select the 'Reset last access information' option, which you also find under the Data Source Management menu.
- Repeat this for all other primary documents that you want to change.

This process is not always foolproof; sometimes the first half page will be filled with nonsense characters. But this can usually be solved by going into the edit mode and deleting those lines. Sometimes the in-built ATLAS.ti editor produces cleaner results than saving a document in Word as rich text:

- You will find the ATLAS.ti text editor under the menu **Tools**. Copy and paste the text from Word into this editor and save the file.
- If you were successful in changing the format for all documents, you can remove the doc or docx files from your project folder. They are no longer needed.

The change path option can of course also be used for other purposes. For example, you can change or add subfolder names, or change from an absolute path reference to the HUPATH reference. This can be useful if you want to change the project structure without needing to access the documents.

Missing converters

This message pops up if you have assigned doc or docx files and the necessary 'doc(x) to rtf' converters are not available on your computer. ATLAS.ti relies on these converters when loading a doc or docx file into the HU editor. Usually such converters are installed on your computer via Word or an Office package. But sometimes users receive files created in Office 2010 when they are still using Office 2003, or they might be using ATLAS.ti in the parallel universe of Windows on a Mac. In such cases it might be that a converter is not available.

The solution for Windows users is to download the latest Office compatibility pack from the Microsoft website. Mac users will need to install an Office package in their Windows environment; the open source version is fine.

<hr />

REVIEW QUESTIONS

Editing primary documents

1 What are the reasons for editing a primary document?
2 Explain the two rules that everyone who edits a primary document in version 5 or 6 should know.

Merging projects

1 What do you need to be aware of when merging two projects?
2 What could create such problems that you need to abort a merge process?
3 What kinds of merge strategies are available? Think of a scenario for each of the four main strategies.
4 How can you find redundant codings?

Backup options

1 What kind of backup options are available for the HU?
2 What kinds of options are available to back up your entire project?

Troubleshooting

1 What can result in corrupted or unloadable primary documents?
2 How can you find out what is causing a problem?
3 What are the solutions for the various problems that might occur?

References

Araujo, Luis (1995). Designing and refining hierarchical coding frames, in U. Kelle (ed.), *Computer-Aided Qualitative Data Analysis*. London: Sage. Chapter 7.

Barry, Christine A. (1998). Choosing qualitative data analysis software: Atlas/ti and NUD.IST compared. *Sociological Research Online*, 3(3). Available at: www.socresonline.org.uk/socresonline/3/3/4.html.

Bazeley, Pat (2007). *Qualitative Data Analysis with NVivo*. London: Sage.

Bazeley, Pat and Richards, Lyn (2000). *The NVivo Qualitative Project Book*. London: Sage.

Bernard, Russel H. and Ryan, Gery W. (2010). *Analysing Qualitative Data: Systematic Approaches*. London: Sage.

Birks, Melanie (2008). Memoing in qualitative research: probing data and processes, *Journal of Research in Nursing*, January, 13, 68–75.

Blumer, Herbert (1969). *Symbolic Interactionism: Perspective and Method*. Englewood Cliffs, NJ: Prentice Hall.

Bodgan, Robert C. and Biklen, Sari Knopp (2007). *Qualitative Research for Education: An Introduction to Theories and Methods* (5th ed.). Boston, MA: Pearson Education.

Charmaz, Kathy (2002). Qualitative interviewing and grounded theory analysis, in Jaber F. Gubrium and James A. Holstein (eds), *Handbook of Interview Research: Context & Method*. Thousand Oaks, CA: Sage. pp. 675–84.

Charmaz, Kathy (2006). *Constructing Grounded Theory: A Practical Guide Through Qualitative Analysis*. London: Sage.

Corbin, Juliet and Strauss, Anselnm (2008). *Basics of Qualitative Research: Techniques and Procedures for Developing Grounded Theory* (3nd ed.). London: Sage.

Cortazzi, Martin (1993). *Narrative Analysis*. London: Falmer Press.

Creswell, John W. (1998). *Qualitative Inquiry and Research Design: Choosing among Five Traditions*. London: Sage.

Denzin, Norman K. and Lincoln, Yvonne S. (2000). *Handbook of Qualitative Research* (2nd ed.). London: Sage.

Dey, Ian (1993). Qualitative data analysis: A user-friendly guide for social scientists. London: Routledge.

Di Gregorio, Silvana and Davidson, Judith (2008). *Qualitative Research Design for Software Users*. Maidenhead: Open University Press/McGraw-Hill.

Fielding, Nigel G. and Raymond, M. Lee (1998). *Computer Analysis and Qualitative Research*. London: Sage.

Friese, Susanne (2000). *Self-concept and Identity in a Consumer Society: Aspects of Symbolic Product Meaning*. Marburg: Tectum.

Friese, Susanne (2011). Using ATLAS.ti for analyzing the financial crisis data [67 paragraphs]. Forum Qualitative Sozialforschung/Forum: Qualitative Social Research, 12(1), Art. 39, http://nbn-resolving.de/urn:nbn:de:0114-fqs1101397.

Gable, Robert K. and Wolf, Marian B. (1993). *Instrument Development in the Affective Domain: Meaning Attitudes and Values in Corporate and School Settings* (2nd ed.). Boston, MA: Kluwer Academic.

Garcia, E. (2005). Keywords co-occurrence and semantic connectivity: an introductory series on co-occurrence theory for information retrieval students and search engine Marketers. Web publication: www.miislita.com/semantics/c-index-1.html.

Gibbs, Graham (2005). Writing as analysis. Online QDA: http://onlineqda.hud.ac.uk./Intro_QDA/writing_analysis.php (accessed 20 January 2011).

Glaser, Barney G. (1978). *Theoretical Sensitivity: Advances in the Methodology of Grounded Theory.* Mill Valley, CA: Sociological Press.

Glaser, Barney G. and Strauss, Anselm L. (1967). *Discovery of Grounded Theory: Strategies for Qualitative Research.* Chicago: Aldine.

Goleman, Daniel (1995). *Emotional Intelligence.* New York: Bantam Books.

Hartmann, Eddie (2011). *Strategien des Gegenhandelns: Zur Soziodynamik symbolischer Kämpfe um Zugehörigkeit.* Konstanz: UVK.

Hinchliffe, S.J., Crang, M.A., Reimer, S.M. and Hudson, A.C. (1997). Software for qualitative research: 2. Some thought on 'aiding' analysis. *Environment and Planning* A, 29, 1109–24.

Hug, Theo (2001). Editorial zur Reihe: 'Wie kommt die Wissenschaft zu Wissen?', in Theo Hug (ed.), *Einführung in die Forschungsmethodik und Forschungspraxis.* Baltmannsweiler: Schneider-Verlag. (Vol. 2, pp. 3–10)

Jefferson, G. (1984). Transcript notation, in J. Heritage (ed.), *Structures of Social Interaction.* New York: Cambridge University Press.

Kallmeyer, W. and Schütze, F. (1976). Konversationsanalyse, *Studium Linguistik,* 1, 1–28.

Kelle, Udo (ed.) (1995). *Computer-aided Qualitative Data Analysis.* London: Sage.

Kelle, Udo und Kluge, Susann (2010). *Vom Einzelfall zum Typus: Fallvergleich und Fallkontrastierung in der qualitativen Sozialforschung.* Wiesbaden, VS Verlag.

Khateb, A., Pegna, A.J., Michel, C.M., Landis, T. and Annoni, J.M. (2002). Dynamics of brain activation during an explicit word and image recognition task: an electrophysiological study. In *Brain Topography,* Spring 14(3): 197–213.

Konopásek, Zdeněk (2007). Making thinking visible with Atlas.ti: computer assisted qualitative analysis as textual practices [62 paragraphs]. Forum Qualitative Sozialforschung/Forum: Qualitative Social Research, 9(2), Art. 12, http://nbn-resolving.de/urn:nbn:de:0114-fqs0802124.

Kuckartz, Udo (1995). Case-oriented quantification, in U. Kelle (ed.), *Computer-Aided Qualitative Data Analysis: Theory, Methods and Practice.* London: Sage. pp. 158–66.

Kuckartz, Udo (2005). *Einführung in die computergestützte Analyse qualitativer Daten.* Wiesbaden: VHS Verlag.

Kuş Saillard, Elif (2011). Systematic versus interpretive analysis with two CAQDAS packages: NVivo and MAXQDA [75 paragraphs]. Forum Qualitative Sozialforschung/Forum: Qualitative Social Research, 12(1), Art. 34, http://nbn-resolving.de/urn:nbn:de:0114-fqs1101345.

LeCompte, Margarete Diane and Preissle, Judith (1993). *Ethnography and Qualitative Design in Educational Research* (2nd ed.). San Diego: Academic Press.

Lewins, Ann and Silver, Christine (2007). *Using Software in Qualitative Research: A Step-by-step Guide*. London: Sage.

Mayring, Philipp (2010). *Qualitative Inhaltsanalyse* (11th ed.). Weinheim: Beltz.

Miles, Matthew B. and Huberman, Michael (1994). *Qualitative Data Analysis* (2nd ed.).Thousand Oaks, CA: Sage.

Morse, Janice M. (1994). Emerging from the data: the cognitive process of analysis in qualitative inquiry, in Janice M. Morse (ed.) *Critical Issues in Qualitative Research Methods*. Thousand Oaks, CA: Sage. pp. 22–43.

Morrison, Moya and Moir, Jim (1998). The role of computer software in the analysis of qualitative data: efficient clerk, research assistant or Trojan horse? *Journal of Advanced Nursing*, 28(1), 106–116.

Muhr, Thomas (2000). Increasing the reusability of qualitative data with XML [64 paragraphs]. Forum Qualitative Sozialforschung/Forum: Qualitative Social Research, 1(3), Art. 20, http://nbn-resolving.de/urn:nbn:de:0114-fqs0003202.

Novak, Josef D. and Cañas, Alberto J. (2006). The theory underlying concept maps and how to construct and use them. Institute for Human and Machine Cognition. http://en.wikipedia.org/wiki/Concept_map (accessed 11 December 2010).

Novak, Josef D. and Gowin, D. Bob (2002). *Learning How to Learn*. New York: Cambridge University Press. (First published in 1984.)

Okeley, Judith (1994). Thinking through fieldwork, in Alan Bryman and Robert G. Burgess (eds.), *Analyzing Qualitative Data*. London: Routledge. pp. 111–28

Prus, Robert C. (1996). *Symbolic Interaction and Ethnographic Research: Intersubjectivity and the Study of Human Lived Experience*. Albany, NY: SUNY Press.

Richards, Lyn and Richards, Tom (1994). From filing cabinet to computer. In Alan Bryman and Robert G. Burgess (eds.), *Analysing Qualitative Data*. London: Routledge. pp. 146–72.

Richards, Tom and Richards, Lyn (1995). Using hierarchical categories in qualitative data analysis, in U. Kelle (ed.) *Computer-Aided Qualitative Data Analysis*. London: Sage. Chapter 6.

Riessman, Catherine K. (2008). *Narrative Methods for the Human Sciences*. Thousand Oaks, CA: Sage.

Saldaña, Jonny (2003). *Longitudinal Qualitative Research: Analyzing Change through Time*. Walnut Creek, CA: AltaMira Press.

Saldaña, Jonny (2009). *The Coding Manual for Qualitative Researchers*. London: Sage.

Schmieder, Christian (2009). Computergestützte qualitative Datenanalyse: Technik der Legitimation – Legitimation der Technik. Eine qualitative Studie zur Verwendung von MAXQDA in akademischen Forschen. Magisterarbeit. Available at: www.freidok.uni-freiburg.de/volltexte/7082/pdf/schmieder_caqdas_dec.pdf (accessed 11th December, 2010).

Seale, Clive (1999). *The Quality of Qualitative Research*. London: Sage.

Seidel, John (1991). Methods and madness in the application of computer technology to qualitative data analysis, in Nigel G. Fielding and Raymond M. Lee (eds.), *Using Computers in Qualitative Research* London: Sage. pp. 107–16.

Seidel, John and Kelle, Udo. (1995). Different functions of coding in the analysis of textual data, in: U. Kelle (ed.), *Computer-Aided Qualitative Data Analysis*. London: Sage. Chapter 4.

Seidel, John V. (1998). Qualitative data analysis. The Ethnograph v5.0: A Users' Guide, Appendix E. Colorado Springs, CO: Qualis Research), www.qualisresearch.com (accessed 20 January 2011).

Silverman, David (2000). *Doing Qualitative Research: A Practical Handbook*. London: Sage.

Smith, Beverly A. and Hesse-Biber, Sharlene (1996). Users' experiences with qualitative data analysis software: neither Frankenstein's monster nor muse, *Social Science Computer Review*, 14(4), 423–32.

Strauss, Anselm L. and Corbin, Juliet (1998). *Basics of Qualitative Research: Techniques and Procedures for Developing Grounded Theory* (2nd edn). London: Sage.

Strübing, Jörg and Schnettler Bernt (2004). Klassische Grundlagentexte zur Methodologie interpretativer Sozialforschung, in Jörg Strübing and Bernt Schnettler (eds.), *Methodologie interpretativer Sozialforschung: Klassische Grundlagentexte*. Konstanz: UVK. pp. 9–18

Welsh, Elaine (2002). Dealing with data: using NVivo in the qualitative data analysis process [12 paragraphs]. Forum Qualitative Sozialforschung/Forum: Qualitative Social Research, 3(2), Art. 26, http://nbn-resolving.de/urn:nbn:de:0114-fqs0202260.

Wolcott, Harry F. (1994). *Transforming Qualitative Data: Description, Analysis, and Interpretation*. Thousand Oaks, CA: Sage.

Wolcott, Harry E. (2009). *Writing Up Qualitative Research*. London: Sage.

Index

Tables and Figures are indicated by page numbers in bold.